Emotion and Gender

Gender and Psychology

Series editor: Sue Wilkinson

This international series provides a forum for the growing body of distinctively psychological research focused on gender issues. While work on the psychology of women, particularly that adopting a feminist perspective, will be central, the series will also reflect other emergent trends in the field of gender. It will encourage contributions which are critical of the mainstream of androcentric or 'gender-neutral' psychology and also innovative in their suggested alternatives.

The books will explore topics where gender is central, such as social and sexual relationships, employment, health and illness, and the development of gender identity. Issues of theory and methodology raised by the study of gender in psychology will also be addressed.

The objective is to present research on gender in the context of its broader implications for psychology. These implications include the need to develop theories and methods appropriate to studying the experience of women as well as men, and working towards a psychology which reflects the experiences and concerns of both sexes.

The series will appeal to students of psychology, women's studies and gender studies and to professionals concerned with gender issues in their practice, as well as to the general reader with an interest in gender and psychology.

Sue Wilkinson is principal lecturer and head of the psychology section at Coventry Polytechnic.

Also in this series

Subjectivity and Method in Psychology
Wendy Hollway

Feminists and Psychological Practice
edited by Erica Burman

Feminist Groupwork
Sandra Butler and Claire Wintram

Motherhood: Meanings, Practices and Ideologies
edited by Ann Phoenix, Anne Woollett and Eva Lloyd

Emotion and Gender

Constructing Meaning from Memory

collectively researched
and written by

June Crawford, Susan Kippax, Jenny Onyx,
Una Gault and Pam Benton

SAGE Publications
London · Newbury Park · New Delhi

SAGE Publications Ltd
6 Bonhill Street
London EC2A 4PU

SAGE Publications Inc
2455 Teller Road
Newbury Park, California 91320

SAGE Publications India Pvt Ltd
32, M-Block Market
Greater Kailash – I
New Delhi 110 048

Cataloguing in Publication data

A catalogue record for this book is available from the
British Library.

ISBN 0 8039 8309 3
ISBN 0 8039 8310 7 pbk

Library of Congress catalog card number 92–54094

Typeset by Photoprint, Torquay, Devon
Printed in Great Britain by Hartnolls Ltd, Bodmin,
Cornwall

Contents

To our mothers

Acknowledgements

We wish to acknowledge the interest, encouragement and help given in many ways by many people. In particular we mention Sue Wilkinson, editor of the *Gender and Psychology* series, and our editors at Sage, Sue Jones and Karen Phillips. Sue Wilkinson has encouraged the project from its inception and continues to do so. Sue Jones provided a very detailed, knowledgeable and encouraging critique when our first proposal was submitted. Karen Phillips has latterly helped to influence the shape of the completed work.

Di Miller at Macquarie University has typed many drafts, and drafts of drafts, and has helped us to reconcile the vagaries of three word processing systems of varying compatibility.

Thanks are due to Darien Midwinter, Sue Rowley and Jillian Trezize for the provision of data and preliminary analyses from the women's memory-work group they set up. We also wish to thank for their interest and hard work all the men and women who cooperated as co-researchers (rather than as 'subjects') in the memory-work groups. They worked under a promise of anonymity that we have at all times endeavoured to observe.

Finally, the encouragement and forbearance of friends, families and interested colleagues is acknowledged with gratitude and love.

THE SPUJJ COLLECTIVE

June Crawford, Susan Kippax, Jenny Onyx, Una Gault and Pam Benton have worked collectively since 1986 on the material reported in this book. They called the collective SPUJJ from the initial letters of their first names. Their work focuses on emotion, and is based on writing memories, mostly of their early childhood experiences, and theorizing this material. Sue, Pam, Una, Jenny and June, like everyone else, constructed themselves and continue to reconstruct themselves in the process of reflecting on past experience. They were thus transformed from little girls to grown women.

1
Introduction

We are academics, and psychologists, and women. We have come together through the production of this book, as academics and as psychologists, to reclaim our experience as women. We report here a project which has grown to be something very different from the usual academic exercise, which pursues a radically different way of doing psychology, and which engages us as women.

We began as an informal study group four years ago. We were five women leading busy lives, who came together out of a common need and interest. Over the years we have sustained regular meetings and the huge time commitment involved in writing a book. We have met in the interstices of full-time paid work and the endless work of caring for young and older children and sick or ageing relatives, of overseas study and travel, of political commitments. To do that required more than the desire for academic distinction. We have been sustained by the intellectual stimulation and excitement, and by the sheer pleasure of what we are doing. We have become close friends. We have found a voice to articulate our disquiet with traditional psychological treatments of topics like emotion. Most of all we have become excited by the possibility of doing psychology in a collective, feminist way. In this book we are as interested in sharing the process as much as the product. The method is radical – and it is fun.

Memories of our Meeting

Pam visited Sue in Oxford in October 1984, and they talked into the night about academic psychology and its discontents. They spoke of Pam's desire as a feminist to explore the possibility of psychological knowledge being constructed in liberating rather than oppressive ways. Sue suggested they organize a reading group on their return to Australia.

In 1985 Pam and Sue started early morning swimming, and the reading group idea resurfaced (*sic*). Sue recalls:

> We were sitting in my car talking. Pam spoke of the isolation she felt from academic and intellectual work. I thought about what Pam had said; I too felt isolated. For although a member of a large psychology department, I found that there were few people with whom I could share my thoughts on the state of the art in social psychology.

Sue and Pam thought about whom else to invite. A group of kindred spirits – other women like themselves with whom Sue and Pam would feel comfortable was needed: 'men have a tendency to take over'. June, Jenny and Una each had a keen and critical interest in psychology and needed no urging. The study group was born. We did not start as a cohesive group; some of us knew each other but in a variety of very different relations. Gradually we became close friends (and formed a cohesive group identity).

Who are we? We are white women whose ages range from the late forties to the early sixties. Each of us was born and educated in Commonwealth countries. Some of us live alone, some with partners, and some of us have children. Although coming from a variety of backgrounds, we could all be described as middle class. None of us has any strong religious affiliation; some of us were raised as Catholics and some as Protestants.

We are all psychologists and we have all worked and taught in a tertiary education institution. More importantly, we all felt and perhaps have always felt isolated and marginalized in our academic work. We felt marginalized because we are women:

> In common with many women working in the academic world, I have always found it difficult to specialize in any narrow field. I remember when I graduated my professor said to me 'it is now time to stop spreading outwards and start building upwards'. In other words, to specialize. This advice I have never taken . . .

We also felt isolated from the academic concerns of many of our colleagues:

> I went to Macquarie University in 1975 . . . a little earlier I had read Mischel's *Personality and Assessment* [1968], and this book . . . and my contact with the more 'human' interest of the psychologists at Macquarie, together with the interdisciplinary emphasis of the School of Behavioural Sciences, disabused me of any remaining enthusiasm for positivism . . . I turned my thoughts to sociology, interaction, dialectics, reconstructing social psychology, and other movements in psychology at the time – (but not the 'third' movement of humanism, Maslow and the like). I have continued in this direction, having less and less interest in (conventional) psychology and not caring much that I am getting quite stale on what might be considered current trends, with more and more interest in the history and philosophy of ideas, including psychology, wider fields of science, and feminist theory.

We were making connections between our alienation from academic psychology and our feminism:

> Perhaps underlying all my other interests and concerns was a strongly feminist orientation. My concerns were twofold: first, I perceived

mainstream academic psychology to be conservative in that it supported the pervasive oppression of women in our society. Second, I strongly believed that a woman-centred analysis of human social life had a great deal to contribute to our human understanding. It made a great deal of sense, therefore, to work with women, to explore alternative methodologies that were both rigorous and non empiricist, and to work towards developing a critical analysis of the ways in which women construct their emotions within our society.

We usually met in each other's houses about once a month on a Monday night. We did not begin with emotions. Initially we listened as each of us talked in turn about her current dominant intellectual concerns. These were diverse. Our commitment to feminism, however, provided a common bond. Pam wanted to explore new perspectives in the developmental literature, particularly the work of Walkerdine and her colleagues (Henriques et al., 1984). Sue was interested in Rom Harré's book *Personal Being* (Harré, 1983) and the perennial problem of the relationship between person and society. Jenny, working in community studies, wanted to consider applications of psychology to oppression and racism. June had a strong interest in feminist theory and a long-term interest in memory. Una brought to the group a strong expertise in motivational psychology and an interest in developing a more adequate theory of emotions.

We found ourselves constantly wanting to cross disciplinary boundaries, to juxtapose unlikely topics and ideas, to move back and forth between the theory and our own lives. In those early months we read and explored the work of Harré (1983) and Coulter (1979). We discussed Manicas and Secord's recent article on the new paradigm in social psychology (Manicas and Secord, 1983), the work of Gilligan (1982), and the collection of papers in *Changing the Subject* (Henriques et al., 1984). We grappled with Foucault (White, 1979).

Not long after we began to meet, Frigga Haug came to Macquarie University as a visiting scholar. She is a socialist feminist who trained as a psychologist but moved into sociology. June, Una and Sue attended most of her seminars and responded with a growing sense of excitement, unease, enthusiasm and laughter. Frigga Haug's work both challenges and liberates, partly because it is genuinely – indeed startlingly – interdisciplinary and integrated. Her ideas transcend traditional boundaries and distinctions, for example, those between psychology and sociology, Marxism and feminism, teaching and research, theory and practice, subject and object. She insists that experience itself is a resource; that it can and indeed should be acknowledged as the basis of theory and research.

The methodology was particularly intriguing – it was empirical but not empiricist. There was real revelation for some of us in confronting a feminist theory that was more than a critical analysis of existing society, one that incorporates its own method for empirical research.

Her method, memory-work, allows the investigation of processes which involve the social construction of selves, and is not individualistic. Working at the interface between the individual and society, looking at ways in which individuals construct themselves, involves doing research in an area which both sociology and psychology might claim, but for which neither provides fully adequate tools. Memory-work has elements which derive from both. In one sense, memory-work is an off-shoot of consciousness-raising: women working together to understand their own experience. Memory-work provides a way in which to set down, to formalize and theorize our experience. The method not only questions the production of knowledge within the phallocentric framework but also provides an alternative mode. With this alternative mode, women are able to acknowledge their powerlessness as individuals but recognize their own strength as a collective.

June, Sue and Una introduced Frigga's work to the rest of us and suggested that we might like to try some memory-work ourselves. We needed little persuasion. The method in particular appealed to us. We liked the feminist political orientation. We liked the collective way of working. We were intrigued by the collapse of subject and object, by theory and method, by the idea of becoming our own subjects. We had a sense of taking a huge step, of working against the rules of empiricist method, of defying the imperatives of our training. But we also had a sense of potential, of being able to treat ourselves as whole people, of being relevant. Could we also remain rigorous?

But what memory-work should we do? Frigga herself had applied memory-work to the issue of female sexualization (Haug, 1987). In this work, she and her research collective discuss the ways in which they, as women, construct their own sexuality; the ways in which they grew into their female bodies. We were interested in a developmental focus, in tracing the social construction of ourselves as women. We sought a topic which would enable us to do this.

Una suggested emotion. For years she had explored and taught in the area of motivation. She had a particular interest in emotions, but thought that traditional academic psychology had never adequately come to grips with the topic. She had never been convinced by the various attempts to derive a taxonomy of emotions or to establish some as primary and others as secondary. She felt that she had never been able to resolve satisfactorily the motivational status of emotion. The rest of us agreed with her concerns; it made little sense to us to think of children entering life with a set of emotional givens. The topic appealed to us as feminists too. After all, as women we are supposed to understand emotions. And we are constantly told that women are 'too emotional' – whatever that means. Yet the literature on emotions does not seem to connect with our own lived experience. We began, then, by questioning conventional psychological knowledge.

We spent the next four years researching emotions. This book is the outcome of that process – an illustration of the process of collective knowledge construction. As part of that process we talked and argued – we reminisced about our own lives and those of our friends. We argued about agency, autonomy, repression, psycho-analysis, semiotics, intersubjectivity, feeling, the body and, of course, the various emotions. We re-read some of the accepted theories of emotion and tried to identify our dissatisfaction with them (see chapter 2). We thoroughly explored and extended social constructionism in relation to emotion (see chapters 2, 7 and 9). We examined some of the developmental literature, and explored the relationship between morality and emotion. We looked at what psychologists had said about emotions, but we also read anthropo-logical and sociological accounts of emotion and turned, too, to the philosophers. As well as those writers referred to above, we drew on the work of Arnold (1960, 1969, 1970), Averill (1985, 1986), Bedford (1962), Bruner (1986), Harré (1983, 1986), Levy (1984), Lyons (1980), Peters (1970), Ryle (1963) and Shotter (1984, 1986).

We encouraged our friends and students to set up memory-work groups to explore their own emotions; we applied for grants and set up memory-work groups to explore sexuality in the context of AIDS. We set up memory-work groups amongst men so that they could explore emotions similar to the ones we ourselves had researched. But most importantly we became our own subjects. We wrote our own memories of remembered childhood events, or sometimes of events experienced as adults. These memories became the raw data for our collective theorizing, a process that continued for many months. Finally we felt ready to pull together some of that data and the theorizing into some kind of coherent structure – that which is offered in this book.

Our Memories: an Introductory Sample

Here is a sample of some of the memories we produced. We present them as stories of five young girls – Margaret, Ann, Marie, Liz and

Fay – who grew up to be Una, June, Sue, Jenny and Pam. We have used pseudonyms in our recounting of the memories, and we have rotated these from time to time. Not only does this give us and our colleagues some anonymity but, perhaps more importantly, it helps resist the temptation to write biography. We offer a few of the actual memories at this point to give something of the flavour of what we did. We leave the detailed presentation of data and discussion of method and results to later chapters.

We began by exploring our early childhood memories relating to wrongdoing. The trigger for the first memory was 'saying sorry'. We expected to find accounts of shame and guilt and were surprised that they did not emerge. So we tried the trigger 'transgressions'. Here is one of the memories produced at that time:

> Margaret was 5 years old and in kindergarten at school. She didn't like it and didn't like her teacher, a woman, who used to make the class do silly things like tear paper into thin strips without breaking them. Margaret's always broke. Her teacher one day was cross about the children sucking 'cherries' out of burst balloons. Margaret remembers the crossness and the class being told that they must not suck cherries because if the cherries burst in their mouths the balloon piece might stick in their throats and they might die. Margaret did not really believe this and she did not quite know what dying was. She went home that afternoon . . . she cut up a balloon and ate some of it . . . she didn't die . . . she felt her attitude to the teacher was vindicated. She also felt somehow that what she was doing was wrong; she closed the bedroom door. Her bedroom which she shared with her younger sister was at the end of the corridor beyond the kitchen at the end of the flat. It always seemed to Margaret that it was a long way from where everything happened. Margaret didn't get into trouble. No one knew what she had done.

After analysing these transgression memories we decided we needed a change of mood. This time we decided to use an emotional label as the trigger to see what difference that would make to the type of memory produced. We chose an early childhood memory of 'happiness'.

> Ann was about 4 and went shopping on Friday evening with her Mother and Dad. Her Dad was carrying her piggy back on his shoulders. She had a sudden and very intense feeling of love and joy – a fullness about being there with her father. This was quickly followed by feeling sorry for her mother because she loved her father more than her mother. No words were spoken.

In the following months we experimented with different kinds of approaches. We looked at 'anger' as another direct but contrasting emotion. We looked at 'praise' as a contrast to 'transgression'. We looked at 'play' to see if that situational trigger would produce reports of 'happiness'. While exploring culturally different occasions of pleasure, we decided to look at 'holidays'. This time for a change we decided to produce adult memories and childhood memories as well. Here is one of those adult memories. Most of the adult memories like this one tend to be much longer than childhood memories, and full of clichés:

It is January . . . Liz is about 26. She is working at a children's hospital . . . Her mother has had two long spells in hospital for eye operations for glaucoma. She is debilitated, run down, and Liz takes a week of her annual leave to take her to the seaside. Most mornings they take the bus to North Beach. Liz surfs and her mother sits on a bench under a tree. She can see well enough to make big stitches and embroiders two cushion covers in coarse cotton while they are there – occupational therapy, sort of. Some days for a change they take bus trips to places further afield.

On the occasion of this episode they have been to North Beach in the morning and are at lunch in the hotel dining room. Cold cuts and salad – that sort of thing. The dining room almost deserted – a few other couples and solitary people at other tables.

Suddenly a party of four enters and goes to a table – quite a fuss in the quiet room. A young man and a young woman and two older women. They are quite formally dressed, not holiday clothes, the young man in a suit or jacket and trousers, shirt and tie. He sees his women folk seated but has looked across and seen Liz and comes to her table where she is with her mother, before he sits down. He seems delighted to see her. 'Why Liz, what a surprise meeting you here! Are you having a holiday?'

Liz is rather taken aback, being 'accosted' by this stranger. But she feels she has to be civil. 'Yes, just for a week. This is my mother, Mrs — by the way . . .' (She can't introduce him, she doesn't know his name). He doesn't supply it, so she tries to keep the conversation going, as politeness seems to demand. 'Are you staying here too?' 'No, we're just on a day trip, driving further down the coast, and thought we'd stop here for lunch.'

They exchange a few more remarks – the weather, the beach. Liz keeps it general, to cover up her complete ignorance of the context in which they are supposed to know one another. She sees his people casting glances in their direction. He has behaved rather badly, and 'left them in the lurch'. She has the feeling that he is 'over reacting' and drawing undue attention to them both. She decides to draw it to a close, dismiss him. 'Well, I hope you enjoy the rest of your trip.' He takes the hint. 'Thanks. Enjoy your stay. Good-bye' (to her mother). He goes back to his own table. Her mother is intrigued. 'Who is that? He seems to know you well?'

'I haven't a clue. As far as I can tell, I've never seen him before in my life. He must be a student I've taught. One of the ex-service lot. There were hundreds of them.' She is less dismayed now, more amused, and relieved that in this minor social contretemps she has managed to 'keep her end up'. When she and her mother leave the dining room, he sketches a good-bye wave from his seat at the table with the others. To this day, she has no idea who they were.

During this period we started to get some memories from other women's groups, and from the men's groups. The topics did not always overlap, but some of them did, and we became increasingly intrigued at what looked like gender differences. One of the men's groups had decided to produce memories of 'fear' and 'danger', and we decided to follow suit, again to see if any obvious differences emerged. These were among the last memories we produced. Here is one of our danger memories:

> They sit at the dinner table – Ann, her mother, her aunt, her brother, her father. The room is dim, yellow light bulb or late summer evening without the light on. There is lots of dark wood – floor, table, picture rail. Any talking is in low voices – requests for salt and bread. Her mother and aunt exchange glances but few words. Her brother is in trouble. He will be punished by her father in the bathroom at the end of dinner. Ann knows she must be very careful and quiet. It is hard to eat. She feels sick, her stomach tight, her face hot. Ann and her mother and her aunt hear the bathroom door close. They try not to hear the crack of the leather razor strop and Graham's cries.

These memories that we and others produced illustrate and raise a number of issues which we focused on over the years, and which set the agenda for this book. Each will be discussed in detail later; here we simply indicate what they are.

We are working with memories and not events. We assume that each memory refers to some real event in time. But the memory is a construction of that event, a construction that changes with reflection, and over time. It is the construction that we are interested in, not the event, because the construction tells us something about the way the person relates to the social. Furthermore, we assume that we continually reconstruct our memories as we find new or different or more satisfying meanings according to our later life experiences and the changing social order in which we live. We retrospectively shed new light on old events; we reinterpret old events from new knowledge. We note for example the effect of the women's movement on our changing consciousness of childhood events. We assume that this process of memory reconstruction continues throughout our lifetime.

Emotions do not appear to be bounded things. A single episode is likely to evoke not a single emotion but many different emotions. Nor is any single emotion likely to be triggered by a particular type of situation; much appears to depend on the social context and the meaning the episode has for the individual. There is clearly no one-to-one relationship between situation and type of emotion. Indeed emotion may be more accurately described as a process not a state.

What appears paramount in our memories is a search for meaning, an active attempt by us to make sense of our experience. Our emotions are not simply automatic responses to a situation, or simple biological states of being. Certainly biological correlates play a part; the body is clearly present and important. And certainly there is an intensity of remembered feeling. But in almost all our memories, whatever the trigger or the emotion, there is an active attempt to understand and explain. We are constructing a meaning of events and of our own response; we are searching for intelligibility.

Some memories appear to be more accessible than others. We may conjecture that we tend to retain as memories those episodes which were problematic at the time. We retain them to ponder them, to reflect on them. Our memories are often of occasions where the responses of others were not congruent with our expectations. There is some contradiction in the event. It is in our attempts to resolve these contradictions, to wrest meaning from the incongruities, that we construct our emotion.

Some memories have more detail than others and their meaning is relatively clear. At least the manifest meaning is clear. Other memories are retained dimly and in a somewhat sketchy form. These are usually the ones comprised mainly of imagery rather than narrative. The narrative memories have more detail, and deal with more complex material. All the memories seem to contain both manifest and latent meaning. The latent material creates a potential problem that we must address (see chapter 9). Are some events in our lives so problematic that we have repressed them so that they are not accessible at all? Can these be retrieved at some later point? What are the implications of this repression for the construction of emotions? What are the implications for our method?

Much of the material in our memories, however, is easily accessible. Here we find the social, the taken-for-granted of everyday life. This material, and particularly the emotional descriptions within it, appears to reflect our childhood struggle with the social order, even as we accept the social definition of our responses. So while the memories are about us as individuals, they also say much about the social order in which we constitute ourselves. This is particularly so when the language we choose is the clichéd language of the mundane. This language provides insights into the moral order of our social world; by deconstructing the language of clichés we may get at some of the underlying unquestioned assumptions of that moral order.

Emotion, as we demonstrate, is constituted in the intersubjective: it is constructed in interaction between people and in our self reflection. When we reach an understanding of common social meanings of events, we are able to use this knowledge to understand others' experience. It is these common, socially derived definitions of emotions that make communication possible. It is this same intersubjectivity that is reflected in the collective process of the memory-work group. The meaning that emerges out of the group theorizing is itself constructed out of our own intersubjectivity – the 'we-ness' of the collective analysis.

In our memories we seem to adopt two quite different ways of resolving the conflict or contradiction, and these two different ways reflect two images of the self. On the one hand, we seem to acquiesce, to take on the social definition of the event or of our actions. On the other hand we resist. Sometimes we actively question, argue, reflect, explore, defy and create our own meanings against the social definitions. There is a dialogue between Mead's 'me' and 'I' (Mead, 1934). We thus construct ourselves and our emotions out of the raw materials of our particular experiences which occur at particular historical times and in particular social contexts and places. In so constructing ourselves, we sometimes acquiesce and take on the social meanings, and sometimes we resist and transform these meanings.

We have been particularly interested in relating our memories to our experience as women. We think we observe in our memories the ways in which we cooperate in the reproduction of our oppression as women. But also, and simultaneously, our memories show the ways in which we resist the process of subordination. We see here a potential for ways of transforming our responses individually and collectively.

Writing the Book

On some occasions, at one of the meetings of our collective, a first draft for a chapter was taken down by a scribe, listening and participating as we talked. Other first drafts of chapters were transcriptions from tapes of our discussions. Others might be prepared by two or three members of the collective, then submitted as multiple copies of a draft to the group. Further discussion and revision in the group meetings would ensue. Individual tendencies to be terse, prolix, didactic, flippant, or oracular were smoothed out in our aim to achieve a common style. We aimed at a style that is accessible to readers who are not psychologists, but which neverthe-less retains the ideas and presents accurately the argument that we developed.

Usually, any individual scribe was not asked to attempt more than one revision of a joint preliminary draft. If further work proved to be necessary, others continued the task, in order to avoid staleness and frustration and to free the original scribe for other necessary work (we were all still heavily engaged in other duties – various sorts of academic and administrative work, to say nothing of commitment to families).

Finally, completed chapters, then the book as a whole, were read in plenary meetings. Coming to this final stage after intervals for sundry visits overseas, attendances at other seminars, conferences and meetings, as well as the performance of the more ordinary duties mentioned above, a commonality, we found a 'flow' in our writing which we own for ourselves, together.

At some point during this procedure the name for our collective was born: it is the only inclusive pronounceable acronym that we can build from the initial letters of our first names. SPUJJ is Sue, Pam, Una, June and Jenny. Somewhat to the mystification of family, friends and colleagues, SPUJJ became a person about the place.

We now present our work as a whole. In chapter 1, Introduction, we have so far described the origins of our project and accounted for the choice of our topic, 'emotion', and our method, 'memory-work'. In this chapter, some samples of our memory-work show how various 'seeding' topics or 'triggers' suggested themselves, and how we extended and theorized the work.

In chapter 2, Understanding Emotion, we consider both everyday understandings of the term and the definitions given in some psychological approaches. After commenting briefly on three memories written in response to the cue 'being praised', we lead discussion finally to the social constructionist view. Social constructionism is the position which we took as our own major theoretical framework for the consideration of 'gendered' emotion. The social constructionist view of emotion incorporates many popular ideas about emotion but goes well beyond them.

In chapter 3, Memory-Work: Theory and Method, we outline the background for our choice of memory-work for the analysis of texts about our experiences of emotion. We state the phases (at least three) that we discovered underlying the process of doing memory-work. Reflection and intersubjectivity are seen to be central to memory-work, which is thus well suited to exploration and development in a feminist context.

Chapters 4, 5 and 6 introduce the beginnings of our research. Chapter 4, Saying Sorry and Being Sorry, introduces a variety of data. We chided each other in early meetings for being too apologetic, 'saying sorry' to each other. This seemed an appropriate beginning point from which feminists might begin an analysis of emotion, and a pool of written memories was assembled. Examples of our discussion and analysis are included. The extension of the research to episodes of 'transgression' and to some memories of childhood obtained from other groups (younger women and young men) was arranged, and some implications for the beginnings of theorizing about gender are indicated here.

In chapter 5, Happiness, we used a named emotion as trigger. As well as our own memories, we make reference to memories of others – the memory-work groups of younger women and young men, as well as other student memory-work groups. We find, generally, that happiness is constructed in positive self definition.

In chapter 6, which explores memories of Fear and Danger, we examine the emotion that has formerly, probably, been regarded as the prototype of emotion. Our sources were four memory-work groups – those previously referred to as well as a group of women who constituted themselves specifically to examine fear. The other groups examined both fear and danger, or just the less specific trigger, 'danger'. Our analysis again suggests that emotion, perhaps especially the emotion of fear, is gendered.

In chapter 7, Emotions and Agency: The Construction of Self, there is a return to theory. The data from previous chapters is reviewed in relation to the notion of social construction of self, bearing with it the implication of morality, although in our analysis the latter is not to be viewed as merely a normative process of socialization. People 'grow into' their emotions. In their appraisals of the situations in which they find themselves, they appropriate the cultural rules and norms, but not in a passive way. Our memories contain the conditions for further self development as agents. We reflect on our emotional experience in order to resolve contradictions and to produce intelligibility, as identity is constructed.

In chapter 8, Holidays: Emotions in Childhood and Adulthood Compared, we hoped that by looking at what was different in our lives (holidays) we would see more clearly what was ordinary, the taken-for-granted. For the first time in our work, adult memories were contrasted with childhood memories, in order to explore elaboration and acculturation of memory. As well, we could inquire whether the problematics of holidays found in the adult memories extended from childhood or were different. We found that for us, as little girls, there were similarities; the problematics of holidays could begin early, but for adults there could be many overlays, for example, of cliché and self justification. For this chapter we also sought and obtained memories of holidays in childhood from the young men's memory-work group. These provided interesting contrast for our further collective theorizing of emotion and gender.

Chapter 9, Remembering and Forgetting, addresses the question of the selectivity of memory itself, and related questions concerning accuracy, veracity and reality of memories. We consider the selectivity involved in the construction through memory of the problematic, and three kinds of forgetting are identified – automatic (of the mundane), motivated suppression and repression. Considering them against the theories of Darwin and Freud, we conclude that the memories we produce in our memory-work represent a biased selection. They are biased because selected from the problematic, the 'unfinished business' of experience. In the detailed examination of one memory involving both suppression and repression we saw that intelligibility in terms of a defined social context or 'trigger' can become available as required. It may, then, be quite possible to retrieve, reflect upon and reinterpret material long forgotten, at any stage of our lives. The relationship between the two (or perhaps more) versions of the self that are represented at earlier and later times is revealed in the way the material is constructed at these times.

In our last substantive chapter from our memory-work research (chapter 10, Anger), examples of a specific named emotion are gathered and considered together. The connections between anger and aggression and/or violence, anger and crying, anger and victimization are canvassed. Anger and hurt, anger and suppression, anger and injustice are features of our analysis. We believe that the experience of anger in women and girls is very likely to be different from that of men, despite some studies which find little evidence for gender differences in self-reported anger. But we agree that the gendered nature of anger is complex and is not wholly accounted for by power relationships alone.

Our final chapter (chapter 11, The Gendering of Emotion) draws together from preceding chapters threads of argument central to the stated aim of our book, conveyed in the title *Emotion and Gender*. The construction of gender differences in all the emotions previously treated is examined, particularly in relation to several central themes. Among these, responsibility, autonomy and agency are at the core. Others that emerge are competence, power, identity and the moral self, and the testing of boundaries. As remarked in referring to anger above, the relationship of gender and power is not a simple one and this is taken up here. The significance of new paradigms, such as the methodology adopted here, for the development of psychological theory and feminist theory is raised anew. Are feminists able to continue to work within conventional as well as new-paradigm methodologies, and would they wish to do so? The way forward is seen through the collective understanding opened to women by the collective method of memory-work. Such an approach allows us to evaluate our understanding in the inter-subjective realm, to explore resonances with the experience of other women. Working collectively with other women in finding alternative women-centred ways of doing psychology and engaging in political action at every level of social life, we are powerful.

2
Understanding Emotion

In our work on emotion, we consider both everyday commonsense understandings of the term and the definitions in psychological approaches. Although dissatisfied with traditional psychological theories of emotion, we recognize that our own understandings have been influenced by psychology, both because of our training as psychologists and because psychological theory has influenced common understandings and has been influenced by them. The definition of emotion in the *Macquarie Dictionary* (Macquarie Library, 1981) demonstrates this:

> 1. an affective state of consciousness in which joy, sorrow, fear, hate, or the like, is experienced (distinguished from cognitive and volitional states of consciousness). 2. any of the feelings of joy, sorrow, fear, hate, love, etc. 3. a state of agitation of the feelings actuated by experiencing fear, joy, etc.

This can be compared with the classic psychological definition of Woodworth (1922/42) 'a stirred-up state of the organism' (p. 410). There is conceptual richness in some psychological theories of emotion, but there is also conceptual confusion. Sometimes emotion is deemed to include, for example, mood, affect, affective state, sensation, feeling, sentiment, interest and temperament, and sometimes emotion is distinguished from some or all of these. As will become evident, we view emotion as something that comes and goes. It is not a mood or state, rather it is a process. Although it is an affective process, it is not to be equated with affect.

In this chapter, we present a brief consideration of some of the important issues in the area of emotion which have remained influential on ideas about emotion. We examine first some of the psychological approaches which feed into popular ideas about emotion. Next, we look at psychological theories which seem particularly important for our work, and finally we present the social constructionist view which we took as our major theoretical framework. The social constructionist view of emotion incorporates many of the popular ideas, but goes well beyond them.

The discussion of emotion in this chapter represents to some extent the reason why we undertook to study emotion. The theory and empirical research in psychology seemed conceptually confused and very limited. The social constructionist view was appealing but insufficiently worked through. In chapter 7 we will present a new theoretical analysis of emotion which is grounded in the data which we report in part in chapters 4, 5 and 6.

Early Theories

At the end of the nineteenth century, there were rich theoretical contributions to the conceptualization of emotion by thinkers such as Wundt, Stout, McDougall, James and Mead. James (1890/1922) stressed the bodily aspects of emotion, although he did not ignore cognitive or perceptual aspects. McDougall (1908) described emotion as the expression of an instinctual response or inner striving. Others, including Mead (1934), argued that while gestures do reveal emotion, this does not mean that their entire function consists in giving expression to emotions. In his elaboration of Wundt's (1921/ 1973) analysis, emotion was said to be both expression and communication.

The ideas of emotion as expressive of some instinct, as bodily response, as a signal or gesture to others, as built on perception and cognition, are important to our use and understanding of the concept. So too are memory, reflection and evaluation.

Emotion as Irrational

The first issue we consider is also one of the oldest, namely the opposition between emotion and reason, the view of emotion as 'passion'. This view originated in philosophy and theology, as Solomon (1983) points out:

> Since the earliest of Western thinking, the meaning of human existence has been sought in the calm reflections of rationality . . . The passions, on the other hand, have always been treated as dangerous and disruptive forces, interrupting the clarity of reasoning and leading us astray. (p. 9)

Solomon also tells us 'in Aristotle, the passions were allowed their place, but always subservient to reason'. In most of Christianity the passions in general were denied even a subservient place – distractors from belief – though selectively admitted in emaciated form as faith and love.

For early 'faculty psychology', the legacy of religion-based philosophy, experience was regarded as a function or activity of the soul, where the soul included mind and 'reason'. Reason was the only part of the soul that was under our control. Passion, being that part of the soul inherited from the animals, was viewed as an 'inferior' faculty that must be mastered. Solomon pointed out that in the

Romantic movement of the late eighteenth and early nineteenth centuries there was a reaction against the hyperrationalism of the Enlightenment and the mechanical conception of the universe in the 'Newtonian revolution'. But even the Romantics could not disagree with the underlying assumption of rationalism – that reason and passions are firmly opposed.

The opposition of reason and passion or emotion is paralleled by the opposition of male and female. Men are seen as rational and women as emotional, lacking rationality. Genevieve Lloyd (1984) traced this opposition in Western thought:

> From the beginnings of philosophical thought, femaleness was symbolically associated with what Reason supposedly left behind – the dark powers of the earth goddesses, immersion in unknown forces associated with mysterious female powers. (p. 2)

Maleness is associated with order not disorder, with the mind not the body, with knowledge and the subjugation of nature.

The polarization of rationality and feeling that has been characteristic of Western rationalist thought has pervaded and limited psychological theorizing. After Descartes, 'mind' was the theoretical object of Western philosophy, which treated it as the 'unitary rational subject' (Venn, 1984). This unitary rational *subject* became also the theoretical *object of science* and, in particular, the object of psychology (Hollway, 1989). Hollway goes on to point out that:

> Experimental psychology has been interested in aspects of *mind* (perception, cognition, attention, memory, learning, meaning) but has sought to deal with them scientifically. In the early laboratories of Wundt and Titchener, introspection was adopted as a method, or tool. (p. 122)

The emphasis of psychology on the objective scientific approach, together with the view that rationality and emotionality were in opposition and could not co-exist, created a problem for psychologists.

Psychologists after Watson excluded notions of agency and introspection became discredited. As Hollway (1989) noted, 'the "subject" of behaviourist experiment became the object, passive, lacking choice, reason or insight'. The body ousted the mind as the focus of psychological study. It was to the body that psychologists turned when they came to explore emotion. Emotions were treated as physiological responses of the body over which humans have little if any control or mastery. The view of emotion as an individually experienced bodily perturbation was confirmed.

Now, although the mind has been revived in psychology, at least in the guise of 'cognition', emotion is still viewed by most psychologists as irrational and essentially of the body.

Emotion as Physiological

If asked to describe an emotion, people will usually refer to the bodily sensations involved, such as sweating, tension, flushing, pallor, heart pounding, weeping, desire to defecate. Some of these processes are observable by other people, other processes are observable only to the person experiencing them. In general, these processes are described by those experiencing them as uncontrollable, though some may be controllable to some extent.

Physiologists have investigated the bodily mechanisms which produce sensations relating to emotion. These include the brain and the central nervous system, the autonomic nervous system and the endocrine system. Indications of the physiological signs of emotion include changes in blood chemistry, salivary secretions, electrical changes in the skin surface through sweating, rate and depth of respiration, heart rate and electrical activity in the brain. Measures of these physiological processes are referred to as psychophysiological measures of emotion.

The influence of physiological theories of emotion on psychology gave rise to many investigations attempting to tie particular emotions to a particular pattern of physiological response. This conceptualization of emotion as a physiological process accorded well with behaviourism and with a psychology which sought to study those aspects which human beings share with lower animals. However, attempts to tie a particular emotion with a particular set of physiological responses were largely unsuccessful, though the issue did not go away, as we point out below.

One of the most influential of the physiological theories of emotion and the one that is most widely accepted in popular accounts of emotion is the Cannon–Bard 'emergency' theory (Cannon, 1927 in Strongman, 1973). Cannon argued on the basis of studies of Bard that there was no one-to-one correspondence between a particular organic or visceral response and a particular emotion. Rather, the organism was prepared for a *general* 'fight or flight' response.

Others, such as Elizabeth Duffy (1962), went further and tried to theorize emotion out of psychology. These theorists explained aspects of behaviour that had been referred to as 'emotion' in terms of a generalized theory. Duffy suggested that two concepts, 'activation' (covering all degrees of physiological arousal, however recorded) and 'direction' (the selectivity of expectations of the organism, whether learned or innate) were sufficient for the 'complete description of behaviour' (Duffy, 1962, p. 13).

Emotion as Instinct

McDougall (1908), in his linking of emotions to primary instincts, sought to differentiate among emotions on their physiological bases. Although his account fell out of favour because the quest for physiologically differentiated emotions was unsuccessful, many of his ideas have been incorporated in modern theories of emotion: for instance, his argument that some emotions are primitive but that social experience leads to a further differentiation of emotions; and his recognition of the important link between emotion and motivation.

McDougall sought to develop an evolutionary 'instinct' theory like that of Darwin which would explain modern social organization. All human social behaviour would be accounted for by the modification of a limited number of innate impulses. This would be achieved in the course of social experience. Social experience, including learning and symbolism would alter the innate initiating sensations and would also extend the individual's repertoire of response. As primary instincts McDougall listed flight, repulsion, curiosity, pugnacity, self-abasement, self-assertion and parental instinct. The perceptual and motor (striving) aspects of these instincts were modifiable, but at the core of each a characteristic emotion – fear, disgust, awe, anger, positive and negative self feeling, and love, corresponding to the instincts listed – provided the impetus for striving.

Izard's (1977) theory of emotion has strong ties with McDougall via Darwin. Here, however, emotional differentiation is tied to differential expression of emotion. Darwin (1872), in his evolutionary theory as it applied to the emotions of animals and man, sought by careful observation and research to stress the utility for survival of much animal emotional response. He examined vestigial signs of this adaptiveness in the emotional behaviour of higher animals and humans. For example, the hostile canine bares its teeth for menace and attack; the person curls the lip in a sneer that also exposes the teeth. A smile is the antithesis of a readiness to attack, and expresses the contrary emotion. But Darwin found in humans other expressions of emotion not easily referrable to present or past patterns of adaptation for survival. He concluded that these must be associated with a general excitedness of the nervous system when the person is reacting emotionally.

Following Darwin, the importance of facial expression as one of the integral components of emotion was stressed by Izard (1977) in his influential theory of differential emotions. He hypothesized that during the course of evolution facial expression developed into a system of social communication of information about internal states. The facial expressions of the fundamental emotions were genetically programmed and were species-common behaviour patterns which showed some continuity from animals to man. Under ordinary conditions, facial expression and/or tension in the appropriate facial muscles were said to lead to experience of emotion.

Although this description of Izard's theory suggests that it stresses the importance of the fact that emotion is built from and contributes to social processes, the theory is itself resolutely physiological:

> The cortical integration of facial feedback produces the specific emotional experience. In short the face provides the data for the activation of qualitatively distinct emotions, but it may be less critical in sustaining emotions. The activity of the striate muscles of the body and the smooth muscles of the viscera amplify and sustain emotion and tell us something about its intensity. (1977, p. 60)

Izard proposed ten discrete emotions as distinct experiential/motivational processes. They were interest-excitement, joy, surprise-startle, distress-anguish, anger, disgust, contempt-scorn, fear, shame-shyness and guilt. This classification is one of many that have been proposed, and moreover much investigation of the dimensional structure of emotions has been carried out before and since Izard's attempt, for example, Wundt (1911), Woodworth (1938), Schlosberg (1941), Davitz (1969).

Cognitive Aspects in Organismic Theories of Emotion

Theories that are also classified as physiological theories of emotion include the very early James–Lange theory, proposed at about the same time by William James (in 1884) and Carl Lange (in 1885). This theory is still influential in psychological thinking, although some aspects of it are not immediately obvious. The version proposed by the physiologist Lange is truly physiological, but James recognized the central importance of perception and appraisal of the event which initiates the emotion. His theory may be viewed as an antecedent of modern re-evaluations of emotion, including both its cognitive and social components.

> My theory is that the bodily changes follow directly the perception of the exciting fact, and that our feeling of the same changes as they occur *is* the emotion. (James, 1890/1922, p. 100)

Although emotion for James *is* the sensation of organic changes, emotion is produced via the 'perception of the exciting fact'. Further, in his writings on emotion there is an acknowledgement that emotions are more than visceral or bodily responses. This is evident in his recognition that there is no set of 'natural' emotions, and in his acknowledgement of the possible role of learning and cultural context (though he does not phrase it in these terms) in how bodily sensations may be classified. It is also evident in his avowal that 'such a question as "what is the real or typical expression of anger or fear?" is seen to have no objective meaning at all' (James, 1890/1922, p. 104).

James was interested in the question of whether emotion could be experienced when enacted professionally on the stage. From anecdotal surveys he concluded that the visceral and organic part of the expression could be suppressed by some, but that others were overcome by the emotion of the part when they were playing it well. He also thought that a final test of his theory would be to study persons who through injury or other cause would be unable to register any bodily sensation. Such cases, he predicted, would be unable to experience any 'real' emotion. Thus although James did not limit the experience of emotion to bodily sensations he did regard such sensations as the *sine qua non* of emotion.

The cognitive component of emotion is not generally part of popular or commonsense views of emotion. However, it is not usually difficult to persuade people of the need to take it into account. The notion of appraisal of the situation before or concurrently with the experience of the emotion accords with everyday experience, and does not seem inconsistent with the irrational or passionate character of the experience or action that may follow.

Other theorists who stressed the cognitive aspects of emotion were Schachter and Singer (1962, see also Arnold below). They accepted Cannon's view that emotions could not be identified on the basis of physiological responses, and they added 'interpretation' to the concept of activation to develop their theory of emotion. Their theory is essentially a 'labelling' theory. It holds that emotion does not occur without physiological arousal but in the presence of physiological arousal we seek to interpret the arousal and identify the emotion from the situation in which the arousal occurs. Arnold summarized Schachter's work as follows:

the artificial production of physiological changes ordinarily occurring in fear will not necessarily produce this emotion. Since this emotion depends on appraisal, the actual emotional reaction will depend on the way in which the situation is evaluated, and the artificially produced physiological changes (e.g. by an adrenaline injection) will form part of the total situation. Hence the findings reported by Schachter (1970) can be explained easily: a subject will act the fool if he appraises the situation as ridiculous *and* is in an aroused physiological state: he will be aggressive if he finds the situation aggravating *and* is aroused physiologically. In contrast, if he is informed that the physiological state is the effect of the drug injection, he will discount his organic sensations and remain unmoved. (Arnold, 1970, p. 184)

The work of Schachter explained how emotions could be differentiated from one another without recourse to identity theory claiming a one-to-one correspondence between physiological responses and emotions.

Frijda (1986) summarized these efforts to differentiate emotions as follows:

> studies that did compare different emotions tended to demonstrate different patterns in these different emotions; a few such responses were found consistently. The evidence distinctly contradicts Cannon. It does not necessarily support James–Lange . . . judging from the available evidence different emotions tend to differ in their physiological response patterns; they do not differ, however, to such a degree and consistency that the response patterns could serve to define or identify the respective emotions; nor are the patterns always there when the given emotions can be assumed to be there or are felt by the subject. (1986, p. 162)

A recent cognitive account of differential emotion is that put forward by Oatley and Johnson-Laird (1987). They proposed five basic emotions: happiness, sadness, anger, fear and disgust which may be accompanied by specific patterns of reaction, as proposed in Izard's earlier (1977) theory. They also proposed that all the various emotions are based on a few distinctive mental states, accompanied with some bodily perturbation, that go with readiness for action. Each is set off when an event is evaluated in relation to the person's goals, especially when they are frustrated, delayed or threatened in some way.

> They [emotions] arise when something unexpected happens, a situation to which we are not fully adapted, an event at which two different concerns clash, or when someone else does something more or less than we expected. (Oatley, 1989, p. 20)

Oatley goes on to point out that 'because some events are both important and unanticipated, we might want to reprogram ourselves in the light of whatever new knowledge we have acquired as a result of these events' (p. 20). Hence, reflection is involved in the construction and/or modification of emotion, although Oatley's view

view is that it is 'involuntary . . . reverberation'. Their theory, which the authors designate as a cognitive, conflict theory of emotion, is very reminiscent of McDougall's theory.

All the above are organismic theories. They are essentially biological. The organismic model defines emotion as mainly a biological process. For Darwin, and we would add McDougall and Izard, it is instinct; for James, and we would add Schachter, it is the perception of a physiological process; and for early Freud (whom we have not yet mentioned) it is libidinal discharge. In these organismic theories, the emotion is assumed to have priority, to exist or come into being without reflection. The manner in which one labels, assesses, or manages an emotion is seen as ancillary or extrinsic to it.

Emotion and Appraisal

There is, however, another psychologist who addressed the cognitive aspects of emotion in a somewhat different way. Physiological responses were not denied, but Magda Arnold (1960, 1970) saw them as ancillary to emotion. Arnold is credited with being one of the most influential theorists to emphasize the cognitive nature of emotion. She believed that emotion has two components:

> one static, the appraisal, which is a mere acceptance or refusal of the expected effect of the situation on us; another dynamic, the impulse toward what is appraised as good, and away from anything appraised as bad. (Arnold, 1970, p. 176)

Thus, Arnold linked emotion to motive, something to which we shall return in chapter 7.

Of primary interest here are the cognitive aspects of Arnold's theory – appraisal and memory. Appraisal is essential to the production of emotion: 'a psychological interpretation of the situation is necessary' (1970, p. 172). This aspect of Arnold's theory, that is, the link between appraisal, memory and emotion, is of particular relevance to our work.

Arnold's theory of emotion is as follows: she began by ascribing emotional behaviour, including physiological changes, to an introductory shock that is succeeded by a more or less rapid interpretation of its cause. The physiological and psychological shock together with the interpretation produce the emotion and determine the appropriate action. The interpretation is a *cognitive* act because 'only a few stimuli, for instance, a sudden loud noise, an electric shock, etc., can directly produce extensive physiological changes'

(1970, p. 173). What is needed is an association between the shock and its cause (the stimulus), and such association, Arnold argued, depends upon memory.

> In interpreting a situation, we do not merely know it as here and now, for instance when we are still at a safe distance from some danger; nor do we ascribe a vague cognitive 'meaning' to it. We *remember* what has happened to us in the past, how this thing has affected us and what we did about it. Then we *imagine* how it will affect us this time and *estimate* whether it will be harmful. (1970, p. 174)

In Arnold's conceptualization, the evaluation or estimate may involve deliberate reflection, but need not. Arnold believed that even where there is a deliberate appraisal, there is also an immediate intuitive estimate or evaluation which inevitably produces an impulse to action. It is important to note, however, that although this 'immediate intuitive appraisal' is not instinctive or hard-wired, it is non-deliberate and automatic. Both sorts of appraisal are cognitive; intuitive appraisal is, she argued, greatly influenced and on occasion determined by affective memory; deliberate appraisal involves reflection.

For Arnold, emotion is born of a personal reaction within a matrix of experience. The following example may elucidate her account. A child is bitten by a dog. It is a painful experience and is remembered. What is remembered is not only the pain but the context in which the pain occurred. The child's affective memory of the episode, the reliving of the original situation, hardens over time into an attitude of acceptance and approach or rejection and avoidance. This influences and may determine the immediate intuitive appraisal the child makes of her future meetings with dogs.

> Since affective memory is a reliving of the original acceptance or rejection in a new though similar situation, the resulting feeling carries no date line so that we are completely unaware that our here-and-now appraisal is really a prejudgment (literally, a prejudice) dictated by affective memory . . . Indeed affective memory is ubiquitous yet intensely personal because it is a living record of the emotional life history of each person. (pp. 176–7)

In the example, the child comes to *fear* dogs automatically. So although the appraisal is immediate and the emotion produced immediately, it is produced via affective memory, that is, cognition is involved. Indeed it is possible to forget the details of the original circumstances which gave rise to the emotion but one does not, however, forget the affect – the affective memory. Arnold comments that 'it seems safe to conclude that it is affective memory as such that has the effects Freud ascribed to repression' (p. 177). Repression, for example, is motivated and affect-laden. We deal with repression and other forms of forgetting in a later chapter. Arnold also allows for reappraisal and reflection. The immediate intuitive appraisal which gave rise to fear may be counterbalanced by a reappraisal that this dog is on a chain or very small. The fear may give way to relief and a willingness to remain in the presence of the dog. Or the immediate appraisal may be countered by an appraisal of a different sort which gives rise to a different desire, a desire to be brave, for example. In the latter case, the emotion is educated (Peters, 1970).

In Arnold's account the emotion which is a felt tendency, a desire, will proceed to action unless further appraisal or reflection interferes with the execution of that action. Emotion and motive are linked.

Arnold's work laid the foundation for the truly cognitive approaches to the study of emotion and, as will become evident, her conceptualization of emotion has been invaluable for our own understanding of it. Although her work is individualist in focus, it leads, via Peters (1970), towards a more social account for the study of emotion.

Psychological Theories of Emotion

Let us take stock of where we are. A modification of the four-component model of Harré et al. (1985, p. 133) provides a useful summary. The first three points made by Harré et al. are:

1 With many emotions there is a characteristic bodily agitation, though more than one emotion may be related to it.
2 Many emotions are manifested by typical behavioural, especially facial, displays. Such displays may be strongly influenced by cultural conventions and/or instinctual repertoire.
3 The cognitive activity of seeking and assigning a cause for one's perturbation is crucial in producing the emotion. Reflection and appraisal are two of the important cognitive activities involved.

These components summarize much of the work we have discussed in this chapter. We will consider Harré's fourth component later. Another way of summarizing the theorists discussed so far is as follows:

McDougall:

meet a bear ⟶ flight
                    fear

James:

meet a bear ⟶ appraise as dangerous ⟶ flight and ⟶ fear
                                          physiological
                                          arousal

Schachter:

meet a bear ⟶ general bodily ⟶ interpret
                  perturbation   the context ⟶ fear

Izard:

meet a bear who growls, menaces ⟶ flight
                                    fear

Arnold:

meet a bear ⟶ appraise as dangerous   ⟶ fear ⟶ flight
                  based on previous experience
                  (affective memory)

Some of the conceptualizations of emotion we have examined make sense, that is, are congruent with our everyday understanding. But when psychologists turn to study emotion empirically much of what makes sense in these theories is lost.

**Psychological Studies and the Argument for
'Common Sense'**

Emotion is defined in part by the way psychology has studied it. Often when psychologists write about emotion they have a well-reasoned view. However, when they study emotion empirically, they take a much more limited view. We referred earlier to physiological measures. Here we turn to survey-based studies of emotion. Studies such as those reported by Frijda (1969, 1986) have sought to define the social meaning of emotion by means of models based on cluster analysis of adjective check lists. Scherer, Wallbott and Summerfield (1986) have used questionnaire data to investigate cross-cultural patterns of emotion words and descriptions. Averill (1982) has studied anger and aggression by asking respondents to describe situations in which they have experienced the relevant emotion. As discussed below in the section on social construction-ism, Averill's work represents an approach that we find somewhat more useful than that of much of the other research referred to, particularly his work on romantic love (Averill, 1985).

Some of the ways in which psychologists have most frequently studied emotion provide examples of the discourse surrounding emotion as most psychologists have understood it. Many studies of emotion have been extremely artificial. Woodworth, Schlosberg, Davitz and others drew on the cultural designation of emotion names often without a thorough conceptual analysis. Ekman, Levenson and Friesen (1983) examined people who were attempting to act emotions, in a study reminiscent of James's survey of actors (1884). Ax (1953) and Schachter (1957) attempted to frighten and anger medical students in laboratories. Lacey and Lacey (1958, 1970) studied subjects mainly in task-oriented situations. Subjects' own reflections on their emotional states were usually not taken into account (though there were some exceptions).

Few studies within psychology have examined what is understood by emotion in commonsense terms. An exception (Davitz, 1970) was one in which people (specifically non-psychologists) were asked to write descriptions of how they felt when experiencing different emotions. At the end of the article, we find the following paragraph:

It would be presumptuous, I believe, to suggest that anything like a general theory of emotion could legitimately be derived from the kind of data discussed here. But while a careful hearing of what nonpsychologists have to say about their emotional experiences has not led us to a serious contradiction of previous work, it has resulted, at least for me, in clarifying some of the words commonly encountered in discussions of emotion and opened new lines of inquiry for further investigation. Therefore, although I do not recommend speaking to nonpsychologists outside of the university as a steady diet, an occasional conversation now and then can be refreshing. (Davitz, 1970, p. 258)

This paragraph in apologizing for itself carries a message of arrogance and timidity, though it is possibly partly ironic. What if the discussions with non-psychologists (outside of the university no less!) had led to a serious contradiction of previous work? Would the article have seen the light of day? We would rather commend the researcher for his good sense in investigating emotion experiences as they occur, and suggest that the commonsense experience of emotion is a prime source for understanding it. Davitz noted that most people are quite clear about what they mean by various emotional labels:

[I]t became clear that when most people used a phrase such as 'I am happy' or 'I am sad' they were referring to *experiences* – not to behaviors, not to situations, and certainly not to measures obtained from an electroencephalogram or a galvanometer. It was in terms of the *experience* of happiness, the *experience* of sadness, hate, or love that my informants defined the meaning of these words. (1970, pp. 251–2)

We agree with this observation, although we point out below that Bedford (1962) stated that emotion is different from experience. It is important, however, to be clear about what variety of experiences should be included within the term 'emotional' experience. It is quite clear that anger and fear are emotions, but what about depression, pain, hunger, frustration?

Empirical studies tended to take psychologists away from commonsense understandings. Conceptual analyses of emotion provided by philosophers helped us back to a more social sense. Those whom we found most useful in providing us with understanding of emotion in the way we as psychologists wished to study it were Bedford (1962), Peters (1970) (much of whose argument was informed by the psychologist Arnold), Averill (1980) and Harré et al. (1985), to whom we now turn.

The fourth component of Harré's four-part model is the most strongly social. It is:

4   The involvement of the 'local moral order', both in the differentiation of the emotions and in the prescription of particular emotions on particular occasions indicates a fourth component. (Harré et al., 1985, p. 133)

This involvement of the moral order carries the conceptualization of 'emotion' into the social realm.

Social Psychological Theories of Emotion

In his analysis of the ways in which human beings use the word 'emotion' and related concepts, Bedford (1962), a philosopher, laid the groundwork for the social constructionist view of emotion. In the analysis he distinguished a number of usages such as being angry from feeling angry and being angry from acting angrily. The more relevant of these distinctions are discussed below.

Emotion and Feeling

First we take the difference between being angry and feeling angry. Bedford (1962) argued that it is inappropriate to use the recognition of the special qualities of the (phenomenological) experience of the emotion as the criterion for identifying the emotion: 'the traditional answer to the question "how do we identify our own emotions?" namely, "By introspection", cannot be correct' (p. 113). Bedford argued that we identify our own emotions in exactly the same way as we identify emotions in others. We do this according to our knowledge of the social context. We realize that someone *is* angry, and assume (perhaps wrongly) that he or she feels angry.

The feeling associated with the emotion is not to be equated with the emotion. Emotion is more than this, although it may include the feeling. Bedford considered the difference between feeling pain and feeling angry. One way to distinguish the two is to note that a question such as 'Do I feel pain?' is meaningless in a way that 'Do I feel angry?' is not. In addition, statements such as 'He was angry but did not feel angry' is meaningful whereas 'He was in pain but did not feel pain' is not.

Emotion and Behaviour

The second distinction Bedford made was between the emotion and the expression of the emotion. He argued that the behaviour associated with the emotion is neither necessary nor sufficient to characterize the emotion. 'He raised his voice and began to thump the table' is a statement of a different kind from 'He was very angry'. The second statement goes beyond a behavioural description. It may explain behaviour, or it may be irrelevant to behaviour. What is needed in order to understand or judge the accuracy of an emotion statement is some knowledge of the social context involved. The behaviour described would be interpreted quite differently if the context was a debate or a theatrical performance or a political speech. Thus the statement about the emotion would be appropriate if the table-thumping followed on an insult, or indeed even if no observable behaviour followed.

Statements about emotion, then, are not statements about feelings nor statements about behaviour. They are statements which are judicial. To say 'he is angry' implies an understanding of the social circumstances surrounding 'his' actions. To say 'I am angry' implies the same understanding. Although knowledge of the social circumstances of oneself will be more complete than knowledge of the social circumstances of another person, the emotion statement is based on the same kind of knowledge in both cases – and in both cases may be mistaken. For example, Warner (1986) (whose analysis of anger is discussed in chapter 10) described certain emotions as involving self deception.

Emotion and Evaluation or Judgement

Bedford stated that emotion statements are always evaluative. Most involve moral judgement or moral evaluation. This is seen most clearly in the case of certain important emotions, namely guilt and shame. Evaluations other than moral evaluations are involved in other emotions, but not all evaluative statements are emotion statements. Bedford distinguished between emotion statements and other evaluative statements (such as feeling statements) by considering the appropriateness of questions about 'ought'. Thus it is perfectly appropriate if someone says 'I feel ashamed' to ask whether that person 'ought' to feel ashamed. It is less clearly appropriate but nevertheless meaningful to question whether someone 'ought' to feel angry, afraid, resentful, regretful etc.

Bedford concluded that 'emotion concepts are not purely psychological: they presuppose concepts of social relationships and institutions, and concepts belonging to systems of judgment, moral, aesthetic and legal' (Bedford, 1986, p. 30). We might argue with Bedford regarding the limited scope of 'the psychological' that this statement implies, but would agree with his analysis. The special importance of moral judgements and their relation to agency is discussed more fully in chapter 7. In general, as we noted above, Bedford's conceptual analysis sets the stage for the social constructionist view of emotion.

Social Construction of Emotion

The social constructionist approach to emotion has been put forward by Harré (1986), Coulter (1979) and Averill (1980) amongst others. A similar view is put by a sociologist, Denzin (1983). To return to the example of 'meeting a bear' which we used earlier in this chapter, the social constructionist approach is the following:

[meet a bear $\longrightarrow$ appraise as $\longrightarrow$ feeling or $\longrightarrow$ flight]
dangerous   affect

As indicated by the enclosing square brackets, the whole – situation, cognition and related behaviour – in context, IS the emotion. As Averill noted:

> An emotion is a transitory social role (a socially constituted syndrome) that includes an individual's appraisal of the situation and is interpreted as a passion rather than as an action. (1980, p. 312)

The individual who experiences the emotion fear interprets his/her meeting the bear, appraising the danger, flight and the accompanying physiological responses as fear. The emotion is a syndrome in which each and every one of these aspects, behavioural, physiological, affective, cognitive, social context . . . may play a part. The emotion is not an uncontrolled response or for that matter a cold colourless appraisal. As Denzin (1983) notes, emotion is a social, interactional, linguistic and physiological process that draws its resources from the human body, from human consciousness, and from the world that surrounds a person. Emotion must be defined and studied as a lived, interactional process.

Denzin also noted that although emotions are embodied experiences, the body does not call out its own interpretations of internal somatic states. His argument is in many ways reminiscent of that of the psychologist Arnold: 'These interpretations are given in the field of consciousness by the person, reflectively, through self-interactions' (1983, pp. 403–4).

We now present our own view of emotion as it relates to a number of aspects of social constructionism. Before doing so, three memories are offered, which were written in response to the cue 'being praised'. This situation has not been extensively analysed elsewhere in this book. The dominant emotion in most of the memories produced was embarrassment (see p. 62 n. and chapter 5). But in the memories here reported, as well as the embarrassment ('humiliation') reported in the first memory, we see indications of self-appraisal, and of the nascent emotion, pride, in a very young child and the development of appraisal, with increasing self-validation, in the older girls. It is perhaps no surprise that these three memories refer to experiences about reading and school.

Liz was in primary school, 8 going on 9 years. It was winter and she was decked out in full new school uniform – tunic, soft cotton blouse, V-necked sweater, 'Doctor' flannel blazer, brown lisle broad-ribbed stockings, shoes. Her class took sewing with the 'big' girls from High School, probably a Third Year class, there weren't many of them. The 'big' girls sat quietly at the back, getting on with their sewing, and Miss B got on with teaching the younger class about fabrics. She called Liz out to the front and started pointing to her various garments and saying 'What material is this? Is it woven or knitted? What fibre?' etc. The little girls didn't know the answers and she told them. When she got to the shoes and stockings, nobody knew. By this time she was holding Liz by the sleeve of her blazer, which she had asked about earlier. Liz started wriggling in her grasp and muttering 'I know, I know'. Miss B gave her a shake, rather affectionate, and said 'I know *you* know, that's why I picked you for this,' and all the 'big' girls giggled. Liz felt humiliated by the shake, the teacher's remark, and the giggling. She knew it wasn't going to make her popular with the class.

Fay:

She was 4 years old. She was standing in the kitchen looking at the canisters on the shelf over the stove recess. . . . The canisters were dark bluish green with gold and black, fairly ornate, lettering on them. They were far from new, stained by smoke from the stove. Her mother was cooking and her father was standing behind Fay – talking to her mother. It was early evening, before tea-time. Fay asked what was written on the canisters and her father began to teach her how to recognize the words. She distinctly remembers the word 'sugar' and knowing that somehow it was not spelled the way it was pronounced – probably that is one thing her father explained to her. As her father explained to her how to recognize the words, Fay got the message very quickly and demonstrated that she could actually read. Her father was very happy and pleased about this.

On some later occasion, Fay overheard her mother and her aunt talking about her. Her mother told her aunt that Fay was extremely clever and could read already. The aunt said 'Oh, it's just because Jim keeps pushing her.' Fay's mother replied, 'You can't push kids to do things that they aren't capable of.' Fay overheard this conversation. She realized that her mother was actually quite proud of what she could do.

Margaret (in secondary school):

When Margaret left the school . . . she was called into the head nun's office; a goodbye. She liked the head nun and felt that the nun liked her. They had a 'grown-up' talk. The thing that stuck in Margaret's mind about that talk was the discussion of Margaret's temper. The head nun had seen Margaret lose her temper on a couple of occasions and presumably had heard of other occasions from other teachers. The head nun commented on Margaret's temper and then said that it was a sign of good character but that Margaret must learn to keep it under control. Margaret was both pleased and very puzzled by this. She usually – but not always – got into trouble when she lost her temper and yet here was someone she respected telling her it was a sign of a good character. Margaret was pleased, too, because it was a validation of herself and her behaviour.

[The author of this memory added a comment, continuing to 'theorize' her memory – 'there is something here about the validation of the emotional intensity. That to feel something deeply and strongly is O.K., and this was important to me. The importance of this story may also be tied to the head nun's reserve. This person who spoke of temper and good character never showed any emotion at all.']

These memories reveal the social nature of emotion and some of its complexity. They all differ markedly from emotions dealt with by psychologists, to whom we have just referred. Social constructionism offered a stronger theoretical alternative.

Our Starting Point

Our view does not differ markedly from the social constructionist position, although we elaborate and extend it (see chapter 7). Like the social constructionists, we believe that there are an indefinite number of emotions. That is, societies mould and shape many different emotions. In the English language there are more than 550 concepts that refer more or less directly to emotions. Joy, happiness, delight, awe, wonder, fear, grief, sadness, anger, pride, shame, guilt, surprise, envy are such names for emotions. However, sensations such as throbs, palpitations and twitches are not emotions; nor are sensations or feelings such as pain, taste, or startle reflexes. Emotions may include such sensations and responses or reflexes, but they are not to be equated with these sensations or affective responses.

Appraisal/Cognition
We emphasize appraisal and memory. Emotions have objects. One is not simply angry or annoyed, rather one is angry at someone, about something. One is not simply overcome by grief, one grieves for someone. Emotions occur in specific contexts. This is what distinguishes emotion from mood. Thus 'depression' is sometimes used by people to refer to a mood, 'I feel depressed', and sometimes to an emotion, 'I am depressed about my exam failure'.

As Bedford's analysis showed, cognition is as important as affect. However, as in the case of affect, there is no one-to-one correspondence between certain events, episodes or situations and certain emotions. Contrary to Peters' (1970) use of appraisal, we would not equate appraisal with a particular emotion. A situation appraised as dangerous may evoke fear, but in some circumstances, as our empirical investigation points out, it may evoke exhilaration.

The inclusion of appraisal in defining emotion implicates meaning and language. As Coulter (1979, p. 133) noted: 'the capacity to experience genuinely either shame, or guilt, or remorse, hinges on a mastery of a natural language involving cultural knowledge and reasoning conventions'. The social constitution or construction becomes evident. This social aspect of emotion is also important with regard to the behavioural component.

Behaviour
Emotions have characteristic expressive and instrumental responses, as already noted. Some of these responses may be innate, others socially acquired. Fear, which may be accompanied by a pounding of the heart, a dry mouth and trembling of the limbs, is often expressed by flight, an instrumental act. Anger, which may be expressed by flushing, shouting and clenching one's fist, is often acted on in terms of aggression, while some people under some

circumstances express anger 'coldly' by narrowing the eyes, compressing the mouth and becoming increasingly controlled. In the social constructionist view, the diversity of behavioural response as well as the generality indicates social acquisition. Averill (1980) suggests that emotional development requires the acquisition of social norms and rules that provide the component expressive responses with their meaning and coordination.

Affect/Feeling

Most emotions, perhaps all, involve affect or feeling. Some experiences which we deem emotional involve intense feelings – the death of someone we love; others involve minimal affect – the impatience we feel when the traffic lights are slow to change. It is unlikely, however, that there are specific physiological correlates for each and every emotion. As pointed out earlier, many emotions have very similar physiological correlates, and some people describe the same emotion as having different phenomenological physiological sensations.

Nevertheless, feelings are important to most emotional experience. The arguments of both James and Izard make sense, and social constructionism includes them. We are aware of our dry mouths and trembling knees, and this feedback is clearly part of our emotion. Emotion, however, as we have argued earlier is much more than such responses.

Emotion is all of these and more. The syndrome to which Averill refers, the emotion, is the set or sub-set of inter-related components; the physiological changes, the bodily actions, the appraisal and evaluation of the situation, the expressive responses, the subjective experience . . . and the instrumental actions. These are coordinated and integrated within the interpretation given them by the actor, the subject, of a 'passion' or emotion. The ways in which these components are organized into coherent syndromes is determined primarily by social and not biological evolution. Emotions conceptualized in this way are socially constructed, usually but not always in one's childhood and youth. They are, however, open to modification and transformation.

Origins of Emotion

But why, one might ask, are emotions constructed, or under what circumstances are the components integrated and coordinated? Is it the case that we simply, at the appropriate times and on appropriate occasions, take on the prescribed social role? The social constructionist account of emotion runs the risk of being equated with social learning – learning how to respond to particular stimuli, albeit a complex set of stimuli. But it should not be so equated. As Averill noted: 'As adults, emotional reactions are likely to proceed automatically and in the absence of any verbal mediation. It is therefore easy to overlook the amount and kind of prior experience that is required for the proper enactment of an emotional role' (1980, p. 321).

The nature of the prior experience which is implicated in the origins of emotions is always problematic. Whether or not there is a hard-wired or instinctive component, we stress the importance of intersubjectivity. As mentioned earlier, Oatley (1989) describes how emotions arise when the unexpected happens. He presupposes a knowledge of what is unexpected.

Oatley recognized the need for evaluation, but ignored the social. We argue in the remainder of this book, and especially in chapter 7, that this appraisal and reappraisal takes place in the social realm. The constructing of emotions, although done by individuals acting in and on their world, can only be accomplished in interaction with others: the appraisals and reappraisals, or what Averill refers to as monitoring, first order and second order, involve engagement with social meanings.

The construction is modifiable; it may continue throughout one's life. The emotions can be re-educated (Peters, 1970). It is here that the moral aspect of emotion comes into its own and where the relationship between emotion, agency and self is most obvious. As Denzin noted: 'Behaviour becomes emotional only when it is so interpreted by the person and brought into self-interactions or reflections' (1983, p. 404).

Emotions are self-feelings. Agency is recognized in the part played by the subject in the interpretation of the components. There is reflection – both immediate intuitive appraisal on the basis of affective memory as Arnold noted, and in many cases deliberate reappraisal and reflection.

This self-reflection is often overlooked. If the significance of self-reflection in the origins of emotions, and their modification and elaboration, is overlooked, then as we noted in a previous paper (Kippax et al., 1988), agency may be underplayed.

So, although we generally agree with the social constructionist view of emotion, as shown in chapters 4, 5 and 6 our work extends this view in two important respects. One is the emphasis we place on the role of self as agent, as moral evaluator. The second is to point to social specificity as well as generality. In particular, we find that women's position within the social structures may lead to their constructions of emotions and moral evaluations, which differ from

those of men, that is, emotion is gendered. The theoretical implications of these issues, together with the relationship between
emotion, agency and self and the relationship between emotion and
motive are taken up in chapter 7.

Emotions are socially prescribed; their presence demonstrates the
person's commitment to the cultural values exemplified in particular
situations and episodes. They are 'communications to ourselves and
to others about our moral state . . . tropes . . .' (Mary Parlee,
personal communication, 1988).

Conclusion

As noted earlier in this chapter, we found that psychological theory
on emotion was limited in both scope and contents. Such limitations
are reinforced by the ways that psychologists have chosen to study
emotion. Even social constructionists such as Averill (1980, 1985,
1986) have chosen methods such as questionnaires which fail to
capture much of the richness and complexity of emotional experience. A method is therefore needed which will recognize that
emotion is constructed in interaction, both self-interaction and
interaction with others, and will enable development of theory
which encompasses such interactions.

3
Memory-Work: Theory and Method

The method 'memory-work' (Haug, 1987) seemed to offer not only a way of exploring human experience but also of capturing and documenting its production. The way in which we decided upon memory-work was not, however, typical of psychological or socio-logical research, for we decided upon the method first, and the topic to be explored, emotion, second.

As we noted in chapter 1, we had come together initially to talk about our disquiet with traditional psychology and its methods. Memory-work, we believed, would enable us to move beyond the constraints of a traditional psychology, to make links with the exciting and radical ideas emerging from feminism and the new paradigm of social constructionism.

Emotion was chosen as the 'topic under discussion' because, as noted in chapters 1 and 2, emotion is women's business; in as much as it is associated with intuition, it is foreign to Western male thought. The topic was also chosen because, as we argue below and in chapter 7, emotions are produced in people's attempts to make sense of their world, in their efforts to appropriate and resist the structures of their everyday lives; they are the stuff out of which people construct and evaluate selves.

Theory and Method of Memory-Work

Memory-work was developed by the German feminist and scholar Frigga Haug (1987). The strength of her method is that it is integral to her theory of socialization, of how persons become selves and the part persons themselves play in that construction. The underlying theory is that subjectively significant events, events which are remembered, and the way they are subsequently constructed, play an important part in the construction of self. Because self is socially constructed through reflection, Haug's theory dictates memory-work as method. The initial data of the method, memory-work, are memories, which are reappraised collectively to uncover and docu-ment the social nature of their production.

Haug's theory of social construction of self captures much of what was and remains central to our own approach. We were confident, therefore, that memory-work, the method she and her co-researchers had used so successfully to study female sexuality, would work in researching emotions. We believed that memory-work was likely to reveal the processes of the construction of emotion. We began to explore it as a way of investigating emotions and in the process we, inevitably, modified and elaborated it.

The theoretical underpinnings of memory-work are essential to an understanding of the method itself; the method is not merely a technique for data collection, but includes analysing and theorizing the data, interpreting and re-interpreting them in the light of the overall theory. We examine the special relations between memory-work and the social construction of emotions more fully in chapter 7.

We begin our exposition of memory-work by comparing it with other methods, namely collection and analysis of accounts, and case history methods. These methods of enquiry are dictated by the respective underlying theories. All three take seriously the subject and what the subject has to say. They share an epistemological basis in treating the subject and the object of knowledge as correlative and co-constitutive and reject the view that 'subject' and 'object' designate independent entities. Meanings are constituted in action and action in meanings.

Accounts and case histories are coloured by subjectivity; they concern what is, and what has become subjectively significant. They tell the stories of attempts to make sense of the world, to make familiar and understand, to resolve contradiction. The 'talk' of these texts, broadly conceived, enables communication between selves and, more importantly in this context, it provides a way of reflecting on and evaluating behaviour for self and others.

The initial 'texts' of memory-work are written memories. As such they have two special advantages: the first is that memory-work enables an engagement with the past. The initial memory texts, the memories themselves, differ from narrative accounts and to some extent case histories, in that they describe what was subjectively significant; memory-work texts focus on past events and actions. These reflections of what occurred then, provide the starting point for memory-work, now. Memory-work is based on the assumption that what is remembered is remembered because it is, in some way, problematic or unfamiliar, in need of review. The actions and episodes are remembered because they were significant then and remain significant now. Their significance lies in the continuing search for intelligibility necessitated by the unfamiliarity of the episode, the conflict and contradiction that might have been present, and the lack of resolution.

The second advantage of memories is that individuals' memories provide the medium in which their actions are given direction and evaluated. As Shotter (1984, p. 212) explains, the process of using one's own past experiences in structuring one's own further actions is very familiar. What perhaps is not so familiar or obvious is that the relation between oneself and one's memories of one's past experience is similar to the relation between other agents and oneself. One's self engages with one's memories, has a conversation with them, responds to them, as another responds to oneself. Memories are essential to the duality of self. The 'I' reflects back on the 'me' and together they constitute the self. Memories contain the traces of the continuing process of appropriation of the social and the becoming, the constructing, of self.

In their attempt to wrest meaning from the world, persons construct themselves; and in their struggle for intelligibility they reflect. They remember the problematic, which is itself socially produced, in terms of the resolution previously sought if not achieved. Memory-work thus is intimately bound up with the uncovering of the processes of the construction of self. As Haug (1987, p. 50) argues: 'Our basic premise was that anything and everything remembered constitutes a relevant trace – precisely because it is remembered – for the formation of identity.' Memories are fundamentally important as constitutive of self in a way that the 'talk' of accounts and, to a lesser extent, case studies cannot be.

The method focuses on uncovering the processes of social construction captured in the memories and reflections of individuals. Its first focus is the individual reflections and the ways in which they indicate the processes of construction. For example, when reflecting on a happy experience, Ann remembered:

Ann was about 7. Her dad was factory manager of a concrete block factory. They lived in a house on the premises. There were stacks of concrete blocks near the house. Ann climbed among them and by moving some blocks (just possible) was able to fashion a rather grand fort. No one could see her if she so chose.

Happiness for Ann, as discussed in chapter 5, was experienced with respect to control and choice with regard to space. Other memories, written in response to the cue 'play', elaborate on this theme.

Amy:

The four children were sent outside to play as usual, and the parents got stuck into talking. A was worried about them forgetting lunch. Outside it was surprising. Down the back of the yard it looked like a jungle. J said it was her special place and she took the others into it. There were leaves and branches everywhere and the girls pretended they were explorers. Then they found the treasure for the day. Slung from one tree trunk to another was a hammock. It looked to A like a raft to use to discover the strange tangled world they were in. With delight all four of them hopped onto it and it quivered and trembled with their weight.

Tim:

His Dad was building a cubby house for him and his younger brother. It was on stilts, with steps going up to it. On a really hot day in summer he, his little brother, and two family friends were playing in it, pretending it was a helicopter. There were no walls on it yet, just a frame, so it was like those helicopters with big bubble windows that you can see everything from. He was having a lot of fun because it was just like a real helicopter, in the back yard of his house.

The three memories contain references to childhood spaces, spaces in which to act out fantasy, spaces separate from the adult world and over which the children have control. The common meanings, in this example of the constructing of happiness and delight through a sense of 'my place', are the second and equally important focus of memory-work.

This second focus is on those same memories compared and contrasted with each other and appraised and reappraised by self and others, the co-members of the memory-work group. In memory-work these reflections are reflected on again, reappraised, within the memory-work group, where the common elements become evident. The individual members of the memory-work group, each of whom has written one or more memories, come together and collectively interpret, discuss and theorize the memories. New meanings are reached, but they are reached by the co-members themselves, together; there is a striving for a 'common' sense.

The two foci of memory-work, which we refer to as phase 1 and phase 2 in our description of the method itself below, capture something of the duality of self. The self talking with itself, is phase 1, and responding to itself as others respond to it is phase 2. The meanings reached or arrived at by the group are a function of the meanings as negotiated then at the time of the remembered event and those now collectively theorized. Meanings are negotiated until a 'common' sense is achieved. The process of the struggle for intelligibility is revealed. The task of memory-work is to uncover and lay bare the earlier understandings in the light of current understandings, thus elucidating the underlying processes of construction involved.

Thus, memory-work is, we believe, a method *par excellence* for exploring the processes of the construction of self and understanding the ways in which emotions, motives, actions, choices, moral judgements, play their part in that construction. It gives an insight into the way people appropriate the social world and in so doing transform themselves and it.

We will consider further the relationships between reflection and memory, the striving for intelligibility and the construction process in chapter 7. But here we will discuss the memory-work in the context of hermeneutics, and then describe the method itself in more detail.

Hermeneutics as an Alternative to Empiricism

Memory-work is firmly positioned against empiricist methodologies of mainstream social science. Whereas empiricism is essentially atheoretical and claims that knowledge is self-evident, a hermeneutic approach is theory-laden and acknowledges that knowledge depends upon interpretation. Hermeneutics does not observe the positivist imperative of the separation of the subject from the object of knowledge. As pointed out above, the co-researchers act both as subjects and the objects of knowledge, producing the data (in the form of memories) and subjecting these data to a progressive process of critical reading and theorization.

This collapsing of the subject and object of research, the 'knower' and the 'known', constitutes or sets aside a space where the experiential can be placed in relation to the theoretical. Haug argues that memory-work is possible only if subject and object of research are the same:

> The very notion that our own past experience may offer some insight into the ways in which individuals construct themselves into existing relations, thereby themselves reproducing a social formation, itself contains an implicit argument for a particular methodology. If we refuse to understand ourselves simply as a bundle of reactions to all-powerful structures, or to the social relations within which we have formed us [ourselves], if we search instead for possible indications of how we have participated actively in the formations of our own past experience, then the usual mode of social-scientific research, in which individuals figure exclusively as objects of the process of research, has to be abandoned. (1987, pp. 34–5)

In issuing this plea for subjectivity, Haug raises the issue of generalizability. Haug (1987, p. 44) argues that: 'Individual modes of appropriation of the social are frequently conceived as personally unique; . . . this involves an underestimation of the sociality of human beings.' The range of actions accessible to any given individual is limited by the structures in which the actions occur and by which they are restrained. The range of possible actions can be viewed in research as general possibilities. Thus, each individual mode of appropriation of the social, of engagement with the structures, is potentially generalizable. 'If therefore a given experience is possible, it is also subject to universalization' (1987, p. 44).

Hollway, who makes a similar plea for subjectivity, deals with the issue of generalization as follows: 'The concern for mass generalization and the requirement to use large numbers for statistical manipulation together produce knowledge which does not address the complex conditions of people and their conduct, either in their uniqueness or their commonality' (1989, p. 15). She goes on to argue, as does Haug, that information derived from any participant is valid because the account given is a product of the social domain.

Certainly on the occasions when we have presented our work, the response to it has indicated that people recognize their own experience in what we have said and written; they find it plausible. The credibility of our work is one marker of its generalizability and its representativeness. Further, as emotions are socially constructed, then the notion that the findings of our work are or should be generalizable to peoples of other places and other times is misconceived.

There is a sense, however, in which the question of generalizability must be answered. Until memory-work groups other than the ones in which we have been involved are established, then it is possible, although we believe highly improbable, that our findings are relevant only to us and the groups with which we have worked. In this sense, the question of generalizability and, indirectly, representativeness, becomes one of concern for heterogeneity. Confidence in the relevance of the outcome of memory-work to persons other than those taking part in memory-work groups can best be achieved by ensuring the heterogeneity of the groups themselves.

Whatever the outcome of further empirical work, a method such as memory-work enables the exploration and analysis of experience in a manner which is radically different from empiricist methods. Memory-work can do this because, like other methods with which it shares a common hermeneutical epistemology, it does not give priority to either subjective experience or theory; rather it sets them in a reciprocal and mutually critical relationship. Hermeneutics is, of course, not new. Dilthey is credited with its introduction to the human sciences (see Messer et al., 1988; Greenwood, 1989).

Psychologists and sociologists as well as historians and literary critics are participant observers who inevitably use their empathic responses to understand events and actions. Further, if human beings understand only that which they have made, as Vico has argued (see Lana, 1979; Shotter, 1986), then an experiential as opposed to an evidentiary epistemology is necessary.

It is not only because of this sharing in a common hermeneutic epistemology, but also because of Haug's theoretical compatibility with our own position, that we knew our application of memory-work to the study of emotions would work. In this sense our adoption of memory-work was not entirely serendipitous. What was unexpected, what overwhelmed and excited us, was the strength of memory-work in enabling us to ground emerging theory in our data and their analysis. We found that memory-work worked even better than we had anticipated.

Memory-Work as Method

Memory-work involves at least three phases. First, the collection of written memories according to certain rules. Second, the collective analysis of those written memories. There is also a third phase in which there is further reappraisal; a reappraisal of the memories and their analysis in the context of a range of theories from academic disciplines. We are still involved in that third phase; in writing this book we have reappraised much of our work in the light of theories of emotion as well as the memories and memory-work of other groups. In the process we have also reappraised the theories.

Subjects/Researchers
Before memory-work can be done, however, a group of co-researchers or co-workers must be formed. Memory-work is carried out by a collective. The memory-work groups may be formed in a number of ways: they can be formed with one or more of the researchers as full members of the group, or with one or more of the researchers as facilitator(s). The use of a group facilitator is not discussed by Haug. Status differences in group membership are very likely to damage each member's freedom in reaching towards what is truly common to the group. That said, however, the presence of a skilled facilitator may be useful on occasions.

The way we began was to form ourselves into a memory-work group. We were our own subjects; the distinctions between researcher and 'subject' disappeared. Our memories were our raw data. This initial group was, in many ways, the most satisfying and productive; most of the data and analysis presented in this book come from this group.

Other memory-work groups consisted of four, five or six people, including one or two of us, the researchers, as full and active members. In an important sense, the work of these groups becomes indistinguishable from that of the initial group. We set up a number of memory-work groups in this way.

We also formed memory-work groups of which we were not members. The groups remained independent of us. We explained the rules for both writing and analysing their memories and left them to it. That is, we encouraged other groups of four or five or six people to be both researchers and subjects. The men's groups referred to in this book as well as other women's groups were set up in this way.

Finally, we also set up memory-groups in which one of us has acted as a facilitator. Although, as noted above, this is not a preferred option, this variation on the memory-work group is a good one if the topic to be explored is one that people find embarrassing or difficult to discuss and/or where the group loses direction. A skilled group facilitator may be able to relieve anxiety. enable the writing of memories and the collective discussion, and re-direct attentions. In these groups, however, we were always aware of problems created by our presence. The group facilitator becomes the leader and the sense of collectivity is diminished.

In all these examples, each particular memory-work group itself has carried the major weight of the analytic work. We have, however, reappraised many of our own memories in the light of the memories and memory-work of these other groups.

In general, we have preferred to set up groups in which the individual members are reasonably homogeneous on some criterion which, a priori, we regarded as relevant. For example, in exploring emotions, the memory-work groups were of 'older women', 'younger women' and 'young men'. In our experience, groups of close friends work well together, although groups in which the individual members were strangers were also successful. The main criterion for success is mutual trust, which is essential if the groups are to meet for the necessary time. Many of our memory-work groups met for months or longer, an indication that the memory-work groups had found the experience rewarding and stimulating.

Phase 1
The memories are written according to a set of rules. The rules we used were based on Haug's injunctions but as our work continued we developed and modified some of them. The rules we used are

described below. The first five are essentially the same as those recommended by Haug (1987).

1   Write a memory
2   of a particular episode, action or event
3   in the third person
4   in as much detail as is possible, including even 'inconsequential' or trivial detail (it may be helpful to think of a key image, sound, taste, smell, touch)
5   but without importing interpretation, explanation or biography.
6   Write one of your earliest memories.

The force of rules 1, 2, 3, 4 and 5 is to ensure that the co-researcher writes a description of a particular event or episode rather than an account or a general abstracted description. For example, if one is asked to write a memory of 'arguments with your partner' then it is likely that an account justifying and explaining such arguments would be written. The written memory is likely to contain characteristics of all arguments – or at least the more serious ones. On the other hand, if one is asked to write a memory of the 'first' or 'most recent' or 'most serious (or trivial)' argument, given the rules above, a description of a particular and significant event is more likely to be written than an account which typically includes warranting and justification.

But which event or episode? What topic? The process begins by the co-researchers choosing a topic (or trigger). Each co-researcher writes a memory of an episode evoked by the trigger. Some of the triggers we used were 'saying you are sorry', 'crying', 'saying no', 'danger', 'holidays', 'being praised' . . . The trigger chosen depends, of course, on the topic under investigation. The choice is extremely important and some triggers do not produce the expected. For example, as documented in chapter 4, 'saying you are sorry' does not always produce memories of guilt or shame. Such memories were in the minority; anger and a sense of injustice were the emotions which coloured the memories commonly written in response to this cue or trigger. The trigger 'secrets' did, however, produce memories which revealed guilt and shame.

We also found that starting with the obvious was not always helpful. Haug (1987, p. 53) noted that: 'any set of ready-made questions is likely to be firmly rooted in popular prejudice' and we found that obvious questions produced obvious and somewhat over-rehearsed responses. The memories were rounded and smooth, they lacked any sense of contradiction; their meanings in general were glib. For example, in a study related to women's sexuality (Kippax et al., 1990), triggers such as 'initiating', 'touching' and 'penetration' produced counter-intuitive and more illuminating descriptions of sexual episodes than 'first love' or 'loss of virginity'. The latter triggers produced memories of episodes which represent sex and love in their least problematic form.

The importance of the ways in which the episodes are triggered cannot be over-emphasized. In a later chapter (chapter 10) we discuss work reported by Campbell and Muncer (1987) which used a method similar in some ways to memory-work, namely group discussions focused on particular episodes. In their study Campbell and Muncer explored the social representations of anger and aggression by asking their respondents to talk about recent experiences of anger and/or aggression. It is unclear what the actual instructions were but if the researchers asked the group members to discuss recent memories of when they felt angry, what the group members will produce is a set of episodes in which anger is represented in its clearest and least problematic form; episodes which are filed away under the heading 'anger'. The method Campbell and Muncer used can document the social representations of anger as it is, but it may not reveal much about the way anger came to be constructed.

Asking for detailed description, including 'inconsequential' detail, avoids evaluation; '. . . we attempted both to denaturalize existing value-judgements, by describing our memories down to the very last detail . . . and to disobey the precepts they embody' (Haug, 1987, p. 49) Detail is important because in detail we recognize the constraints placed on our understandings by the notion of 'relevance'; the so-called 'irrelevant' aspects of episodes or events point to the hidden moral and normative aspects of our actions. A good example of the importance of detail comes from one of the groups of students which we set in train.

The following memory was written in response to the cue 'doing something silly':

Melissa, age 19, is minding her boss's house while she is on holiday. Melissa was standing in the bathroom. It was immaculately designed and maintained although very sterile. She was getting ready for work that afternoon, was already dressed, applying make-up and blow-drying her hair. She was also smoking a cigarette.

Melissa placed the cigarette on the vanity counter-top, with the lit end hanging over the edge. The vanity was a lovely cream with deep colours swirled through it, with gold taps and accessories.

When Melissa had completed whatever she was doing, she picked up the cigarette, horrified at the burn mark she had left. She panicked, imagining her boss's face when she returned to see a big black stain, obviously marked on the vanity top. Melissa tried everything to remove it. Nothing worked. She felt so stupid and got angry at herself whenever she thought about it. Melissa hasn't smoked since.

The white of the bathroom, its cleanliness, is contrasted with the black mark which the cigarette burns into the woodwork. Smoking is unclean, particularly by subordinates in their boss's bathroom.

The following memory, given in full in chapter 1, was written in response to the cue 'fear':

> They sit at the dinner table – Ann, her mother, her aunt, her brother, her father. The room is dim, yellow light bulb or late summer evening without the light on. There is lots of dark wood – floor, table, picture rail. Any talking is in low voices . . .

The details speak of dread. It is dark, dim – not 'soft' voices but 'low' voices. Fear is apprehension and dread of what is to follow: they 'hear the bathroom door close. They try not to hear the crack of the leather razor strop and Graham's cries.'

As well as this request for detail, the injunction to write in the third person also helps to avoid the warranting and the justification which is characteristic of accounts. Writing in the third person enables the subject to have a 'bird's eye view' of the scene, to picture the detail. The subject reflects on herself/himself from the outside – from the point of view of the observer, and so is encouraged to describe rather than warrant.

If interpretation is avoided then the smoothing over of rough edges, covering up the absences and inconsistencies, is also avoided. For this reason, too, biography and autobiography are to be avoided. Biography represents linear constructions whereby earlier actions and events lead to and determine later ones. Haug warns against the coherence which biography brings; the coherence of the reinterpretation of past events as antecedents of what follows, that is, of what we 'know' to be the consequences. Coherence hides resistance and in this way works against the method: a method in which the analysis 'has to be seen as a field of conflict between dominant cultural values and oppositional attempts to wrest cultural meaning and pleasure from life' (Haug, 1987, p. 41).

The first rule listed above – 'write a memory' – we found puzzling at first. Writing, we thought, is more likely to lead to a construction of coherence and logic and some inevitable loss of richness than a verbal articulation. However, we followed the rule and became convinced of its correctness. Writing has a number of advantages. Writing gives one permission not to bother to make things 'normal' or proper.

> Writing is a transgression of boundaries, an exploration of new territory. It involves making public the events of our lives, wriggling free from the constraints of purely private and individual experience . . . As an alternative to accepting everyday events mindlessly, we recalled them in writing, in an attempt to identify points in the past where we succeeded in defending ourselves against the encroachments of others. (Haug, 1987, p. 36)

The writing provides a discipline to the memory-work group. Another advantage is that talking is far more likely to involve self presentation; it is difficult not to get caught up in justification and interpretation when one is identified as the speaker. Writing from the third person point of view encourages description and discourages interpretation. Writing also provides a fixed and permanent record. A final advantage is that written text gives the everyday experience of our lives, the 'unimportant and uninteresting', a status, a significance that is worth exploring. Writing is, in this way, of special significance to women. Women see writing as an impossibility, because they believe there is nothing to write about. The everyday of women's lives is thought to be insignificant, unworthy, banal. Writing helps to counter this impression.

The final rule, which we used in our work on emotions, was to write an early memory, a memory from childhood. For each memory we decided to write a memory of the earliest episode. In most cases, this produced a memory from early childhood. This rule was of our own making and we adopted it because we were interested in capturing the processes involved in the construction of emotions, something thought to occur early rather than late in life. Early memories, we thought, would reveal more clearly the processes of construction. This and related issues will be discussed in chapters 7 and 8.

Individual members of a memory-work group follow these rules in writing their memories, a process which often requires a week's gestation. Our own experience was that, in general, about a week was needed. Sometimes a cue would trigger a number of memories. Sometimes, some cues were slow to trigger a memory. Very occasionally for one or more of us, the trigger did not work and we could write little in the way of a memory.

Phase 2
Having written their memories, the co-researchers meet to read and analyse all the memories. The rules or guidelines for this phase of the memory-work are given below. Once again, in our work we did not adhere to all of them strictly.

1 Each memory-work group member expresses opinions and ideas about each memory in turn, and
2 looks for similarities and differences between the memories and looks for continuous elements among memories whose relation to each other is not immediately apparent. Each member should question particularly those aspects of the events which do not appear amenable to comparison. She or he should not, however, resort to autobiography or biography.
3 Each memory-work member identifies clichés, generalizations, contradictions, cultural imperatives, metaphor . . . and
4 discusses theories, popular conceptions, sayings and images about the topic.
5 Finally, each member examines what is not written in the memories (but what might be expected to be), and
6 rewrites the memories.

The analysis aims to uncover, in the first instance, the 'common' sense, the common understandings, contained in them. The memories are theorized as a cross-sectional example of common (social) experience. In this regard, as noted above, it is important that autobiography and biography which emphasize individual aspects of experience be avoided. What is of interest is not why person X's father did such and such but why fathers do such things. The aim is to uncover the social meanings embodied by the actions described in the written accounts and to uncover the processes whereby the meanings – both then and now – are arrived at.

In examining each memory for absences, contradictions, clichés and cultural imperatives, the collective reflection and theorizing of the episode, as remembered and written, exposes the processes involved in the making of a 'common' sense of the actions described. The taken-for-granted of everyday life is uncovered in, for example, the cultural imperative to 'enjoy holidays', the clichés surrounding 'walks in the country', the absence of peers from women's childhood memories. The collective reflection and examination may suggest revising the interpretation of the common patterns, and the analysis proceeds by moving from individual memories to the cross-sectional analysis and back again in a recursive fashion. Exposing these processes of construction raises the possibility of modification and transformation of the common-sense understandings. In this way, the method is reflexive. It generates data and at the same time points to modes of action for the co-researchers.

Typically, at this stage in the analysis, new triggers or cues are suggested by the group members and Phase 1 is set in train again. In the ideal case, the process continues until the members feel that the topic or they are exhausted. In reality some memory-work groups are constrained by external factors such as limitations of time.

The knowledge of processes of construction that memory-work generates comes from two sources: first, each co-researcher's reflective activities, that is, how each co-researcher 'talks to her/himself' about her/his own experiences; and second, how co-researchers 'talk to each other' about their own and others' actions and experiences. Reflections on (memories of) a particular episode or event are based in the meanings arrived at and available then, at the time of the event or episode, and now, at the time of the theorizing. Members of the collective are thus regarded as 'experts in everyday life' (Haug, 1987, p. 54). The collective theorizing, in Phase 2, involves the co-researchers in a reappraisal of these meanings in the light of their common experience.

We adhered to the guidelines listed above with the exception of the last. We experienced some difficulties in rewriting our memories and found that such rewriting was unproductive for us. On reflection now it seems obvious that the difficulty in doing so relates to our decision to focus on a memory of an early event or episode. With regard to our 'emotion' memory-work, we worked almost exclusively with memories of young girls and boys, where by definition, we and they were still learning the social rules and were still involved in the appropriation of the social with all its contradictions. We found it difficult to rewrite the memories of then, given our position as adults now.

The rule to write memories of early events had another impact on Phase 2. There were gaps and absences and conflict and contradiction in our memories but, as we discovered when we wrote our adult holiday memories, there were far fewer clichés and cultural imperatives in our childhood memories. We had not yet learned them.

These two points, of course, raise the whole issue of the extent to which the reported memories are from then rather than now. At one epistemological level they are obviously now by virtue of being memories. However, we experienced a strong sense of distinction between the quality of different memories: those which were immediate and those which felt much more worked over as if they were the product of experience subsequent to the reported event or episode. Many of our childhood memories had the quality of 'immediacy' and it was this quality that made them difficult to rewrite. It was also this quality that was associated with the reduction in clichés and cultural imperatives.

Immediacy is not to be confused with questions of accuracy. The memories are true memories, that is, they are memories and not inventions or fantasies. Whether the memories accurately represent past events or not, however, is irrelevant; the process of the construction of the meanings of those events is the focus of memory-work. This point will be taken up in chapter 9 (Remembering and Forgetting).

Phase 3

There is yet further analysis in Phase 3, when the material provided in Phases 1 and 2 is examined and further theorized. We compared and contrasted the memories produced in response to a number of cues and our discussions of each of those memory-topics. In the case of our work on emotions we wrote memories to a large number of cues over a period of three years. The theorizing of the memories that were written in response to the early cues, our early memory-topics, influenced our theorizing of the later memory-topics. We also incorporated insights gained from the theorizing of these 'late memory-topics' back into our review of the earlier topics. A similar process of comparison took place as we compared our memories and our theorizing with the theorized memories of other memory-work groups.

Further, we read and listened to the group discussions and critically examined the themes and commonsense understandings arrived at, relating them to our own understandings of social practice as informed by particular theoretical positions. As we reached new understandings we reappraised our initial analyses of the memories.

This recursive process led us to our own theories of the construction of emotions. As Haug (1987) suggests, we reflected our insights against other theories of emotion, psychological and sociological as well as the 'everyday'. We asked questions about the ways in which women are portrayed as 'emotional' and about the language of emotions. We discussed forgetting and remembering, repression and suppression; we thought about the impact of our gender on the ways in which we worked and theorized as well as on the construction of our emotions; and we wondered about the differences between childhood and adult memories and noted the relative lack of clichés in our childhood memories. In other words Phase 3 is the phase in which we evaluate our attempts at theorizing. Writing this book has led us to reflect once again and to ask ourselves when if ever the process of reappraisal and reflection will end.

Doing memory-work therefore involves the group in these three phases. However, it is necessary to remember that these three phases are recursive; they feed into and off each other. We have written about them as though they are separate but in practice the three phases of the process are not so easily distinguished.

Memory-Work and Intersubjectivity

We have applied memory-work to explore the social construction of emotion. This was our major goal. Because the method is so intimately linked to a theory of socialization, we have also explored the role played by memory and emotion in the construction of self. In particular we explore the social processes underlying that construction.

The memories themselves, written by the co-researchers, provide insights into the co-researchers' search for intelligibility. The reflections comprise episodes of contradiction and contrast, the unfamiliar and the problematic and they provide a key to the ways in which the emotions were constructed within the social and interpersonal interactions of the remembered episodes. The feelings of self, the gestures of others, were and, as we note below, continue to be interpreted within the framework of the unfolding actions of self and others, that is, intersubjectively.

This interpretation is taken up and the episodes reflected on again by the group of co-researchers (for us, both at the time of doing memory-work and now in the writing of this book). The commonness of the episodes and the common sense reached, point to the importance of the social process. Together with each other, the co-researchers reach common and sometimes new understandings of the episodes under discussion. The collectivity of the co-researchers distinguishes memory-work from a somewhat similar use of reflection within psychodynamic therapy. In memory-work, understandings are not sought or reached within a particular psychodynamic or other theoretical framework, but within the commonsense understandings of everyday life. Hierarchical relationships between researcher and researched are avoided.

Reflection is at the heart of memory-work. But although reflection is an individual process, in memory-work it is made public within the collective. Thus, the embracing of subjectivity does not necessarily lead to individualism. In a manner which is reminiscent of Mead (see Joas, 1985) and very similar to that adopted by Shotter (1984), Haug recommends building upon the human ability to recognize the commonality of experience. Thus, as Mead, and Vygotsky and others note, intersubjectivity precedes subjectivity.

Mead (1909) builds his notion of intersubjectivity from the structure of gestural communication, which is connected closely with the body and founded in cooperative action. Human communication is, for Mead, the basis of the social character of consciousness. We stress that when we use 'intersubjectivity' throughout this book we refer to the inclusive notion of intersubjectivity as based on actions and not restricted to language.

In chapters 4, 5 and 6 we take a number of episodes and describe the constructions of a number of emotions. We reflect again on the episodes and focus our attention on the ways in which feelings and emotions enter into our understandings of these episodes.

The meanings of actions are not found in the actor's head but in the common meanings which she/he negotiates in interaction with others – both then at the time of the episode and now in reflection. The memories of events are collectively reappraised. Memory-work makes it possible to put the agent, the actor, back into psychology – in both method and theory – without falling into psychological individualism.

Arnold (1970) who wrote at the time when the mind (or cognition) was not considered a proper object of psychological study, and agency was denied, turned her attention to the cognitive aspects of emotion. As we noted in chapter 2, she recognized the importance of reflection and memory to any study of emotion. Although her psychology remains individualistic and she makes no reference to agency, she ties emotion to memory in a way that foreshadows Shotter: 'We remember what has happened to us in the past . . . we imagine how it will affect us this time and estimate whether it will be harmful' (p. 174).

Shotter (1984, p. 214) makes the ability of humans to reflect the centrepiece of his argument for agency. Indeed he argues that human agency depends on both foresight and memory. It is memory, he claims, that 'is the process by which past specificatory activities are linked to current specifiability – which makes for intentionality, and gives a "directionality" to mental activities.' (p. 208). Our memories contain the conditions for agents' further self development.

It is in this way that memory-work, as we have noted, is a method with which to explore the construction of self. Harré (1979, 1983) argues that human agents are also social beings, persons. Indeed their agency depends upon them being social beings. As Shotter notes:

> human beings seem to accumulate within themselves, not just a history, but a sense of their 'position' in their world in relation to all the others with whom they share it. As persons they must be not just conscious but self-conscious, that is, aware of the function of their own actions in

relation to the social order at large in which they are 'rooted'. (1984, p. 209)

Intersubjectivity is thus central to memory-work. Memory-work attempts to uncover the processes of the production of selves. Selves are the creation of the collectivities in which they live and act. Selves are able through their reflexive powers of self-intervention to re-create themselves. Identities are not formed or maintained through imitation or through any simple reproduction of predetermined patterns. The human capacity for action forces persons to attempt to live their own meanings and find some means of self-fulfilment albeit within a predetermined and circumscribed social space.

Memory-Work as a Feminist Method

The method memory-work was first developed and continues to be developed in a feminist context. It replaces the hierarchy of 'experimenter' and 'subject' by a collective process involving co-researchers. It also differs from hermeneutic methods with which it shares many similarities, as noted earlier in this chapter, in that the collective process does not give priority to the interpretation of an 'expert'. New understandings and meanings are reached by the subjects, the co-researchers themselves. The memories and the 'talk' remain the property of the co-researchers. The method thus has a political force and, in this way, has links with consciousness-raising.

Memory-work offers a way of escaping from some of the problems inherent in traditional psychological methods identified by many feminist writers in the United States and the United Kingdom (for example, Crawford and Maracek, 1989; Gavey, 1989; Hollway, 1989; Kimmel, 1989; Maracek, 1989; Mednick, 1989; Fine and Gordon, 1991; Kitzinger, 1991; Parlee, 1991; Wilkinson, 1991), although doing feminist research using methods which lie outside the mainstream raises its own problems, as Parlee (1991) for example notes.

The method of memory-work transcends the opposition between the individualistic bias in psychological theory and a structural theory that does not recognize human agency. It deconstructs the taken-for-granted in its concern with contradiction, conflict and absences. It facilitates the questioning of existing knowledges which Grosz (1988) characterizes as phallocentric (that is, where 'male' subsumes 'female', and is taken to represent human).

4
Saying Sorry and Being Sorry

The best way of demonstrating how memory-work 'works' as a method is by presenting a sample of the process in detail. In this chapter we describe the ways in which memories of episodes associated with apologies and transgressions and the collective discussion and theorizing of the same memories enabled us to capture the construction of some emotions. It was in this, our first experience of memory-work that we began to discern its power with regard to the analysis of the construction process. When we compared our own group's memory-work with that of other groups, we became aware of the gender differences in the construction of emotions. As our work continued we began to realize the important part played by emotion in the construction of self.

Apology – Saying Sorry

Five memories were produced by our group in response to the trigger 'saying sorry'. The first memory, Ann's, appears in two versions. Both were written prior to any collective discussion. In the second version, which was written after Ann had reflected on the memory-work 'rules' about focusing on 'absence' and rewriting, she retrieved her mother's participation. Members of the collective had differing responses to the power of the two versions. They are included here as an example of the method in action.

Ann, apology, version 1:

It is evening. She is playing on the floor in the lounge room. Her father reading the paper in an armchair nearby. She notices that he's fallen asleep, his arms above his head. She creeps up to tickle him, a frequent reciprocal game. At the first touch in his armpits he comes awake, startled, and simultaneously hits her across the face. 'Don't you *ever* do that again' he shouts. She is sobbing with fright and surprise: 'I'm sorry, I'm sorry'.

Ann, apology, version 2:

She was aged between 4 and 6. It was evening, her mother in the kitchen cooking dinner. She was playing on the carpet near her father's feet. He was reading the paper, sometimes talking to her, sometimes responding to her questions or comments. It was a warm night, he had taken off his suit coat. Absorbed in her game she didn't notice him falling asleep until he failed to respond to one of her remarks. His hands were tucked behind his head, his mouth slightly open, he was snoring lightly. She crept to him giggling to herself, anticipating his delight as she initiated one of their tickling games, watchful as to whether he was *really* asleep. He pretended a lot. At the first touch on the cotton shirt covering his armpits his eyes startled open, his mouth erupted an 'ugh' of anger, his hand stung across her face: 'Don't you *ever* do that again'. She cried, loudly enough so her mother heard (or perhaps she heard him shout) and came in. 'What happened?' And after the explanation: 'She didn't mean to upset you.'

This memory shows sharpness of detail: it is evening, a warm night etc. A number of fairly strong emotions are reported in quick succession. For Ann there was first 'giggling . . . anticipating with delight'. This was followed rapidly by fright and surprise. Although not reported in the memory there is the implication of shock and bewilderment and, just possibly, a flash of anger, quickly internalized into a cry of 'I'm sorry, I'm sorry'. The father was startled and his emotion remembered as anger. None of the mother's emotions are reported. However the memory implies that Ann's mother is concerned to placate her husband. 'She didn't mean to upset you.' On first reading she appears to play a minor role.

The emotional tone of the episode is one of sharp contrasts and contradictions. The tickling game is a 'frequent reciprocal game' and Ann approaches a loving and playful father who unexpectedly erupts with sudden anger and violence. Her own delight is transformed into fright and surprise.

The episode as remembered throws into high relief the discrepancy in power between Ann and her father. She initiated the game; he responded with anger and violence. The message appears clear – if it is a 'reciprocal game' then it is one in which he sets the terms. She was wrong in assuming the right to initiate the game.

In discussing the episode later, Ann reported that she said 'sorry' as a kind of 'don't hit me again' response, 'because my father was a very angry man who punished my brother a lot . . . he never hit me at any other time that I remember . . . there's a lot of confusion in my recollection. I was afraid of ever inciting him again . . . maybe I'd heard my brother say "I'm sorry" as a way of deflecting his anger.' The 'sorry' then does not seem to imply an acceptance of guilt but an acceptance of the father's power.

The intervention by Ann's mother was weak. Role relations between mother and father are implied in the social clichés: she was 'in the kitchen cooking dinner' while he sat 'reading the paper'; she emerged from the kitchen to defend Ann, 'she didn't mean to upset you'. But the defence was two-edged. As we later theorized: she did *not* say to Ann 'he didn't mean to hurt you'. Indeed by apologizing on the child's behalf to the father she appears to be acknowledging Ann's responsibility for his discomfort. So both parents supported the unacceptability of Ann's actions: 'don't *ever* do that again'. Ann, by initiating an action that he was not prepared for, was responsible for his discomfort. She was powerless but responsible.

Ann's memory, and each of the others in this group of memories, was analysed at three levels following the method outlined in chapter 3: the textual, the cross-sectional and theory at a more general level. Having written as early a memory as possible around the specific trigger situation of 'saying sorry', we then analysed each individual memory in itself – the text was examined for clichés and contradictions, for sequences of actions and role relations, for statements made and for absences, for emotion stated and implied. This is the first level of analysis, the textual analysis, the construction contained within the memory itself.

Having examined each individual memory, we then looked across the memories written in response to the same trigger, and later across other groups of memories written by ourselves and by others. At this stage we sought common patterns.

We looked at similarities, recurring themes and differences. What did the episodes mean to us as little girls? Why did we remember these particular memories? What were we learning? What emotions were described? What do the memories tell us about the way we construed our social world and our place within it? This is the second level of analysis, the cross-sectional, with emphasis on the *pool* of memories.

The third level of analysis turned us to psychological theory, and we used our insights drawn from the collective theorizing of the memory pool to inform our critical reappraisal of psychological constructs. How did our theorizing of emotion challenge everyday notions? How did our data fit or challenge psychological discourse and everyday notions?

We did not proceed neatly and stepwise from one level to the next and then finally to the more general theory of level three. Our progress was inevitably more haphazard than that. We constantly moved back and forth across levels as insights from one level raised new questions at another.

In our analysis we were looking for the recurring patterns that might tell us something about the way in which women's emotions are socially constructed. Indeed many of the issues (themes) that emerged from Ann's memory are repeated in those that follow

below. Note that Liz's memory differs from the other early childhood memories in many respects, and hence serves as a contrast.

Margaret:

She was 3 or 4, maybe a little more, and was staying with her
grandmother. Her mother was ill or perhaps her little sister was ill.
Anyway, she was with her grandmother and her mother wasn't there.
They were together, she and her grandmother in Yass. It was not her
house (Margaret's house). She was going to bed and her grandmother
whom she called Nana, asked her to go to sleep. Margaret said 'No,
because I haven't said my prayers' and her grandmother was very cross
with her for saying 'no'. Margaret was very upset and explained that she
had said 'no' because she had to say her prayers before she went to sleep.
Her grandmother was still cross because Margaret had said 'no' and
asked her to say she was sorry. Margaret said she was sorry but was hurt
and didn't understand why her grandmother was so cross.

Fay:

It was late afternoon; it was summer. She must have been bored, doing
little or nothing, waiting for meal time. Her aunt arrived home from
work. This aunt was about 40 years old, small and slight. She wore a dark
blue dress, no hat. Her brown hair was carefully arranged close to her
head in a style that was more fashionable in the 1920s or 1930s than in the
1940s. Her facial expression was as usual one of martyrdom. She (Aunty)
went into the bedroom she shared with the grandmother, and deposited
her handbag and basket on the bed. Fay was aware of all of this, and
noticed that her aunt had brought home an evening paper. When Aunty
joined the rest of the women in the kitchen, Fay picked up the
newspaper, took it into the dining room and began to read it.

The bedroom belonging to Aunty and her grandmother was not large.
It held a double bed, a wardrobe and a dressing table (which at that time
Fay knew as a duchess). The bed cover was worn, made of some textured
pale pink material ('I think it was dyed' – Fay remembers at some stage
all the aunts, including her mother, dyeing that bedspread).

The next thing she knew, her mother asked Fay to go into the bedroom
(her mother's). Her mother told Fay that she should not have taken the
newspaper to read until after the aunt had finished with it. Fay was
puzzled by this. She could see no reason why she should not read it if
nobody else wanted it at the time. She argued with her mother, pointing
out that she was not doing anybody any harm. Her mother became quite
upset, though she spoke quietly (as usual). She tried to explain that the
person who buys the newspaper or magazine has the right to be the first
one to read it. She also made it clear that this tendency of Fay's to
appropriate every bit of reading matter which came into the house was a
defect in her personality and the cause of annoyance on more than one
occasion. She told Fay that she must be careful not to annoy the aunt
who earned the money to pay the rent on the house they all lived in. She
told Fay that she must apologize to the aunt.

Fay was not very happy about this. She really felt a great sense of injustice in it all. She did not believe that she had anything to apologize for, and felt self-righteous and unjustly treated. However, after arguing with her mother for a while, she agreed that she would apologize.

She sought out her aunt who was in the kitchen; she said she was sorry for reading the newspaper without asking permission. The aunt had no choice but to accept the apology, though Fay felt that she (the aunt) was uncomfortable about it. Although the aunt said little – 'That's all right' or some such phrase – Fay definitely got the message that her behaviour had been once again the cause of annoyance to the aunt. Instead of feeling repentant or forgiven, she just felt that once again whatever she did was the wrong thing. This aunt (alone among the six aunts plus grandmother) always made her feel this way. She knew that she was not alone in finding her aunt hard to please; all the cousins were united in this belief, and even the other aunts treated this aunt as someone difficult, judgmental, but to be accepted cheerfully as the cross they all had to bear.

Marie:

She was about 10 or 11 and a tomboy. The house was on the edge of a built-up town – less than a block away was country. There were large fields with scrub bush along the edges. Some good spots for hideouts. Certain bushes made good bows and arrows. Good climbing trees. She often explored these places with two or three others – all boys slightly younger than herself. There weren't many girls her age – the few there were were sissies. She could climb the highest in a tree and hang upside down by her heels – a feat few could match. It gave her a certain status, respect in the neighbourhood.

A kid lived in the house nearest the field – there was a large yard and a real club house – a single room wooden hut. Marie admired and envied that place – though the kid that lived there was a wimp. She organized a club with the neighbourhood kids with the club house as headquarters – there were to be challenges and medals of achievement for racing and hanging from trees by the heels – and archery.

One day there was some sort of trouble – alien kids wanting to move in to the club house. The details are vague – perhaps the wimp who lived there wanted some friends – anyway there was some sort of confrontation – words exchanged and a few stones. Marie almost certainly was in the centre of the controversy but did not throw stones.

Later at home a serious confrontation, the other kid had complained to his mother who had complained to Marie's mother. She was sent to her room. Then summoned and given the strap. Details are vague – probably three or four lashes with a belt – probably on hands, legs and/or bottom.

In the confrontation at home Marie admitted to the incident of the other kids trying to muscle in on her club. She did not feel guilt at the incident – only indignation at being pushed out of her place and then (falsely?) accused of stone throwing. And now the parents took the side of the enemy by belting her. She received the belting sullenly – she felt unjustly betrayed, pursued and defeated – humiliated and without alliance or support. Yet she remained hurt but defiant.

At no time during the incident did she feel, or express, 'sorry' except for herself.

Liz:

Liz was about 10 or 11 years. She had seen a woman (who seemed to her very old – grey haired, a 'bun' at the back of her head, tall, spare, severely clad) pass from the street into the school grounds and then into the school, and remarked 'Who's that old hag?' It was the mother of one of her schoolmates, who took the story home. The mother complained and Liz later sat in class with her schoolfellows while the teacher read them all a general lecture on courtesy and the dangers of gossip, having recounted the episode complained of 'without naming any names'. Liz experienced all the feelings of shame and mortification, but no apology was required.

We had expected that this trigger 'saying sorry' would, according to the cultural stereotype, produce dominant emotions of guilt, shame, repentance or regret. Such was not the case. Each episode as remembered produced not a single focused emotion but a variety of contrasting emotions. And, of all the memories produced, only Liz's memory showed the expected guilt/shame.

Margaret's memory is dominated by a similar sequence to that of Ann's given at the beginning of this chapter (note the similar ages). That is, first an expectation of *pleasing* the grandmother by saying prayers, followed by a feeling of being 'very upset', 'hurt' and 'confused'. She did not understand why her grandmother was so cross. The dominant emotion in the powerful grandmother was anger. As we later theorized, Fay's and Marie's memories make explicit the sense of injustice only implied in the memories of Margaret and Ann.

Fay's memory (slightly older) recorded a rich array of emotions, with a similar sequence. First she felt 'bored' and so took the newspaper to read. In response to her mother's chastisement she was 'puzzled' and could see no harm in what she had done. Puzzlement was replaced by feeling unhappy, feeling self-righteous and unjustly treated and finally defeated. 'Whatever she did was the wrong thing.'

Marie's memory was also that of an older child. She was involved in a children's fight for which she was held responsible. Her emotions included scorn and indignation. She received the belting sullenly and felt unjustly betrayed, humiliated, hurt but defiant.

Liz's memory by contrast displays no emotion up to the remark 'Who's that old hag?' However, she experienced strong feelings of shame and mortification when her action was subjected to 'a general lecture on courtesy'.

These five memories formed the first pool for our collective theorizing about the memories as a whole. In this cross-sectional analysis we found several common patterns. The episodes described by Ann, Margaret and Fay (Marie less so) contained the same sequence. In discussing the memories we all reported much the same complex of feeling – surprise/confusion, a sense of injustice or betrayal, indignation, humiliation, defiance, perhaps embarrassment and some anger, but rarely guilt. Here is an excerpt from our early theorizing.

Una: Where was the emotion in all this?
Jenny: It is full of emotion.
Sue: I was hurt.
June: Yes . . . I didn't report that but I would say that I felt a bit ashamed or embarrassed – that I had contravened a rule . . . I don't know what the emotion is – not anger – self-righteous indignation is the nearest I can get to it – I've got some very vivid memories like that when I contravened a rule that nobody told me was there.
Jenny: We've all got the same words: indignation, humiliation, defiance, embarrassment – that same congruence – not direct anger.
June: Yes, I was angry, bloody minded, defiant
Jenny: The same betrayal
. . .
June: What we're talking about as women is this relationship with authority and other people don't respect you as a person because you're already in a state of being oppressed
Jenny: I think it has something to do with agency – how important autonomy is as a personal value. If that's not particularly relevant you probably don't have so much at stake. There is a logical incompatibility between making your own decisions and having your decisions made by an authority
Sue: We've moved from saying we're being prejudged to saying
Jenny: Prejudged by whom? Prejudged by authority – we rebelled against authority
Sue: What we were saying in our stories was that we were wrongly judged and reacted with bewilderment, indignation
June: But the thing we have to theorize is why were these events remembered from our childhood? Why was that the common theme?
Jenny: I'm saying that was the basis, that I recognize now in writing memory-work – that it was events like this that formed the basis of my rebelliousness. At that stage you don't rebel, at that stage you are struck
Sue: By the strangeness – the injustice of it all.
Jenny: Yes, first it's strange, then it's indignation and then an awareness of injustice. Then perhaps there is some kind of resolution – an incipient defiance.

If there was a dominant emotional response in our memories, it was not guilt but something we found hard to name; a sense of injustice, of righteous indignation, of betrayal. There was a feeling that our sense of worthiness as autonomous individuals was threatened by those who were most important to us, a sense that we had been betrayed by those we trusted.

In some of the memories we were trying to impress adults and peers, even to 'show off'.[1] In our 'saying sorry' memories there was no intention of doing something 'naughty'. Quite the contrary. Ann was playing a reciprocal game, Fay was reading a newspaper, Margaret was saying her prayers. Neither Marie nor Liz was aware of wrongdoing at the time they acted. All of us, except Liz, were trying to be 'adult'. We each in our own way had taken the initiative, believing ourselves to be quite in order within the social rules as we understood them. In fact we were eager to demonstrate our knowledge of the rules and were confident of a favourable response by others. Our actions were appraised differently. At one level we were not taken seriously as individuals of worth, but at another level we were taken *too* seriously. As we later theorized:

> A child seeks recognition, seeks to demonstrate a knowledge of the rules, and feels sure the demonstration will evoke a favourable response – she is therefore surprised and hurt when the recognition fails to materialize.

Indeed our attempts to be adult had the effect of challenging existing power relationships, as elaborated below. Our theorizing brought to light a related contradiction. The transgressions in our stories concerned relatively trivial events. We were young. In the chastisement we received we were made to feel our own special insignificance. But if we were so insignificant why did our trivial actions have such serious consequences? We appeared somehow to have disrupted the social order and to be held responsible for potential chaos. Such an ability to disrupt indicates that we or our actions were deemed *significant*. The key to understanding the events and others' responses to our actions appears to lie in the nature of the social relation in which our actions are embedded. We decided to examine these more closely. Fay's 'sorry' memory is particularly poignant. It reveals the way in which our own and others' emotions are simultaneously embedded in and constituted by a network of gender relationships.

Fay lived in a female-dominated house during the war years with her mother, grandmother and two aunts, one of whom was the

---

[1] We have a collection of memories of being praised for 'being good' which we did not analyse exhaustively. The dominant emotion in most of these memories was embarrassment (but see chapters 2 and 5).

breadwinner for the household. There are two strong but contradictory themes expressed through the story. The first is that of women living together, sharing the joys and the hardships, all one together. Herein lies the significance of dyeing the bedspread. Fay elaborated later:

> That is a very vivid memory, a very happy occasion . . . [the cloth was] boiling in a copper – there was rationing and everyone was poor. I remember everyone laughing and giggling and making messes. It was a real *event*.

Yet in contradiction to that ethic of sharing there is the other theme of the stern, martyred aunt, the breadwinner, the person who bought the paper and has the right to be the first to read it, who was not to be annoyed, who 'earned the money to pay the rent on the house they all lived in'.

Against these themes, Fay's actions came as a direct challenge to the aunt's selfishness and the others' acquiescence. Fay was puzzled, she could see 'no reason why she should not read it if nobody else wanted it at the time'. But as Fay herself later theorized 'Was she really puzzled or did she know all along what she was doing? Was this all a set-up to show how unjust and unreasonable everyone was?'

Fay's challenge could not go unnoticed. For the sake of 'oiling the social mechanism' it was essential that Fay be made to apologize; that her own insignificance be reinforced, that the aunt be placated. So the existing web of relationships, once challenged, was restored. Note that the contradiction between the collective sharing and the need to placate the powerful aunt was partially resolved by a common agreement among the kin that the aunt was 'difficult'.

Fay's challenge was similar to Ann's. Both initiated an action which was defined by the powerful other as a challenge to their authority. The other person responded with anger and the child was chastised. In both cases the mother was not the powerful other but supported the authority of the other (and not the right of the child to initiate action).

In a very similar way, Margaret initiated an action that she thought would be pleasing to the powerful other, in this case her grandmother. Again, however, this initiating action was interpreted as a challenge to the other's authority (perhaps it was intended as such?) and provoked anger and chastisement. In all three cases 'saying sorry' appeared to be a necessary step in restoring the existing web of social relationships.

But that is not all that was happening. We were being taught not to challenge authority. We were also being required to take responsibility for the effects our actions had on other people. We were made to feel that we were (are) somehow responsible for the well-being of others. We were expected to say 'sorry' because our trivial actions had caused discomfort to others. We were also learning about anger in others as discussed in chapter 10.

Here is another excerpt from our collective discussion at the time. We had been talking about 'responsibility' and it led to this insight:

> *June*: Where do we get this sense of responsibility?
>
> *Jenny*: Yes, where do we get it? I've been watching all the adult women I know saying sorry, sorry, sorry, taking responsibility for all the cares of the world, but
>
> *Pam*: Because it's unjust. We had to say sorry when it wasn't our fault and we were made to take responsibility when it was not our fault. We're made to feel that we are somehow responsible for the happiness of others. Ann was responsible for her father's discomfort . . .
>
> *Jenny*: And Marie was responsible for those kids fighting.
>
> *June*: And Fay was responsible for Mother's getting unhappy . . . we didn't see this before when we wrote the stories separately, only when we see (read) them together . . .
>
> *Sue*: What's the relationship between responsibility and autonomy? . . . The other thing was, feeling our autonomy was being violated
>
> *Jenny*: They're not exactly opposites but when you're taking responsibility for others you're expected to do so regardless of your own feeling
>
> *June*: Self-abnegation imposed, but it's resented.

It was in this context that we as little girls were learning about the importance of saying sorry. Marie refused to say sorry in her story, despite the belting, because she did not believe she had done anything wrong. Ann said 'sorry' as a kind of 'don't hit me again' response. Fay and Margaret were required to say sorry though they did not want to. In our theorizing, and with reference to Marie's obduracy, Una commented:

> It seems ungracious to me . . . The other [response] is more hypocritical but says 'All right, what's done is done. We'd better make the most of it'. (These are clichés.) That involves some hypocrisy and oiling of social mechanisms . . . That's what happens all the time and you deny or abrogate your individuality to the extent that it is important.

Perhaps then these episodes, and others like them, are the beginning of the burden shared by most adult women. We feel responsible for everyone else's emotional well-being, and are constantly apologizing for others' discomfort. We do this even when we clearly have no part in the cause of that discomfort and no real power to correct it.

We learned the lesson of apology, said without contrition, for smoothing over social interactions involving conflict. Our private assessment of our own rightness remained at least partly intact – we did not feel guilty. There appears to be simultaneously an appropriation of the social order and a resistance to it: we both accepted and defied.

That raised other questions. Did we always resist? Did we not have memories of 'real' transgressions? Why was Liz's memory so different? We did not focus much on Liz's 'old hag' memory during our initial discussions. We did note that it contrasted with the other stories, primarily because Liz *did* feel ashamed. She was not required to apologize, thus was not given the opportunity to make reparation. But the powerful other (in this case the teacher) subjected her behaviour to public condemnation. The key difference between this memory and the others is that Liz appeared to accept the judgement of the teacher, to believe that she was in the wrong, and that she had failed to meet standards of adult competence. Liz acknowledged the competence of the adults involved and accepted their authority. By implication the rest of us in our memories did not.

Transgression – Being Sorry

To explore these themes further we gave ourselves the task of writing memories of real transgressions, that is, where we acknowledged doing wrong. The memories produced fell into two patterns. Some of our stories seemed to be like the 'saying sorry' memories only more extreme. In these stories the sense of injustice was replaced by, or developed into, a deliberate defiance. The second pattern involved guilt, shame and mortification.

Margaret's memory of transgression from chapter 1 was a good example of the first pattern.

> She didn't like her teacher, who used to make the class do silly things. Her teacher was cross one day about the children sucking 'cherries' out of burst balloons. Margaret remembers the crossness and the class being told that they must not suck the cherries because if the cherry burst in their mouths it might get stuck in their throats and they might die. Margaret did not really believe this and nor did she quite know what dying was. She went home and that afternoon . . . she cut a balloon and ate some of it. She didn't die. She felt that her attitude to the teacher was vindicated. She also felt somehow that what she was doing was wrong; she closed the bedroom door.

Shirley's memory was similar (it is given in full in chapter 10). At the age of 10 she was in hospital, reading her magazine:

Shirley was reading her film star magazine. Sister Leslie was in her office. . . . At about 20 minutes to nine, Sister Leslie came into the room. She saw Shirley was the only one reading, and said she was turning out the light. Shirley said, 'It's not time yet'. Sister said, 'Don't speak to me like that.' She took Shirley's magazine, turned out the light, and went back to the office. Shirley stood up in bed, leaned over so that she could see the office, and saw Sister sitting at the desk reading the film magazine. She could also see the clock, which still said something between 15 and 20 minutes to nine. She was so angry . . .

Shirley labelled her transgression as being angry.

These stories represent an extension of the apology memories. There is a strong sense of injustice, things are not as they should be. The powerful authority is wrong. The competent adult appears incompetent. The adults in these memories do not obey the rules that they had created and required us as children to obey. The child challenges the incompetent authority, in the first case secretly, in the second case directly. We were defiant of an irrational social order, though well aware of our own 'transgression' in being so. While we remained powerless to change the rules, we none the less strongly objected to incompetent use of them, and self-righteously asserted our own autonomy. We reserved the right to make our own judgements and to act accordingly. Note that in these and other similar 'sorry' incidents we acted alone, without allies or outside support. As in our previous memories there was usually neither shame nor guilt.

The second pattern of transgression memories was quite different. On some occasions we did feel acute shame, guilt and loss of personal worth, both in our own eyes and those of important others. Liz's memory (age 6–7) is a good example:

Liz woke in her cot, lying on her right side. The big room was very dark but the moonlight was very bright as it streamed in the window past her head and onto the mat beside her bed and across the foot of it. She felt cold and clammy. Out of the corner of her eye, level with the top of her bed and beneath the open window, she could see the cane armchair that always stood there. On it crouched – something – a dark shape, 'head' lowered between 'shoulders' and with 'arms' that stretched along the curved back of the armchair and down its sides. The bulk of the 'body' was heaped on the chair. It loomed black and heavy. She felt cold and small.

Her parents' bed was high and huge on the other side of the patch of light. It was very quiet and still. Beyond that she knew, was her sister's cot, past another open window and sliver of light. But she could not see all that, not the rest of the big dark room. She ventured a whisper, then a call 'Daddy'. There was a stir. 'What is it?' 'There's a man at the window.' 'Nonsense, it's nothing.' 'But I can *see* him, Daddy.' 'There's nothing I tell you, go to sleep.' She lay hunched up trying to see the figure in the chair. Her thumping heart subsided. Perhaps if she closed her eyes . . . She went to sleep. In the morning, when she woke her parents were up and her sister was crooning in her cot. There was a big heavy travelling rug, grey one side, tartan the other, tumbled in the chair.

Her mother came and helped them get up and they went out to breakfast. An ordinary day. But after breakfast her father took her aside and spoke to her. His manner was serious: 'You know you wet the bed last night, don't you?'

Marie's memory has similar ingredients:

She was 7, in primary school. Her teacher (Miss Levy) was a friend of her mother. Her mother also taught at the school in the infants. Marie was in disgrace and felt it – some misdemeanour. Did she answer back maybe? The memory is of Marie loitering behind the hedge after school and jumping out to say 'boo' to Miss Levy. She felt very ashamed and unworthy and wanted desperately to get back in Miss Levy's good books. Miss Levy seemed calm and patient – she smiled – but very distant. Marie was convinced that she (Miss Levy) only put up with her (Marie) for her mother's sake.

In these memories, in contrast to the others, there is an acceptance of the authority of the other, an acknowledgement not only of the other's power but also of their competence and 'worthiness'. Against this standard is measured our own social incompetence – we were not bad, but rather socially awkward, lacking control. We sought social recognition and acceptance but could not achieve it; we felt inadequate and ashamed.

We theorized at this point – while noting the contrasting themes – a generalized relationship between the assertion of a strong sense of personal agency or autonomy from an early age, coming up against the apparent unyielding requirements of a pre-constructed social order imposed by powerful and important others. Our stories repeatedly focus on the point of contact and the pain of that struggle. If we strive for self-assertion and fail we may either accept or reject the adult's judgement. If we accept the judgement of authority we feel shame/guilt. If we do not accept the adult judgement we feel anger/indignation.

To enlarge our own pool of women's memories concerning apologies and transgressions, we obtained four additional stories from a group of young women. This group was initiated by us but the theorizing was theirs – following the method discussed in chapter 3 (see also discussion of relation between these data and our own group's memories above). We examined the stories to discover whether their content confirmed and expanded our own.

Gay:

There was one time when Gay accidentally broke a precious vase of her mother's. It was a brandy balloon shape – large, a golden colour. Gay was about 13 or 14 years old. Gay's mother was very angry and very sad. She sat on the floor in the lounge room and cried. Gay realized how hurt her mother was. She was very sorry she'd broken the vase.

Lou:

It was school holidays and Lou had had a fun day playing with her friends. They'd decided to have a concert at her house as her mother was out at work. They charged the other neighbourhood children a penny to come in. They'd shut the curtains and had lit candles in the candlesticks to show the children around. Lou had sung 'Dream' and they'd sold sweets to the children at intermission. When Lou's mother came home she found candlewax all up the stair carpet and she was very cross. Lou was very sorry, she didn't like to upset her mother, she helped her to scrape it off.

Denise:

Denise was about 7 or 8 years old and had been looking through her older sister's diary in her bedroom. When she saw what was happening, Cheryl screamed and carried on at Denise. The fighting went on for a while but then Denise began saying she was sorry. She was in tears and really was sorry for what she had done. She was also sorry that she had caused the fighting. She also wondered if Cheryl loved or liked her anymore.

Amy:

There was a feeling of suspicion in the house. Amy felt uncomfortable in her tummy again. When no one was around she had gone to her mummy's purse and quickly taken one of the large two-shilling coins. She felt excited and then unhappy, but to put it back wasn't possible because everyone was up and around now.

She took it to school and spent all of it at the tuckshop. The tuckshop ladies looked as though they knew she had taken it from her mummy and she felt sick in her tummy again and the lollies didn't taste good.

When she got home her mummy said to tell her if she had done anything she shouldn't have and that she thought she had more money in her purse and then it wasn't there. She said that Amy wouldn't get into trouble and not to be afraid and just tell the truth and that she was sorry.

Amy felt wonderful and the sick feeling was going and she knew she should belong and feel safe again once she had told her bad secret. So she did.

Her mummy said she knew she had and then yelled at her and smacked her and called her a nasty, bad girl. Amy felt out there and alone again, and her tummy ached with her disappointment as she tried to understand what had gone wrong.

Since that day her mummy never trusted her near her purse again and never believed she wasn't going to be guilty if given a chance, and Amy also felt uncomfortable.

As with our own memories, many and varied emotions were reported within a single episode. Amy's story is particularly rich. Within the single social event we have the experience of excitement, pain, guilt, relief, disappointment, confusion, unhappiness, all in quick succession.

All four stories report an acknowledged transgression against an important and powerful other, usually the mother. All the children experienced guilt, usually acknowledged as feeling 'very sorry'. All expressed regret and a wish for reparation. These stories fall within the boundaries of our second cluster. The girls had failed to live up to adult standards. They were not so much bad as socially incompetent. Consequently they felt inadequate and ashamed.

Only in Amy's story was there any sense of injustice or betrayal. Significantly, the injustice is not identified except in the juxtaposition of statements 'she said that Amy wouldn't get into trouble and not to be afraid . . . her mummy then yelled at her and smacked her and called her a nasty, bad girl'. There is here, not only a negation of the worth of the child as an individual, but also an invalidation of the trustworthiness of the mother.

In nearly all the stories generated by women, the child transgressed alone. The exceptions are Ann's story (giggling together in bed, see below) and Lou's story. Only in Ann's story is there any suggestion of collaboration or 'partners in crime'.

She was about 4 years old, being looked after at a neighbour's house by her brother Alan. Their parents had gone out for the evening with the neighbours and Ann was at the neighbours' house because they had two small sons, one a few months older (Ian), and the other (Peter) two years younger than Ann. Ann's brother Alan was 14.

Ann was supposed to be asleep in the boys' playroom but Ian's bedroom was next door and she and he whispered and giggled to each other. There was a train set on the floor. She crept across the tracks to Ian's room and they sat in his bed 'reading' books by torchlight and eating sweets.

This is how their parents found them when they arrived home. Alan, the babysitter, had fallen asleep. Although Ann and Ian knew they had been naughty, it was Alan who got into trouble.

This story does not fit either of the theoretical clusters. There is no sense of injustice done to her, no questioning of authority. Neither does she report feelings of incompetence or guilt. But she was not alone. She transgressed with another child, a boy. And it was her elder brother who was called to account for the transgression.

This story of Ann's contrasts with all the other women's memories. In our other stories we acted alone; we neither received nor apparently expected support from peers or authority figures. As young girls we were isolated in our transgression and in our subsequent confrontation with authority. Alone we experienced the full weight of adult moral authority. Was Ann's story different because she was with boys? Are men's memories of childhood transgression different from women's? We asked a group of five young men to write their memories of transgression.

Donald:

He was playing with his friend Tim who lived across the road. It was a sunny warm day but they played inside anyway. They played at 'prisoners-of-war' as they often did. This time they were pretending they were escaping by tunnelling. They actually used hammers to knock a hole through a solid double brick wall under a bed. Each time their mothers called out (to find out what they were up to) they stopped 'digging', pretending the mothers were German guards. They were eventually found and dragged out. Spankings and harsh words followed. It was worth it.

Lawrence:

He had been angered by Olga. He was used to dispensing a rough justice whenever it seemed warranted, but on this occasion Olga, knowing what to expect, managed to escape his reach. She ran away and crawled under a bed. He pursued her, but in the enclosed space, found that he could not hit her satisfactorily. He then got close enough to her face to bite her. He became shocked and then slightly horrified when he realized that he had bitten right into her cheek with sufficient force to leave an uneven semicircle of blood on her soft baby skin. She screamed. He got out from under the bed. Their parents came running. They asked him what he had done. He told them as the crying continued to emanate from under the bed. His parents were silent. They stared at him. He was beneath contempt. Their disgust was palpable – he slunk away.

Richard:

It was Easter. He was in second class and had to go to a special church service. He and a friend, bored by the service, were sitting talking and laughing with their feet in the part of the pews that the prayer-books are kept, and on the padded wood meant for kneeling on. A teacher behind them got up and dragged them from the church, infuriated. As punishment, they were made to miss the Easter Hat parade that afternoon.

Patrick:

He was at school in class with two friends. One of his friends noticed that all his things had been taken out of his space under his desk. He was rather concerned about it and went to tell the teacher. She came over and found out who was involved. His stuff had just been moved to another desk but the three of them were all sent to the headmaster for playing. They had to tell the headmaster why they were sent to him. He remembers him giving some sort of lecture about good behaviour. Then, at one point, he told them they were to be punished – be given the strap – so they put out [their] hands and got the strap each and then went back to the classroom.

Alex:

He was at preschool and it was afternoon nap time. He had just set up his foldaway bed, was lying down under the blanket when he heard some bird noises (something like 'coo-coo') made by some of the other kids. He thought this was very clever/daring/fun/naughty and it made him giggle inside. You were supposed to be very quiet during afternoon nap time to let everyone sleep. He made some of these bird noises too. The teacher must have seen him make one of the noises because he heard footsteps and was shocked by a big whack on the bottom. The teacher didn't say anything, just smacked him.

There are some points of similarity between our stories and those of the men, but many points of difference. They, like some of us, were testing the rules, challenging authority. Their memories, like ours, contain a range of emotions. There was boredom, anger, playfulness, shock, defiance, delight. Only Lawrence experienced guilt or shame. One very strong emotion that emerges from these memories is the sense of glee and delight in breaking rules. The memories appear to demonstrate the exhilaration of flirting with danger, of risk-taking that we found in some of the theorizing about our happiness memories. There was no evidence of any such delight in our own apology or transgression memories, except for Ann's giggling in bed and possibly Lou's concert (in the latter there is no textual reference to delight).

In all the men's memories of transgressions, the boys were punished, even though Lawrence merely felt the weight of his parents' disapproval and scorn. The punishment appeared to be expected (although its occurrence was often sudden) and accepted. Only in Patrick's memory is there a sense that the punishment may have been unjust. Even here the injustice does not appear to be central. He does not discuss it, but accepts the punishment with resignation and a certain stoicism. Unlike our own apologies, there was no indignation or resentment or defiance. The men's memories all involve an understanding that their actions would arouse anger in the adult authorities. The adults' responses were also understood and accepted. Yet there was a strong sense, in at least three of the memories, that the pain and punishment 'was worth it', as Donald notes.

The men's own theorizing about their memories led them to conclude that in breaking one set of rules they are obeying another set: the rules of conformity to peer expectations override the adult rules and help to explain the pleasure inherent in disobeying adult rules. Although there is no sense of peer pressure in these memories, the presence and support of peers and their function as audience is an important component of these episodes. This helps to explain Patrick's acceptance of punishment. It is a mark of distinction to be sent to the headmaster and punished, with connotations of bravery and heroism. Again, the single exception to this theme is Lawrence, who did not perform with or for a peer audience, and who, alone, experienced shame and guilt – 'he slunk away'.

In nearly all cases for both women and men, we as children were challenging authority figures who were mostly women. We all experienced powerlessness and punishment at their hands. But the responses of the girls and the boys appeared very different. We as girls (except Ann's giggling in bed) were hurt, angry, confused, defiant, ashamed. The boys (except Lawrence), were gleeful, fundamentally disrespectful, were able to disregard the authority even while accepting the punishment.

It is interesting to note that all reported episodes of transgression involving guilt or a sense of injustice were also lacking in peer support. In all those expressing some kind of disregard for authority, children were either acting as part of a group (team) or were clearly playing to an audience. The differences between women's and men's memories may lie in the greater likelihood that boys seek and use peer support. As girls we stood miserably alone in our transgressions; we felt a sense of injustice or shame.

The men's memories contrast so much with the women's memories from childhood it is as if they came from different worlds. In our culture girls are implicitly (and often explicitly) more constrained than boys. There are both different standards and different expectations of compliance to rules which are ostensibly equally applied. One expression of this is in the adage 'boys will be boys'.

These data raised a number of questions. Why do the boys' memories relate so strongly to peer support? Why were we girls so isolated in our memories? Why do the boys appear basically satisfied with the outcome of their transgression even though they were more likely to be punished? Why did girls report such hurt, indignation, shame? Why do the girls appear so much more powerless?

These questions pursued us from the beginning. We explored the relations of power by considering 'gender reversal' in some of our stories. Going back to Ann's early memory of tickling her sleeping father (see the beginning of this chapter), what would have happened if Ann had been a boy? Would it have been acceptable for him to initiate the game? Would a boy have a 'reciprocal tickling game' with his father? How would the episode have changed if Ann had tickled her mother under the arm while her father was in the kitchen cooking? Turning to the other episodes: would the response have been different had Margaret been a boy and refused to go to bed until he had said his prayers? Or if Liz were a boy and wet his bed – would he have been in the parents' bedroom? Or if Fay's aunt had been an uncle? Many of these reversals seemed incompatible with our childhood experience (father cooking). But some memories already challenged standard gender identity (aunt as major breadwinner).

Of particular interest were those memories where we were required to say sorry or conform against our will. In saying sorry we were restoring the web of social relationships and being required to take responsibility for others' well-being. Would the same demands be as likely to be made of boys? We think not.

We theorized that as girls we had a particular relationship to authority such that others did not respect us as persons (that is, as agents) because we were already in a state of oppression both as children and as female children. Men as boys also experience powerlessness and punishment. They, however, seemed able to internalize the position of authority and identify with it. Perhaps as adults they are therefore less likely to remember the oppression of childhood or identify with it.

Conclusion

Finally, in our collective theorizing we returned to the general issues. What does the total pool of memories suggest? Why are these episodes the ones remembered? What have we learned about the social construction of emotions?

What do the memories of 'saying sorry' and 'transgression' tell us? Our analyses then and our theorizing now suggest that children construct a number of emotions – anger, defiance, glee, shame, guilt . . . in the context of a complex of relations around issues of responsibility and autonomy. In most of the memories discussed, our actions are actions of children trying out our wings, pushing at the boundaries. We try to be adult amongst adults or we try to be one with our peers; we act as we believe others expect us to act, we reciprocate, we test our competence.

Adults often respond to these actions by punishing us. The punishment may be a calm reprimand, tears, a slap, removal from the scene of the crime, a cross and angry voice, a public shaming. Our actions are viewed as irresponsible and incompetent. If they had been viewed by adults as responsible actions we would not have been punished – there would have been no transgression, no need to say we were sorry. Children define transgression in terms of adult punishment. Our autonomy is threatened by the punishment and the implicit (and often explicit) admonition not to repeat the action.

The children respond to this threat in different ways:

1   They accept the punishment, (introject) the admonition and believe that they have acted irresponsibly, incompetently and badly and they feel shame, guilt, hurt, unhappy, sorry. Many of the girls' memories and discussion of them can be interpreted this way.
2   They accept the punishment, indeed expect it. However they do not feel guilty or ashamed and they do not say they are sorry. Instead, because of peer support and because they believe – at some level – that irresponsible behaviour is expected of them, they feel glee, enjoy the fun. Many of the boys' memories and their analysis suggest this.
3   They reject the punishment and the definition of their actions as irresponsible. They believe that they acted properly, appropriately, without malice, and they are angry because they believe that they have been misunderstood, and/or because they believe it is the adult who is wrong or who has acted incompetently. They challenge the adult view of their actions as irresponsible. Many of the girls' memories are of this type.

In all three cases, the children's autonomy is questioned by the adult. In all three cases the children's actions are viewed as irresponsible by the adult. In the first case, the child accepts the adult view and it is only in these cases that guilt, shame, is constructed. The child's sense of self, her/his autonomy is shaken. In the other cases, the child's sense of self as an autonomous person is affirmed via alliances with and support from other children, particularly in the case of boys, or affirmed by beliefs that the adult authority is wrong or in error.

As we wrote about the apology and transgression memories for this book we found ourselves reflecting further about the relationship between responsibility and autonomy, which seemed very differently constructed in the memories of the women and men. For young girls there seemed to be both a positive and negative aspect to responsibility. Sometimes we were proud of the adult expectation on us to behave responsibly (in an 'adult' way) and this expectation enhanced our sense of self as competent, autonomous people. If under those circumstances we ourselves judged that we had betrayed that trust we felt guilt and shame. On the other hand, we often felt we were held responsible for irritating and upsetting the social realm of adults (e.g. Fay upsetting her aunt, Ann her father, etc.) where our actions were intended to have quite other results. This apparent expectation that we were responsible for the well-being of others contrasted markedly with the memories of the boys, which showed no such expectation.

For boys it seemed clear that transgressing adult rules (often the rules expressed by adult females) was an important part of constructing masculine identity, particularly in expressing solidarity with other males (the norms of mateship). We feel that the expression 'boys will be boys' accurately summarizes the differential expectation by adults of female and male children in contexts where rules and expectations are ostensibly applied without regard to gender. Boys are allowed (probably encouraged) to be 'boys'; girls are expected to behave like adults.

5
Happiness

In this chapter we explore a named emotion, happiness. Unlike our discussion in the previous chapter, where the focus was on the range of emotions experienced in the remembered episodes, our analysis in this chapter is focused primarily on the one emotion. The memories analysed here were written in response to the trigger 'being happy'. Also included here are those memories, which contained references to the emotion 'happiness', written in response to 'play', 'holidays' and 'being praised and told good girl'. As well as our own memories, we make reference to memories of others – a memory-work group of young women and another of young men, as well as student memory-work groups.

We were curious to see what sort of memories we would get if we used 'being happy' as a trigger or cue. So as well as using indirect cues, as noted above, we broke our own rules, so to speak, and used a named emotion as a trigger. Although in naming 'happiness' we ran the risk of producing memories which were over-worked and the processes of construction overlaid with cultural imperatives, such fears were not borne out. The clichés of Christmas stories and happy birthdays appeared but they were in the minority. In general, the cue 'being happy' produced some very early and therefore very interesting childhood memories which concerned the security of relationships and love, as well as the excitement of skilling and control.

Early Memories of 'Being Happy'

Having decided to write an early memory of 'being happy', we allowed ourselves, as usual, two weeks in which to write before our next meeting. When we met we were surprised that each of us, independently and without any suggestion or urging, had produced not one but at least two memories to 'being happy'. Our theorizing revealed why we had done this.

For example, two 'being happy' memories from Margaret were:

> Pleasure, but a quiet kind. She snuggled up in bed against Noonie, talcum and light flowery perfume smell, very soft, cuddly, reading stories together.

Roller-skating about the age of 11. Exhilaration at the skill – excitement at the danger (she would go fast along the driveway and have to turn sharply at the gate onto the footpath). Buses thundered along the street (flirting with death?).

Another memory, this one from Liz, contains both themes of happiness in the one memory:

> She was 4 years old. Her mother was in hospital giving birth to her baby brother. She was alone with her father. He gave her a bath, using a large baby bath on the kitchen table. She didn't know why he wasn't using the big bath in the bathroom. He made a game of it, and she enjoyed it mildly. Then she stood up to get out of the bath. Her father held out a towel in his arms and told her to jump into it. She was slightly afraid, slightly exhilarated. She jumped into his arms and knew complete security and happiness.

There appear to be at least two major themes in our early memories of 'being happy'. The memories speak of the happiness of belonging, of being loved, and the pleasure and the thrill of exhilaration. Both themes of happiness refer to pleasure, almost a sensual pleasure.

The fact that we each wrote two memories indicates the importance of two types of happiness: one focused on a quiet yet intense kind of pleasure associated with warmth and love; the other on an active pleasure associated with excitement, with challenge, with a separateness from parents. With the exception of Liz's memory, no parents, adults or indeed any other persons are present in the 'exhilaration' memories, and the episodes are all staged outside. In the 'being loved' memories, on the other hand, adults are the source of the pleasure and the events associated with the pleasure take place indoors. Further, with the exception of Liz's, all the exhilaration memories are memories from late childhood or early adolescence.

The initial analysis of our own memories was confirmed by the memories of the student groups. Two themes of happiness emerge. The primary appraisals reveal a feeling of belonging and love, a feeling of being special as shown in the following memory:

> She was about 4 years old . . . She was feeling happy and contented and special in that she had her mother to herself for the whole day and her mother had bought her a book . . . she had the book and her mother hadn't bought her sisters one and she had had her mother's attention all day. She felt a bit like a princess.

Also revealed in the students' memories are feelings of excitement. Happiness lies in mastery, as in this memory:

> She led Tandi to the saddle shed, saddled up, mounted and started off up the bright green grass-covered paddock, past the dam where a few ducks and pigs were feeding to the 'top' gate – the sense of excitement and joy as the horse and she cantered on across the landscape was a deeply felt experience which is a pleasure to recall now – feelings of freedom, floating, unity, trust, and sheer joy were all present.

Both these themes will be elaborated with reference to our own memories as these were more fully theorized than the memories of the student group. We shall, however, make reference to the students' memories which enlarge on or modify our understanding of happiness.

Security

Liz's memories are very early ones; she is about 3 or 4. Her earlier one, reported below, has to do with security and psychological warmth. She is in bed with her parents on Christmas morning and playing a game with her father.

> It was probably Christmas. She was 3 years old. It was early in the morning, and she had come into bed with her parents. She lay next to her father, with her mother on his other side. Her father was lying on his back with his knees raised under the blankets. His arms were outside the blankets. From somewhere, probably a Christmas stocking, had come two little slippers made of icing (fondant) decorated with sugar flowers. Liz had brought them to show her parents. Her father put one slipper on each of his first two fingers and walked them up the slope made by his knees. Liz found this a source of great joy. Her father was happy to play the game for her, but her mother did not seem to join in or to be interested. Liz sensed that her mother's reaction was not positive and this puzzled Liz. She could not understand why her mother was not also delighted as she and her father were.

Her story carries with it an understanding that security can and may be threatened. There is an awareness of vulnerability. 'Her father was happy to play the game for her, but her mother did not seem to join in or to be interested . . . She could not understand why her mother was not also delighted as she and her father were.'

In her second memory her feelings of vulnerability are more evident. Her father is bathing her and he suggests that she jump into the towel: 'She was slightly afraid, slightly exhilarated.' This is contrasted in the memory with: 'She jumped into his arms and knew complete security and happiness.' This memory is of a more adventurous kind than the Christmas story and as noted above it overlaps, to some extent, with the 'mastery' theme.

Ann's security memory is remarkably similar to Liz's memory of being in bed with her parents.

Ann was about 4 and went shopping with her mother and Dad. Her Dad was carrying her piggy back on his shoulders. She had a sudden and very intense feeling of love and joy – a feeling about being there with her father. This was quickly followed by feeling sorry for her mother because she loved her father more than her mother. No words were spoken.

Ann's early memory in which happiness is associated with security and belonging contains a sense of vulnerability as do Liz's memories. There is an anxiety about this security being disturbed: 'This [her feeling of love for her father] was quickly followed by feeling sorry for her mother because she loved her father more than she loved her mother.'

In all three memories there is an awareness that security and love is something that can be threatened. Liz cannot understand her mother's lack of delight; in her other memory she is afraid that her father may not catch her; Ann is aware of differences in the 'amount of love' one can feel.

Fay had difficulty producing an early memory which involves others but she did remember one which is a memory from her adult life. Although it is different from the three memories discussed above, it does contrast the warmth of companionship with 'the street outside the window'. Fay is doing a 1,000-piece jigsaw with a friend. What she remembers is 'white walls and woodwork, glow of fire, footfalls in the street outside the window, red Westminster carpet, feeling of tiredness, relaxation, warmth, companionship – if there was any communication it was sparse.' Security is found inside. This memory reminded Fay at the time of retelling of something she had recently read: ' "When happiness comes," said my friend, "it's so thick and smooth and uneventful, it's like nothing at all." ' (Garner, 1985, p. 61).

The sensory images of this type of quiet happiness are of warmth, cuddles in bed, the 'glow of the fire'; also there are many references to the sun in the students' memories. The texture is thick. Blankets, the towel into which Liz jumps, and the 'red' carpet to which Fay refers. Smell is also important – the talcum powder that features in Margaret's memory, the 'evening smell of summer flowers'. The voices are warm and resonant; the faces smiling. Happiness is the security that comes with being with people you love and who love you. These people, with the exception of Fay's memory, are fathers, mothers, an aunt. It is a quiet kind of happiness, although it

may also contain references to an unusual and special circum-
stance in which the feeling of belonging is heightened and affirmed.
In the latter case, happiness is associated with an exclusive and,
hence, unusual attention and love, as, for example, in the memory
of one of the students quoted above: 'she had had her mother's
attention all day. She felt a bit like a princess.' This exclusiveness
may be part of the happiness associated with special days, such as
birthdays.

This sense of belonging, of being loved, is contrasted with
possible loss of love, a threatening of security. Our secondary
appraisals suggested that in these children's memories there is a
recognition of vulnerability. The children seem to know that such
happiness is to be savoured; a sense of the unusual. One student
remembered a day spent with her mother with whom she had spent
very little time while growing up:

> It was a warm sunny afternoon . . . She called for her mother to come
> and see the flowers. As they both bent down to examine and admire the
> flower they drew physically closer together, exchanged smiles . . .

The contrast of security and the fear of loss and the accompanying
anxiety is more explicit in Marie's memory. Happiness, here, is an
end to separation:

> Coming home from school when she was 5 to an orange juice made by
> my mother. It was the coming home.. There was a ritual. The orange
> juice was part of the home coming. Marie came home on a bus up Old
> South Head Road. She didn't like school and felt insecure. She had no
> school friends.

Many of the memories collected from the students were about the
happiness experienced at the end of a forced separation, as in the
case of time spent by the child in hospital.

> Sharon was in hospital recovering from a major operation at the age of 5.
> One evening . . . she woke up to find a big, light green fluffy toy dog
> sitting next to her on the bed . . . the nurse told her that her father had
> come to see her, and would come back later . . . Sharon felt upset that
> she had missed him . . . She eagerly awaited her father. An hour or so
> later, she sighted him coming into the ward and felt a gush of emotion.
> . . . spent a happy evening with her father. She felt very loved and
> secure.

A quiet warmth and solidness summon up a sense of pleasure or
happiness which is tied to security and belonging. The happiness
here is closed and cocoon-like. Happiness is being secure in love

and surrounded by those whom one loves. It is a happiness associated with intimacy. This happiness is dependent on others, it is constituted in our attachment to others.

What is of special interest, here, is that in response to a cue which names the emotion, 'being happy', the primary appraisals point to the emotion 'happiness', while the secondary appraisals uncover and/or elaborate the presence of conflict and contrast. The opposite was indicated in the 'saying sorry' and 'transgression' memories in chapter 4. In the episodes described in relation to these triggers, puzzlement and conflict are primary. The emotion, whether it is guilt or anger or a sense of injustice, is constructed in the secondary and further appraisals. The conflict present in the 'being loved' memories points to an awareness that security, which is grounded in being loved, may be threatened.

Mastery
Feelings of exhilaration and excitement are constituted in the unfamiliar, in challenge. Happiness seems to lie in the successful negotiation of the challenge and its mastery. It is associated with a sense of achievement, a skilling, a mastery over the environment, over nature.

The 'mastery' memories, both from our memory-work group and from the other participants, are of two closely related types. One set has to do with a freedom from constraint; there is a sense of happiness associated with a breaking away from dependency. There is a sense of a self as independent of parental control, a growing sense of autonomy. The other memories are concerned with achievement. Typically the achievement is physical and to do with the natural environment. There is mastery here, too, but in this case the mastery is of the environment. Typically, too, the memories are of actions or feats accomplished alone. The conflict or contrast, where it is explicit, resides in the risks involved in trying out one's skills.

The following memory of Ann's captures the freedom and sense of independence and autonomy:

> Ann loved to scale the hills and explore . . . From high up you could see the whole valley, and far away, the harbour. Ann felt exhilarated and free.

Other stories which are concerned with freedom and independence come from the student participants. One memory is of going to the beach during the school holidays. Note that this memory does not observe the 'third person' rule. The child, a girl, is 7 years old:

It was raining and my mother and brother were with me. I remember the intense pleasure of the cold water on my body and the sense of joy and freedom experienced as I raced through the waves. The day was a cold May day. The main feeling was one of freedom, through lack of constraint.

These and other memories concern the invigoration one gets from nature; and from feeling some mastery over it or, at least not being cowed or made vulnerable by it.

Mastery also resides in the skilling of the body. The skilling can be experienced as in the above as a freedom from the guidance or control of parents or it may be experienced as control over the environment. Both types of memory provide a contrast to those security memories above in which safety and warmth were found, inside, in response to a sense of vulnerability experienced, outside. The episodes which describe the freedom from constraint and the skilling of the body are all set outside.

In Margaret's memory of roller-skating, described above, and in the memories of Fay and Marie below, the pleasure is related to achievement. The happiness is associated with a physical mastery. In Margaret's roller-skating there is a clear reference to danger and vulnerability but it is met with excitement rather than apprehension, because there is some control, some skilling. In Fay's and Marie's memories there is a sense of anticipation, although in Marie's memory the anticipation is implicit. There is always anticipation associated with catching a wave; one may miss the wave or one may be thrown off or 'dumped' by it. (Both Fay and Marie broke the rules and wrote their memories from the first person perspective.)

Fay:

Between the years of 16 to 30 or so I was a good surfer – body surfing, I mean . . . For me happiness was – is – judging a wave, then swimming on to it, the sensation of getting your head out ahead of it, the water funnelling through your arched arms and body. The rush to the beach, 30 seconds or a minute perhaps, I never timed it, kicking your legs maybe, a wild feeling like a yell, though you didn't necessarily yell, then the slow drag of your body on the sand, picking yourself up, Pure Joy, then the return to the surf to try it again. As long as your body could stand it. Then return to the beach, towel, return home, shower, lassitude. This was Happiness. Physical. The actual experience – 30 to 60 seconds, I would guess – repeated 4, 5, 6 times if you were lucky, before you tired, and if the Surf was right.

Marie's memory has much less description but it, too, is about the thrill of surfing: 'A thrill that stays with me still. A sense of being at one with something.'

There is a sense of mastery over the sea; one can only catch a wave if one knows how and is able to swim well. Fay also remembered similar feelings and emotions associated with a perfect stroke at golf or a good game of tennis. 'The rally seemed to go on and on, as I raced across the back-line, saving, returning shots . . . That was happiness . . . Mastery and control and mindlessness – supremacy of the body.'

There is great joy in the control of one's body and the natural environment. The memories are full of sensual images, the flavour of which is not warm, not thick and smooth, but cold and brittle. A student's memory of a walk in the bush captures this: 'the brisk morning air . . . the taste of fresh cold flowing water at the side of the track . . . the taste of chewing gum after having eaten nothing since early morning . . . the flavour of gum just seemed to invigorate him.' The pleasure in the memories is keen, sharp and short-lived; happiness here is eventful. The pleasure lies in physical prowess and in the power of the body. There is a strong sensual, even sexual, element.

These memories point also to independence and power. It is through the skilling of one's body and mastery of the environment that power and freedom, in the sense of autonomy and independence, are achieved. Another of Ann's memories, already given in chapter 3, captures the relationship between power and autonomy:

> Ann was about 7. Her Dad was factory manager of a concrete block factory. They lived in a house on the premises. There were stacks of concrete blocks near the house. Ann climbed among them and by moving some blocks (just possible) was able to fashion a rather grand fort. No one could see her if she so chose.

She was in command; not only could she move the cement blocks but she could make a fort and, if she chose to, could hide from the world. The memory speaks of control as does the following student's memory in which he describes the satisfaction he derived from digging holes in the back yard when he was 5 or 6 years old: 'One of the holes I dug was a good deal larger than the rest . . . I remember spending hours finding much pleasure in relishing this latest and greatest achievement.'

Recognition

Although there are two themes of mastery and security, they are not independent of one another. The fact that some of the memories contain both themes, for example, Liz's memory of jumping into the towel, suggests a connectedness.

Benjamin (1983) has pointed out that independence and autonomy are only achieved via the recognition of others. In this way,
autonomy and independence are paradoxically dependent upon
others. The child achieves self differentiation through independence
and mastery but that mastery must be recognized. Further, autonomy and independence are only likely to be produced in a sense of
security and are, therefore, dependent upon it. Security and
autonomy are two sides of the same coin and both are tied to our
experience and construction of happiness.

Other memories, for example, the following one from a student,
concern recognition. The child in the memory is about 4 years old.

> She has recently been given a box of coloured chalks and a blackboard
> . . . On this blackboard she is drawing a picture . . . She is uninterrupted
> in her activity. Her baby sister is content to sit on the rug and play alone.
> As the picture nears completion, Julie's father arrives home from work.
> His delight and enthusiasm for Julie's picture fills her with a huge sense
> of happiness. She looks up at her tall father and feels delight at being his
> daughter and having pleased him. To add to her happiness, her father
> says that he would like to take a photo of the drawing as he believes it to
> be especially good.

The memories and the analysis of them indicate that happiness is
constituted in achieving selfhood. Such achievement is dependent
upon being loved and feeling secure, secure enough to move beyond
the security of childhood to earn autonomy. Such gaining of
autonomy is, in turn, dependent on some mastery. Autonomy, as in
the previous chapter, is an important concept. Its re-occurrence
here points to the centrality of autonomy to the development of a
self and the place of emotions in that development.

Happiness is constructed in pleasure and in sensuality. In the
sunny, warm, textured, thickness of security of being with and loved
by others, inside, and in the invigorating, cleansing, brittle, sharpness of separateness and freedom, outside. The construction takes
place at the intersection of the inside and outside, in the apprehension and anxiety of the move from the warmth of the inside to the
cold of the outside, in the testing of the boundaries and the skilling
of the body. There is always a danger that recognition will not be
forthcoming and that love may be withdrawn.

The emotion of happiness is closely related to bodily sensations.
Indeed, nowhere is the body more evident than with these memories. Pleasure is achieved through the control of the body and the
mastery of the natural environment. There is a sense in which when
a person is happy then that person is physically at one with others or
at one with the world.

Other 'Happy' Memories

Having theorized our 'being happy' memories, we examined our memories written to the cues 'play', 'holidays' and 'being praised' as they, we thought, might throw further light on the construction of happiness. The 'play' memories will be discussed here in as much as they complement our analysis of happiness. Some reference will be made to our 'being praised' and 'holiday' memories. A detailed analysis of 'holidays' is, however, reserved for later (chapter 8).

As noted at the beginning of this chapter, the quality of these memories is somewhat different from the memories discussed above. Although happiness was present in some of the memories, despite the cultural imperatives to be happy on holidays and in play, there is not a great deal of happiness expressed in these memories. Even in those memories where happiness is experienced, the primary appraisal is often one of shock and puzzlement. It is in the resolution of the conflict or contradictions in the memories, that the emotion, happiness, is sometimes constructed. In many of the memories of play and holidays, emotions other than happiness – emotions such as fear, guilt, embarrassment – are the ones constructed. There are very few memories which focus directly or explicitly on the security theme, but some of them unambiguously concern mastery. We will deal first with the memories written in response to 'play'.

Play

The two aspects of the mastery theme discussed above, freedom from constraint or autonomy and achievement, are captured in some of the play memories. These two aspects come together in control over one's own body, in skilling it and gaining some mastery over it.

> Liz (age 5 or 6), Donald and another small boy dug a toilet hole in Donald's back yard. Liz had to (?was dared to) pooh in it ceremonially. She balanced unsteadily on the edge, dress up, pants round her ankles. The boys jumped around laughing and encouraging. She was worried that Donald's mother (her kindergarten teacher) would come out and find her. She wee'ed in the hole and pulled her pants up. They danced around singing 'Mummy is the root of all evil' (a pun on a contemporary song 'Money is the root of all evil'). There was relief, glee.

The second memory is as follows:

> Fay was between 1½ and 2½ years old. She had a celluloid doll called Jackie. Jackie had articulated arms and legs and head and well-modelled features including open eyes with eyes painted blue with whites and black

lines, and hair that was also modelled in the celluloid. Jackie was about 6–8 inches in length, and Fay's mother had dressed her in a dress from the twenties. Some sort of blue and white striped tussore silk with a long straight bodice and short pleated skirt. But Jackie had no pants and Fay was interested in the smooth pink space between Jackie's legs, which she could move up and down so that Jackie could be made to 'sit' as well as 'lie down'.

The third memory is:

> Margaret (age 8 or 9) was sitting on the steps leading to the front door. It was afternoon and the steps were in shadow. She wore a grown-up's dress over her own clothes. It was a dress that was in excellent condition . . . It was made of maroon heavy silk or rayon fabric. There was a collar of the same colour which was made of shiny satiny material. The dress had an opening from neck to waist, fastened with press-studs. There were vertical folds of material on each side of the opening. She was nursing her doll, and she opened up the dress and arranged her own clothing underneath so as to expose her left breast. She sat with her doll, playing at feeding it at the breast. She felt sensuous (sensual?), happy and content. She hummed or sang to the doll. There were other children – her brother, possibly cousins, playing under the house – not far away but not within sight. Her mother opened the front door. 'What are you doing?' she said. Margaret suddenly felt guilty and embarrassed, she didn't quite know why. 'Just playing,' she said. She had the impression that her mother knew what she was doing, and that her mother was amused by it.

In each of these memories, an aspect of the body and its functioning is explored in some way. Either directly, as in Liz's memory, or indirectly through a doll as in Fay's and Margaret's memories. The happiness in the quoted memories is the happiness of coming to learn about and control the body. Both Liz's and Fay's memories concern making the body (either one's own or a doll's) work. In Fay's and Margaret's the happiness is of a quiet pleasure and contentment; playing alone.

The security theme is not entirely absent, it is implicit. The adults who are mentioned in the memories are in the background and that is where the children want them. Fay's mother has provided the doll with clothes and an unnamed adult has given Margaret her dress-ups. Margaret's mother when she appears is 'amused'. The images are of satin and silk, of smooth things that are nice to touch. In this regard, they resonate with the security memories discussed above.

Of the three memories, Liz's has the strongest sense of adventure. Her memory is more like those discussed above under 'mastery'. There are other children present and the reference to an adult is in terms of a worry about the emergence of an authority figure from the house. She is playing in a child's world and adults are not wanted. The emotion present in the memory is 'glee'.

The 'play' memories of the memory-work group of young men are very similar to these three. Happiness was expressed as either 'having fun' with other children, as in Tim's and Stan's memories or, as in the case of Murray and David, the memories were of a contented and quiet pleasure alone or with adults.

The difference between the memories of the men and women rests in the content. The women's memories, in general, concerned the body; the men's concerned the environment. The toys with which they played were footballs or train sets, and the mastery was over these things. The attention to detail in David's memory, of when he was 3 or 4 years old, is reminiscent of the attention Fay pays to the doll:

> It was a sunny, cool winter morning in Hawthorn, Melbourne. He was by himself on the second floor balcony at home, playing with a clip-together plastic train set. . . . He was alone and warm and he had his plastic train set. The track was in pieces. It was the soft, red, chunky plastic and the pieces fitted together like jigsaw pieces. The train had an engine car and several carriages. The wheels and axles were metallic and the bodies were of coloured plastic. Some of the track pieces were straight, some curved, some branched, some tapered off so he could run the train on the track and then off and across the concrete. He made the track into circles and meanders and pushed the train along making 'toot-toot' noises and talking to the passengers. . . . He asked all the passengers to wait while he re-arranged the track and then let the train go on . . .

The mastery here focuses on a knowledge of how a train works. He has control over the train and the passengers.

Tim plays in a cubby-house in the trees with his brother and friends. They pretend it is a helicopter and they take it in turns to be the pilot. Stan's memory too is about skilling and competence. His memory includes a set of instructions about how to climb a particular tree: 'On the way down you can swing from one of the branches and then jump to the ground. This is fun – not just because of the act of swinging and jumping but because your hands slide easily round the branch because the bark/skin is so smooth.'

The imagery in many of the men's memories mirrors that in our own. There are references to smoothness, to sun, and to warmth. But as well in all the men's memories there is an explicit reference to height. Tim's cubby-house is up high – 'you can see everything'. Murray liked watching 'the men kick it [the football] high in the air'. David plays with his train-set on the second floor balcony. In the corner there is a rain water drain: 'it was dark and mossy and he couldn't see the bottom and he dropped the piece [a tapered end piece of the track] in'. Philip's memory is of playing in the quarry in which they climbed to the top . . . The men discussed the thrill they remember when climbing high and difficult trees. Their adult theorizing connected this valuation of height with overcoming the constraints and powerlessness experienced by them as children, although they were a little wary of seeing height as a metaphor for adult power.

Their play memories also concern place. Philip's quarry is a special place, the cubby-house is Tim's domain. Our memories of play also contain references to place – mostly back yards, verandahs and front or back steps. Without exception, play takes place outside the adult domain.

Happiness in play, whether the quiet kind or the more gleeful, adventurous sort, is associated with finding out, with acquiring knowledge and skills; competence enables autonomy and control. The memories suggest that girls gain this competence with regard to the body, boys with regard to material things. Play is preparation for adulthood; modelling and role-playing are involved.

As Mead (1934) notes, play is the way a child steps outside the self and takes on the 'role of the other', the adult. Children learn to understand themselves as children; the adult/child interface is made intelligible through play.

> In the back yard which sloped down to the lake, Ann set up a mass production for mud pies. Mud formed into pies on the table, down the chute to a lower table for the 'icing' to be put on. Then laid out in the sun to dry. Ann's younger brother was assistant baker – not terribly enthusiastic or skilled was he. Ann organized this activity and felt quite pleased with the efficient and effective process achieved.

Play is child's work, a central source of developing identity. Identity is gained in control over actions and in ownership of place. The skilling gives the children a sense of competence, and with it they win freedom from the constraint of adults. Happiness is growing up. Play enables an extension of self, in the safe world of childhood. Play is a metaphor for freedom, for freedom from rules unless one makes them up for oneself, freedom from responsibility, and freedom to explore, freedom to extend and test out one's skills and achievements.

The 'being praised' memories confirmed, again, the mastery aspect of happiness. The happiness here, however, is tied to recognition. Recognition of competence is what being a 'good girl' is all about. Margaret remembered that, when about 2 years of age, when she wanted to go the toilet she would say, 'I want to be a good girl'. Margaret and Liz were praised for 'being brave'; Marie, Liz

and Fay for being clever, intelligent beyond their years, top of the
class, having a good memory. Margaret was praised for being polite
and controlled; Ann for being patient. This was praise for moral
competence. Happiness lies in the acknowledgement by mothers,
fathers, teachers, adults of the competence and achievements of the
children.

Happiness resides in the differentiation of self, in autonomy and
freedom from parental constraint, which in turn is earned by skilling
and controlling the body. The memories indicate that women will
find their happiness in relation to their bodies and their control of
nature, while men will find happiness in respect of material things.

Holidays

Whereas the 'play' and 'praise' memories highlighted the mastery
aspects of happiness, the memories of holidays brought us back to
the 'freedom from constraint' aspect of happiness. As with the play
memories, many of these holiday memories contained contradiction
and conflict. Indeed, the contradictions present in many of our
memories of 'holidays' focused on the lack of the expected freedom
that one associates with holidays, with being away. This sense is
captured by a memory of Margaret's, given in full in chapter 8:

> It was a beautiful day, hot and sunny. The beach was just a short walk
> away, about half a mile. Margaret was dying to go to the beach. But she
> had to wait until her mother had done all the housework. She was asked
> to rock the baby to sleep. . . . Margaret was impatient, she wanted to get
> away . . .

Eventually the baby seems to go to sleep:

> She carefully stopped the rocking and tip-toed to the door. Just as she
> reached it, the baby cried. She had to go back and start all over again.
> . . . She reluctantly returned to the task, and eventually escaped,
> successful at last.

What this memory points up is the way in which holidays are
meant to free one from the arduous aspects of skilling, from
responsibilities of 'growing up'. Margaret is happy playing at
nursing her doll, such play is within her control. She does not want
the task of putting a 'real' baby to sleep, especially as she is on
holiday. The memory is full of anticipation and she 'eventually
escapes, successful at last'. Her escape is to the outside. She wants
to play, and play is associated, as we saw above, with the outside,
and not with the adult world of the inside.

Ann's escape is to the inside. She is fearful and anxious of the
unfamiliar outside. Her holiday memory below, like Margaret's,

points to the tension between the inside and the outside. But in her case the tension lies between, on the one hand, a duty to 'go outside and get some fresh air' and play with the dogs and ride the horses, activities which frightened her, and, on the other, her desire to escape 'curling up in the lounge room and reading'.

Holiday is a metaphor for freedom. Happiness here is doing what you want to do. As children this meant an escape from duties and obligations. In Margaret's case these duties were adult duties, in Ann's the moral obligations of childhood. In Ann's case the freedom may be unwanted; the unfamiliar too testing.

Ann, age 8–9:

> Ann looked forward to the evenings after dinner when she was allowed to stay up for a while. There were often visitors and there would be lots of talk and laughter in the living room in front of the big log fire. They used also to play cards at night – usually rummy or five hundred. Ann's uncle used to gamble madly at five hundred and he was always 'going out backwards'. She loved these evenings when everyone was relaxed and happy. There was lots of talk amongst the adults about wool prices, and the weather, and the state of the nation.

This memory (or *mélange* of memories) is reminiscent of the security memories discussed above: 'She liked the house and felt warm and safe in it.' The security here is characterized by warmth and belonging, but in this holiday memory there is a sense of difference. Ann is being admitted into an adult world; her escape is from the world of children outside. She is recognized and feels happy in her acceptance into this adult world. She feels competent, mastery is present here too.

Conclusions

Happiness is constructed at the intersection of freedom and auto-nomy, on the one hand, and recognition which is grounded in security and love, on the other, as noted by Benjamin (1983). Play and holidays enable freedom and autonomy, they allow excursions into unfamiliar territory. In play that autonomy is explored within a safe domain, parents are physically absent but always on hand. Holidays, too, are supposed to allow freedom and an extension of self, but sometimes the unfamiliar threatens rather than releases the self for adventure and exploration. Michael Gow in his play *Away* (Gow, 1988) examines these and other themes of holidays and we take them up in chapter 8.

Happiness is constructed in positive self definition. The children in these memories are negotiating the interface between adulthood and childhood. They venture forwards, in play, on holidays, on their own, and with other children; when they seek recognition they turn to adults, their parents, and relatives, their teachers. Their successes are marked by happiness.

Happiness is, of course, constructed anew in adulthood. A short story, which we read during the period when we were doing 'memory-work', captured the flavour of the children's happiness discussed above and also described an adult experience of freedom from constraint. The story captures the realization that the recognition by others of one's mastery, control, skills, and achievements is no longer necessary. In the story, the protagonist recognizes that she is free to take control of the direction of her life. Her happiness is produced in the realization that she is free from the constraints of motherhood and she celebrates her growing recognition of selfhood with a song. The story, which is called 'A Happy Story', is by Helen Garner (1985).

> They kiss me goodbye, grinning, and scamper across the road. I do a U-turn and drive back to Punt Road. I shove in the first cassette my hand falls on. It is Elisabeth Schwarzkopf: she is singing a joyful song by Strauss. I do not understand the words but the chorus goes 'Habe Dank'! The light is weird, there is a storminess, it is not yet dark enough for headlights. I try to sing like a soprano. My voice cracks, she sings too high for me, but as I fly up the little rise beside the Richmond football ground I say out loud, 'This is it. I am finally on the far side of the line.' Habe Dank!

6

Fear and Danger

In many respects our culture as well as other cultures (Armon-Jones, 1986) accords fear great importance. It is used as a means (or perhaps even *the* means) of social control. We use fear in child-rearing as a means of controlling and limiting behaviour. In educational settings, fear of punishment has long been viewed as a very effective means for disciplining children. Psychological theory (behaviourism) has shown that 'fear of punishment is more effective than punishment itself' in bringing about behaviour change.

Systems of justice, both criminal and civil, are also built upon the belief that punishment is a deterrent. Imprisonment, fines, withdrawal of privileges (such as driving licences) and the fear of being faced with one of these punishments are supposed to deter citizens from breaking the law.

In chapter 2, we used fear (of the bear) as a 'typical' emotion. Many if not most of the theories we discussed in that chapter assumed that fear was a unitary, non-controversial emotion, universally understood. Theories differ in their definition of what constitutes emotion, but the paradigm of meeting a bear, 'experiencing' fear, and desiring to flee (or actual flight) is taken for granted. It becomes a stereotype or prototype of emotion.

In our work on fear and danger, as discussed in the present chapter, we find that only a few memories involving fear, whether our own memories or those of others from whom we collected them, were of this kind. This is probably not surprising, since we have already pointed out that it is problematic episodes that are likely to be remembered.

Liz, age 8–9:

This is something that must have happened on more than one occasion, but there is one occasion that sticks in her mind. She had been to the corner shop . . . to get to her house she had to go up the hill and down again. At the top of the hill was a large, tall Queensland house and in that house lived a black dog. There was a sign on the gate which said 'Beware of the Dog' and the dog seemed to be bad tempered and dangerous.

On this occasion, the gate was not properly closed and as she approached the house the dog came out of the gate and stood barking and growling on the footpath. She could see him silhouetted against the sky as she walked up the hill. She was very afraid. She knew that you must not show the dog that you were afraid, because that would make him much more likely to bite you. So she slowed down and walked very slowly up to the dog telling herself not to let him know how afraid she was. She seemed to be able to stop her heart from pounding and walked past this fearful animal without running or panicking as she felt she really wanted to. He was a large dog with thick black curly hair and his eyes were red and angry looking. He stopped barking as she got closer and growled ominously. She continued walking slowly but purposefully past him expecting him to spring upon her at any moment, or at the very least to chase her down the road. However he just remained in much the same spot menacing but not moving, and she eventually reached her own yard.

The situation here is very reminiscent of the discussion of the role of memory in emotion that was used by Arnold (1970), to which we referred in some detail in chapter 2. In this memory the process of appraisal is made quite explicit. It is deliberate appraisal. The child is sizing up the situation, deciding whether it is more prudent to 'give in' to the fear and run away 'as she felt she really wanted to' or to remain outwardly calm and walk past. It is reflection which we have argued makes the episode memorable, and this memory describes the reflection explicitly.

The social construction of fear as revealed by our work beyond the above example also points to the importance of power relations, and hence gender. Our analysis of fear and danger memories suggests that emotion, perhaps especially fear, is gendered.

Our sources here are four different memory-work groups:

1 Young men – a group already referred to in chapter 4. This group chose 'danger' as a trigger.
2 A group of women aged in their thirties who constituted themselves specifically to explore 'fear'.
3 A group of younger university students who also used 'fear' as a trigger.
4 Ourselves, who chose to write both 'fear' and 'danger' memories.

We begin with the young men's 'danger' memories because our own memories of 'fear' and 'danger' were produced as a result of the young men's use of this trigger.

Young Men's Memories of 'Danger'

The young men had chosen 'danger' as the last topic in a series of memory-work discussions. It was a topic which grew directly from their exploration of transgression, where, as shown in chapter 4, most of their memories were about the risk-taking involved in breaking rules and/or pushing at the boundaries.

Their danger memories fell into two categories: those of Lawrence and Robert, where the actors got into dangerous situations as a result of peer pressure, and the other three involving 'accidents' or threatening events outside the child's control: a near-choking, a fierce dog, a poisonous spider. In all cases the situation was witnessed and resolved by an adult, all female except for Lawrence's teacher.

Lawrence, age 4¾:

He was at his primary school. He and his good friend Simon were playing in the playground. They came across a painter's plank about 5 metres long and 20 cm wide, propped up against a tin shed. One end of the plank rested on the edge of the roof, while the other sat in the light dust about 3½ metres out from the base of the shed wall, the latter being about 2 metres high. With some trepidation and expectation and no doubt a sprinkle of exhilaration they cautiously climbed on all fours up the diagonal plank and onto the roof of the shed.

After working the situation to the maximum extent, Simon descended backwards down the plank. Lawrence, however, was not so casual. He made numerous attempts to muster the courage, and even considered jumping off the side of the shed, but he could not bring himself to place his body in the vulnerable position which was a precondition for getting (safely) to the ground.

Eventually Simon tired of waiting for him and so went away, luckily to return with a teacher. After much coaxing, the teacher managed to convince Lawrence to trust the skill of his arms.

Robert, age 6–7:

He was in first or second grade and was with his mother down at Balmoral Beach. He met this other kid – Jason – from school who wasn't his friend, but wasn't not his friend, maybe a bit of a bully: a kid that was respected. He suggested swimming to the nets (there was a section of the beach netted off). He had never swum that far before – but said 'yes' anyway. He only just reached the nets – quite a way behind Jason who was a much better swimmer. He rested by hanging onto the nets for a while and then began to swim back. About half way back (it was only about 50 metres to the shore – if that) he began to flounder and grow tired and gasp for air. He struggled on. He was obviously in trouble. He didn't yell for help. His mother had seen him and raced into the water and helped him to the shore. She made quite a commotion.

In the second group of danger memories the danger arose unexpectedly as the boys went about their ordinary daily lives.

Philip, age 6–7:

To understand this memory fully, a little background knowledge is required. Across the road from where Philip lived there was this family and their children who Philip played with. This family had a large German Shepherd who was always kept in the back yard where the children didn't play. It was common knowledge among the children that he was dangerous, and Philip feared him a lot. The fact that he did not have a dog and was not used to them added to his apprehension towards this dog. One day he was walking home from school, he turned into his street and walked up it for a while when he heard some barking and saw the big German Shepherd coming towards him. He began to scream. He knew he couldn't run back up the street away from the dog and he still had three or four houses to pass before he reached his house and was safe from the danger. The dog was between him and safety. He was terrified. He screamed more and more. The dog approached barking threateningly. Philip didn't know what to do. Then his mother appeared at his house's door in her coat. She came out onto the street. Philip had not imagined that his mother would come out with the dog there, but she did and the dog stopped. Philip walked to his mother and was comforted as he was escorted inside.

Howard, age about 7:

He was playing in his favourite place near his grandma's house. It was just up the hill about 20 metres and was a little cleared area surrounded by trees. He and his brother had been 'working' for weeks clearing it up, building 'walls' around the place and moving old car parts that were scattered around. He decided that they needed a seat. Looking around, he saw a piece of iron girder sitting in the grass. It was only a small piece, big enough to pick up. He lifted it up, and peered underneath it. A big spider, a redback,[1] ran up at him and was nearly on his fingers when he dropped it. He ran screaming down to his grandma's house, sliding in the gravel on the road. He screamed for hours because the spider had nearly bitten him.

Dougall, age about 3:

He was eating a carrot after dinner on a summer evening while riding around the back garden. It was balmy and darkening. He rode around on a three-wheeled Dinky sometimes putting sand in the small 'bucket' carrier on the back of the Dinky. Suddenly, he was choking on some bits of carrot. He started coughing and running short of breath. He half-ran inside the house to get help from his parents. He was panicking and began to cry. His parents were very worried and tried to dislodge the caught pieces by patting and glasses of water. He was taken to hospital eventually where he had X-rays on his chest. From then on he was never allowed to be active while eating.

All the memories contain a strong sense of justification, there is a great deal of warranting. The extremity of the danger was insisted

---

[1] A redback spider is regarded in Australia as dangerously venomous.

upon with much detail; the history of the savage dog, the height and angle of the roof, the distance of the swim, the necessity to go to hospital after the choking incident, a *redback*, not just any old spider. The very specific details of measurement '3½ metres from the base', '50 metres to the shore', '20 metres up the hill', which must be retrospective judgements given the youth of the actors, emphasizes how the young men as adults need to rationalize and/or justify their failure of control. This emphasis is connected with the boys' fear of 'losing face', explicit in the memories of Lawrence and Robert at the time.

In their theorizing of the memories, the young men emphasized the importance of the physical challenge:

> *Philip*: I think of danger in terms of physical danger.
> *Lawrence*: Did you realize it was a really difficult thing to do?
> *Robert*: Yes. It was a thrill to do something dangerous, to prove myself.
> *Dougall*: The danger was retrospective.

They also theorized the function of the adults, 'Your mother probably said "You stupid little . . ." ' and emphasized rules prohibiting certain activities. As young men, Lawrence and Robert emphasized how they had experienced combinations of shame and fear at their failure to complete the challenges in front of their admired peers.

What really stands out in these memories is the relationship between what is appraised as dangerous and behaviours like crying, panicking, calling for help, etc. – behaviours that typically define 'fear'. The emotions, however, that are being constructed in these situations are pride and shame. The fear which is present appears to have been constructed earlier. In all memories, the importance of 'face' is paramount, particularly in the memories of Lawrence and Robert, where a peer is simultaneously an instigator of the behaviour, an example of someone who successfully negotiates the danger, and an audience for the failure involved.

Dangerous situations are defined by these young men as situations in which it is appropriate to feel fear. They were objectively physically dangerous situations; there was no doubting that. It was appropriate for them to cry and seek help. Even Robert implies that he would have called for help: 'He struggled on. He was obviously in trouble. He didn't yell for help. His mother had seen him . . .'

Women's Memories of 'Danger'

Our own memories in response to the 'danger' trigger could not be categorized quite so neatly. Liz's memory is most like those of Robert and Lawrence in that it involves peers as audience.

Liz, age 13:

It was the end of the school year and her school class had decided to have a 'breaking up' outing at a place called 'the Oasis'. This was a large recreation area, a popular tourist attraction, with tropical gardens and a beautiful swimming pool.

It wasn't a marvellous day, though hot and steamy there were clouds. There were about 12 or 13 of the children, both boys and girls. Liz had never been in a swimming pool before, and was not really confident about her swimming ability. The others were having fun by climbing onto the diving board and jumping into the water. She really felt that she would love to do this. So she watched the others for a while, and finally decided to give it a try. She climbed up the ladder to the diving board, and went out to the end of it, and looked down. She felt that what would happen if she jumped would be that her legs would not remain sufficiently straight after she hit the water – that being the advice she was given. It all seemed too high and too far down and just too dangerous. She turned around and walked back to the ladder – and then made the mistake of trying to go down frontwards. It was wet and slippery and she slid to the bottom, banging her own bottom on the hard concrete.

Liz's situation in this memory is very similar to that of Lawrence, where he is stuck on a roof. She too has courted danger by climbing onto the diving board, and emphasizes the physical measuring that underpins her judgement – 'it all seemed too high and too far down and just too dangerous'. Unlike Lawrence, however, she assesses the danger quite coolly and accepts her failure to meet the physical challenge matter-of-factly. In fact, the 'coda' of her awkward descent suggests wry embarrassment and contrasts strongly with the dramatics of Lawrence's failure. Peers are implicitly present in Liz's memory, but do not seem to carry the same emotional meaning as for Lawrence.

Margaret's memory involves an active courting of the danger, although it is the exhilaration of mastery rather than fear which is emphasized. In this way, it seems comparable to our 'happiness' memories. (In fact, she used the same situation as one of her 'happiness' memories, rewriting it as a 'danger' memory without remembering that she had already produced it.) In this memory, Margaret successfully confronts danger with only herself as audience, whereas other people are present in all the other 'danger' memories.

Margaret, age 10–11:

There was a straight concrete driveway beside the house which led from the footpath to the back lawn. There was no garage and no car parked there. After school she would take her roller-skates to the grass and attach them to her leather lace-up school shoes. The skates were American, a present from her brother. Instead of straps at the front the skates had metal clips which you wound on to grip your shoes, with a key. If you didn't tighten it sufficiently the shoes would come out of the skates and you were likely to hurt your ankles. If they were tightened too much the shoes would be damaged. The toes of the shoes got badly scuffed when you braked anyway. She adjusted the skates carefully and stood securely on the grass. The gates were open onto the footpath. She clomped six heavy steps across the grass, gathering speed and momentum, then launched herself down the drive, getting faster down the slight incline, then bracing herself for the turn at the gates, the most exhilarating moment because it was a tight turn and if you misjudged you fell over, or rolled onto the road. Each time she repeated the feat she became more confident. She loved the rush of wind against her face and body, through her hair. One time she almost tripped, a bus rumbled past, close to the nature strip.

These two danger memories are most like the young men's memories, but they differ in one important respect. Although there is a clear assessment of danger – 'if you misjudged you fell over, or rolled onto the road', the diving board was 'too high' – there is no panic, no crying and no calls for help. Rather there is a cool assessment of the situation and an estimation made of the risk involved. Peers seem unimportant and face saving is absent.

Ann's and Marie's memories are more like those from the second group of young men, in that they involve dealing with unexpected events.

Ann, age 19–20:

Ann was coming home from university one night on the last or a very late ferry. She had done this many times and was not worried by the dark or by being out at night alone. She got off the ferry and hopped on the bus that used to meet the ferry. She became aware that a man was watching her but didn't take much notice. He got off at her stop and Ann knew as she turned the corner he was behind her. What began to worry her was that while she was walking on the footpath he was walking on the grass verge. Somehow Ann knew that he was getting closer. All of a sudden as he crept up beside her he said 'boo!'. Ann was somewhat taken aback and turned to him. He said: 'You don't frighten easily, do you?' Ann said 'No', and hurried across the road. When she got across the road she began to feel frightened as she had to climb up some steps through the trees to get to her street. But she felt she shouldn't run. As she got to the bottom of the steps, knowing she had not far to go, she began to run. When she got home, she realized how dangerous the situation might have been – she wondered if he had been mad.

Marie, age 11:

In 19. . the family got a new car, ivory colour with green upholstery. One Sunday afternoon the whole family went for a drive. Father's farm was on the other side of town from where they lived. Their father had suspected that sheep were getting out into a neighbour's paddock. It would be autumn or winter (because there was a freshly ploughed and planted paddock involved).

Sure enough, some sheep had got out. At the place where they were found, the road ran along the side of a hill, round a corner and then down a slope to a creek crossing. The sheep would have to be driven along this and across the creek crossing up the hill to a gate to be put back into the proper paddock.

When the family got up to them in the car they ran all over the place. So the father stopped the car and said to the mother, 'You drive along slowly and I'll try and keep them together'. The two sisters were in the back seat of the car.

As they got towards the bend in the road the sheep 'broke' and ran in all directions, some back towards the car, with their father dashing about and waving his arms and hooting at them.

The mother probably wanted to stop the car (she could drive but wasn't used to this new car). Instead, it roared away and at the same time she wrenched the wheel and they went straight through a wire netting fence, hitting a fence post with the middle of the bumper bar and knocking the fence flat. The car roared down hill towards the creek, through a ploughed paddock because she had panicked and was still standing full on the accelerator.

As the car roared on, Marie, who was sitting in the position behind the driver, realized the emergency, dived over the back of the seat and dragged on the handbrake which was in the middle of the front seat. At the same time her sister, who was smaller, also dived over the front and turned off the ignition. It all happened too suddenly to feel frightened, but they 'had to do something'.

By the time they had got upright again the car had come to a halt in the middle of this wet ploughed field, and their Father had come charging down the hill and was looking in the window of the driver's door. The most memorable thing about this episode was the look on his face – it was quite 'ashen'.

All he said was to the mother, 'Move over', and he got in and started the car and drove it back on the road. Then he got out and said to her 'Now drive'. She drove very slowly down the road to the gate where he was putting the sheep into the paddock. Then he drove us all home.

In discussing these memories we initially noted our emphasis on *dealing with* the danger. Marie in the car, Margaret on roller-skates, Ann walking home, Liz assessing the risks on the diving board, are all making judgements which indicate the importance for us of maintaining, or regaining, control. The women attempt to solve the problem confronting them; they avoid the jump from the diving board and work out their capacity to roller-skate at speed, put on the car brakes, and deliberately and carefully maintain control by not showing any fear. In contrast with the young men, there seems a total lack of concern about 'losing face' and a total absence of panic.

Our own memories were of episodes occurring at older ages than those of the young men. Therefore, as older girls in the memories, we had far more experience than the boys in the memories of events and their consequences, on which to base judgements of danger. This raises interesting questions, which we have not explored, about why early or later memories are produced. However, we theorized at first that the main contrast, in terms of gender, was that as boys the young men *courted* danger, whereas for most of us as girls/ women, because we were not consciously testing our limits, there was no chance of a 'loss of face'.

In the memories where 'danger' was defined in terms of the unexpected occurrence, the women's memories, but not the young men's, were concerned with the actions of other people.

Young Women's 'Fear' Memories

The general theme of frightening events just 'happening inadvertently' also emerged in memories of the younger women's group whose sole focus was the emotion 'fear'. The following is only a small selection from the memories generated by this group, on which their analysis is based.

Dee, age 3:

She was sick and was on her campbed in the lounge room. The room was gloomy though it was daytime. Her mother was at her bedside and told her that the doctor was here to see her. The doctor was dressed in black. After looking at her he said he wanted her to roll over and pull down her pyjama pants so he could give her an injection. She was very frightened by this and refused, hiding under the campbed.

Dee, age 4:

Her mother took her down the road to school. It was a sunny day. She had never been before. The school ground was quiet – all the children were inside. She went into a classroom with her mother. The teacher spoke to her and took her over to a dolls' house near the room dividers. Some other girls were playing with the dolls' house. Her mother said goodbye and was gone. She was frightened at being left alone in this strange place. She ran out of the classroom. No one saw. Outside there was a hedge separating the school yard from the street and footpath. There were some workmen digging a hole in the footpath. There was a red barricade around the hole. She hid behind the hedge.

Sandra, age 5:

She is alone. She sits in front of the wood stove in her grandmother's kitchen on a wooden chair. She is getting ready for school but she can't do up her shoelaces. She doesn't know where the adults have gone and she is panicky and afraid they have left her. She can't go out to look for them because she can't do up her shoelaces . . . They come back. They were out the back with the car. The kitchen fills with noise.

Jay, age 7:

She was walking through North Park with another girl. They were on their way home but they were not hurrying. There were two boys in the park that afternoon. Perhaps one of them hailed the girls or perhaps they just met face to face on the gravel path near the rotunda. The larger of the two boys carried a hessian sugar bag. They talked for a while, perhaps they knew each other. Anyhow, she was sitting on the grass when the boy with the bag tipped out a large stumpy-tailed lizard. It was about 12 inches long. She had seen such lizards many times before in the bush and was only mildly curious as it squatted on the grass. But she immediately became apprehensive when the bag carrier picked up the lizard, holding it just behind its front legs and advanced towards her. Her chest tightened, her breathing was almost stilled and her heart shook madly inside her. She did not move. He stopped with the lizard head a few inches from her face. She tried not to think of its scale-like bumpy skin as ugly and watched panic stricken as the filmy eyelid passed over the bulging eye and then back up again. Its mouth opened – 'hah' it breathed and its long tongue shot out almost into her eyes. She let out a screech and leapt to her feet running madly, her smooth-soled shoes slipping on the damp grass, her heart belting against her ribs, her breath cutting into her lungs and her ears pounding. He and the lizard pursued her. She looked back knowing she should not.

Everyone knew that if you looked back you could not keep ahead. 'No' she cried, 'go away' as she ran back round the rotunda and without any sense of direction round and round in the park, she ran crying and gasping back past where she had been sitting. Finally she stumbled and fell sobbing and crying uncontrollably on the grass. The boys stood over her jeering and taunting. Then still jeering they picked up the sugar bag and moved off in the direction they had been going.

In the comparative analysis of their 'fear' memories and the young men's 'danger' memories, the young women's group developed four themes. These are based on the total pool of their own memories, not only on those four cited above.

1 Threat appraisal

All the boys feared physical harm to themselves, which was embodied in *non-human* aspects or processes of the natural world, such as drowning in the sea, choking on a carrot, falling from a roof, being bitten by a spider or dog. The girls or young women all feared physical or psychological subjection by *people*, usually male strangers or fathers. The boys appeared to fear mainly loss of face, due to their inability to master nature/the natural world, whereas the girls'/women's dominant fear was loss of identity or autonomy.

2   Resource appraisal
    Parents, grandparents, or teachers were helpful or saved the
    boys. By contrast, the girls felt they had to face the threat alone,
    the 'others' in the memories (mothers, friends) could not or did
    not save them. They were mostly silent, unable to speak. Dee's
    group found most of their memories located in the home, and
    the boys' in the outside world.
3   Action in response to threat
    The girls were either avoidant or inactive in the face of threat,
    whereas the boys mostly sought adult help. This point connects
    with the differing nature of the threat in the boys' and girls'
    memories, that is, that the threat to the boys was from non-
    human sources, whereas the threat to the girls was from people.
    It is also connected with gender differences in resource appraisal
    noted above.
4   Narrative form
    The young men's memories were action narratives, with a
    quality of abstract precision and a large number of justificatory
    elements. This was in marked contrast to the large amount of
    sensory information and lack of justification in the young
    women's narratives.

Before we comment on these young women's 'fear' memories and
their analysis of them, we turn to our own fear memories.

Older Women's 'Fear' Memories

Our own group also produced a set of 'fear' memories. One of these
has already been quoted (see Fay's memory in chapter 3).

Ann, age 6–7:

She had gone with her family for a holiday. They were staying near the
lake. There was a long pier out into the lake where fishermen used to sit.
Ann and her sister had gone for a walk out along the pier one afternoon.
It was warm but overcast. Suddenly she was aware of a dog – an Alsatian
– in the water. The dog seemed to be watching her and his ears were up.
Ann began to walk back along the pier and then to run – the dog was
swimming to the beach and running up the beach after her. She was
terrified and began to scream out for her father.

Liz's memory of a dog, as noted at the beginning of this chapter,
although similar to Ann's and Philip's, indicates the importance of
control which is gained through appraisal and reappraisal. In
contrast to Ann's memory here and Philip's earlier, in which the

appraisal of the danger appears to be intuitive, Liz's appraisal was deliberate.

The following memory, Clare's, has many similarities with Jay's lizard memory above. It involves fear of reptile-like creatures (eels) but only because some boys are threatening to use them to frighten Clare. Both memories, explicit in the case of Jay's memory and implicit in Clare's, illustrate the recognition by both boys and girls that girls can be frightened (and subjugated) by boys. It is almost impossible to imagine the reverse. The boys in these memories have already assumed power, and the girls recognize it.

Clare, age 6–7:

She was walking home from school and the road crossed a wooden bridge over a middle-sized creek (quite deep) with lots of water weeds, then past the biscuit factory on the left and the plastics factory on the right before reaching her house. It was attached to the tile factory at the foot of the hill. There were eels in the creek, large frightening ones that bite. In order to cross the bridge, Clare had to pass a group of boys from the Catholic school (being Catholic made them more alien). They often congregated there. They never actually attacked Clare but she felt very frightened and vulnerable, especially when they all looked and laughed. They may have made threatening reference to the eels.

If we examine all the memories – our own of 'danger' and 'fear', as well as those of the young men and of the young women, then our analysis confirms the four themes described above. Men's appraisal of threat is associated with physical danger, whereas women's appraisals are associated with both the physical and psychological danger. Many of the women's memories concern the action or inaction of others; they are fearful of being left alone, of others' harassment and incompetence.

The women's 'fear' memories are very similar to the men's 'danger' memories in that it was in 'fear' that women called out for help and sobbed and cried, not in 'danger'. As noted above, the young men identified 'danger' in terms of their panic and calls for help. The narrative form of men's memories includes much precise information to justify and warrant their behaviour.

The data indicate that, in general, women fear loss of control while men fear loss of face. Indeed, some of the women's memories, see especially Fay's 'fear' memory, indicate that much of women's behaviour may be controlled by fear. This difference between men and women in the construction of fear may be related, in turn, to the finding that girls and young women cope with their fear in silence, alone, while boys turn to adults for help.

The young women's group also noted that some of their 'fear' memories were inside (indoors), though some were outside, while the men's danger memories were, without exception, outside. When the situation was inside, the fear tended to be self-generated, it comes from within. When outside, it was 'caused' by something or someone specific. Fay's 'fear' memory is an inside one, as is Marie's memory.

Marie, age 10–11:

She had measles in the last term of the year. Her father believed fatalistically that kids should be exposed to these infections so her sister wasn't isolated but continued to share the bedroom, quite a pretty room for two girls. The window was between the two beds and facing the window was the door which led into the main hall of the house. Opposite this door was the door to the dining room which was really the main sitting room of the house.

On this night Marie's sister was not in the room. It was early evening but quite dark. Marie woke from a sleep, probably feverish, and the light through the half closed door of the dining room across the hall shone through the half open door of the bedroom which was dark. The house was very silent, Marie felt that no one was near.

In the half light, Marie saw something or somebody standing just inside the door of the bedroom. It seemed to be the figure of a woman in a sort of a long filmy gown or sheet standing motionless with its head half shrouded, as with a hood. It stood quite still, half turned away.

Marie was very frightened and cried out. The light came on and her mother came in to see what was wrong. Marie, still frightened, told her about the figure – a woman. Her mother pooh-poohed this and told her it was nothing. Marie was still frightened and begged her to stay there with her. But her mother said this was ridiculous and went out again, turning off the light and saying 'Go to sleep'. But she opened the door of the dining room so that more light shone across the hall and into the bedroom. Marie could hear her mother turning the pages slowly as she read the 'Herald'. The light and the sound of the pages turning comforted her and after a time she went to sleep.

In theorizing, Marie noted that she did have some confused idea at the time that what she saw was a figure of death – maybe out of a movie, or a story. She was probably delirious at the time, and the memory, the figure, the whole situation is like a cliché. We briefly discuss clichés and their function later in this chapter, and in more detail at the end of chapter 8.

It seems clear that there are strong differences in the ways in which girls and boys, women and men, are expected to react to situations defined as physically dangerous or challenging. Further, we reflected that, in psychology, 'fear' is conventionally dealt with as an impulsive emotion, whereas in our memories it is closely tied to the moral order, and seems more conflictive than traditionally viewed. This point is taken up more fully in chapter 7. The moral imperatives surrounding injunctions to 'be brave', that is, not to display fear even when we feel it, also differ between men and women as we show below.

In very few cases is fear described without some involvement of pride, guilt or shame. Even in the relatively unproblematic cases of fear of the dog, or the spider, the actor needs to justify the fear, bravery or courage being seen as of higher moral value than giving in to fear, either by expressing the fear or by asking for help. This theme, either directly stated or implied, is strongest in the young men's memories. Pride in overcoming fear, or shame in giving in to it, are present in most of the memories described so far in this chapter. The major exceptions are those where the fear is engendered deliberately, as in the lizard and eel examples. Here, the conflict is not between the brave and the cowardly response; it is engendered because of the 'no win' nature of the situation. There is really no choice, the girls must escape.

Injunctions to 'be brave' are more strongly enjoined upon boys than upon girls. We note that boys when they give in to the fear make sure that they communicate in extreme terms. 'He screamed more and more.' 'He screamed for hours.' 'He was panicking and began to cry.' Once the fear overcomes them, the boys make sure that others know how terrified they are – extreme reaction seems to be needed in extreme situations. The girls, on the other hand, in similar situations, did not find it necessary to expand upon their reactions. 'She began to scream.' 'She cried out.' 'She ran away.' Only Jay, fleeing from the taunting boys with the lizard, described her reactions in strong terms.

Girls are given more latitude to express fear, and this seems to make it unnecessary for them to describe their expressions of fear in extreme terms.

Young Adult 'Fear' Memory from a Student Group

It is not only in different expectations of reaction to fear that gender differences are to be found. As feminist writers such as Brownmiller (1975) and Bart and O'Brien (1985) have highlighted, women are restricted socially, physically and psychologically through largely justifiable fear of men. Men and boys know and expect this, as shown in the memories of Jay with the lizard and Ann walking home from the ferry above, and use this knowledge in subtle and not-so-subtle ways.

As feminist analyses of many social practices have revealed, there is a contradiction between the ideology of women being persons to be protected and the reality of danger to them. For example, Scutt

(1983, 1985) examines the relationship between criminal assault at home and the 'romance' depicted in Mills and Boon novels and movies like 'Gone with the Wind', as well as pornography. Linda MacLeod (1985) shows how government policy sees police intervention in wife-battering in terms reminiscent of the knight rescuing the damsel in distress.

What is regarded as legitimate fear, how much emphasis on apprehension there is, the importance of control or retrospective justification of 'cowardice', the distinction between feeling and showing fear, seem quite gender-specific. For boys, the presence or absence of peers is crucial in whether fear will produce shame. Fear restricts women's activities, but is an incentive to action for men; for example, contrast Robert's swim and Clare walking home from school. Boys seek danger, girls have it thrust upon them. When they are small, girls are terrified, immobilized by fear, feel vulnerable. As they become older, girls and women begin to overcome their fear and strive for control.

In terms of expressing or showing fear, there are gender differences as well. Under some circumstances, girls and women are expected to show fear of men, such as in Ann's memory above. But they cannot always be sure that such fear is justified. If they display fear before the man 'makes his move' they may well be subject to ridicule. This is one of the ways in which the contradiction that a man is both a potential protector (from other men) and a potential threat serves to restrict women's actions.

Although women may have danger thrust upon them, they may nevertheless feel responsible for having 'got themselves into it', as the following memory from a student group illustrates. This memory and the analysis of it illustrate many of the points just made.

Kelly, age 19–20:

She had been waiting on the corner trying to hitch a lift for hours. It was the longest ever she had had to wait and she was exhausted to the point of tears. It was a public holiday and only three cars had passed her in four hours. She made up her mind that the very next car that came along she would flag down even if she had to pretend it was an emergency. After a few minutes a Holden came around the corner and slowed down as she frantically waved her thumb around. It was a middle-aged man at the wheel who smiled at her a little too sweetly, she thought to herself, but even though she had promised herself that she would be extremely selective in who she took lifts from she didn't care at the moment. The lift was the most important thing at the time. She hopped in and struck up a conversation about sport. Whilst they were travelling, she noted that the stretch of road that they were on was pretty isolated, not a house or car in sight in either direction. Suddenly a hotel came into view and he suggested they stop for a beer. When they finished they went back outside into the car and he made no motion to start the car. He quickly leaned over to her and she realized that he was drunk. He put his arm around her and asked her to kiss him. She was stunned and frightened. She instantly thought about her backpack in the back seat of the car and started to talk her way out of it. She knew she could run for it but wanted to stall him long enough so she could grab her pack without him driving off with it. She was shaking with fear and was raving about how upset she was. She managed to get the pack, slam the door, and run back towards the hotel as he drove off. She burst into tears.

There is a further aspect of memory-work methodology which was applied to this memory, but not to other memories we have used. This is the rewriting of the memory. Part of what we do in memory-work is to expose the restrictions on our actions contained within cultural imperatives often embodied in clichés. We mean by clichés expressions which often embody things which we take for granted. Some of these may appear trite on the surface, having become meaningless by overuse. Others embody socially embedded meanings which are taken for granted. Nevertheless, even the trite and meaningless clichés can reveal automatic and unquestioned ways of thinking which may need to be challenged. An analysis of written memories will look for clichés and examine the meanings they carry. This was the initial analysis of Kelly's memory done by the student group . Following this initial analysis it was possible to rewrite the memory. The process is described in detail here as it is one of the few examples where we found this aspect of memory-work to be of direct relevance to our work.

Kelly's memory is longer than most of our memories of child-hood, and it is full of clichés. As we shall see in chapter 8, our own adult memories were similarly longer and much more cliché-ridden than our childhood ones. We surmise that the rewriting of child-hood memories is not particularly helpful whereas rewriting adult memories forces us to expose and question what we otherwise take for granted and enables experience, memory and hence the self to be reconstructed.

The analysis began by examining the clichés and their function. In setting the scene, the actor feels the need to justify her situation. She has to tell us how desperate she is; she would not do such a foolish thing if she had not been 'exhausted to the point of tears'. Her desperation is underlined by the 'frantically' in her description of how she waved her thumb.

Apart from 'middle-aged', the only description of the man is that he 'smiled at her a little too sweetly'. This absence, together with the cliché, suggests that she does not want to remember any more about him. Her description also suggests that 'she should have known better' – the account already attributes to him some of the characteristics of the potential molester.

The description of the road, the hotel, the situation 'suggested they stop for a beer' are all clichés. They are also contradictory. She does not seem surprised when a hotel appears on such an isolated stretch of road, and agrees to go and have a drink, despite the fact that she seemed to be apprehensive. They went in for 'a beer', but he becomes drunk – no explanation of this is offered.

'He made no motion to start the car' is an ominous cliché under the circumstances. The situation is one of menace, she is 'fearful' and 'stunned', but then at last 'started to talk her way out of it' convinced that 'she could run for it'. Finally, she 'bursts into tears'.

The reader is left with the distinct impression that she feels responsible for what happened to her. She should have known he was likely to attack her when he 'smiled at her a little too sweetly', but she 'didn't care at that moment' even though she should have. She tries to protect herself by 'striking up a conversation about sport'.

Even when he begins to attack her, she gives him an excuse for his action, 'she realized that he was drunk'. Nowhere in the written memory does she blame the man, become angry with the man. Rather she blames herself. She is 'stunned and frightened' not angry and furious. She chooses prudently to run not to fight. She is successful in escaping, even in escaping with her belongings, but she does not feel successful. She 'bursts into tears'.

When the group theorized this memory, they asked questions about *why* the woman needs to justify her actions. Why should she feel that it is unreasonable to expect to be able to accept a ride from someone without being attacked? Even if the outcome of her hitching a ride was a bad one, she should feel justifiably angry, indignant, even afraid, but not stupid and responsible.

When she successfully solves the problem of how to escape without forfeiting her belongings, she should feel pleased with herself. She should feel angry with the man, but elated and relieved that she has escaped unharmed. Instead she feels guilty, ashamed and angry with herself.

The group felt that this memory could now be rewritten in a way that revealed the man as unreasonable and irresponsible and the woman as more powerful and morally justified. Though she might still be a victim, she is acting responsibly. She is not condemned for her victim status, and does not so condemn herself. The following demonstrates the potentially empowering effect of rewritten memories:

She had been waiting on the corner trying to hitch a lift for hours. It was the longest she had had to wait. It was a public holiday and only three cars passed her in four hours. She was glad when a Holden came around the corner and slowed down as she waved her thumb around. A middle-aged man was at the wheel, and she got into the car, grateful for the lift.

She struck up a conversation about sport. They travelled along a section of the road without houses, and there was no traffic in either direction. They approached a hotel, and he suggested that they go in for a beer. She agreed. When they had finished, they went back into the car.

She wondered why he didn't begin to start the car. Suddenly, he leaned over to her and put his arm around her and tried to kiss her. She was furious, completely surprised, and a little frightened. She thought 'I must get out of this situation' and began to talk her way out. She managed to stall him long enough so that she could grab her backpack out of the back seat of the car, and then dashed out and slammed the door, and ran towards the hotel. He drove off. Much relieved, and happy to be out of that car, she resigned herself to another long wait for a lift.

It is significant that on rewriting the memory Kelly left out the sentences about 'bursting into tears'. The omission indicates that Kelly believes, as does the group, that the powerful and those who believe in their actions do not cry. Even in the rewritten memory, however, it is difficult to avoid the imputation that she was responsible. Our society accepts that young girls are always in danger if they accept a lift from a strange man, especially if they 'ask for it'. The 'it' that they are asking for is more than a lift, and they should not be surprised when they 'get it'.

The hitch-hiker memory illustrates the way in which fear, both at an interpersonal level and as an example of social control, acts to limit women's freedom. At an interpersonal level, fear of provoking a more powerful person to anger and/or aggression limits personal freedom and autonomy. At one extreme, such fear can manifest itself in an inability to run away from a chronically fearful situation, such as repeated assault in the home.

The rewritten version of this memory also suggests some important connections between anger and fear. Anger felt by a less powerful person towards a more powerful one is realistically constrained by fear. Given power imbalances between women and men it is easy to see how gendered differences in anger occur, and in chapter 10 we discuss in some detail the relationships we found between anger, power and gender.

Nevertheless, we wish to emphasize that while power differentials are important in the development of gendered emotions they are not the only factor; cultural expectations of nurturance and responsibility also play a crucial role. The analysis in the previous two chapters points to the importance of these expectations.

7
Emotions and Agency:
The Construction of Self

In chapter 2 we distinguish organismic theories of emotion, which give priority to bodily responses, from those which focus on the cognitive or mental aspects of emotion; either emotions are described as physical occurrences, physiological responses to stimuli, or they are described as the result of appraisals or evaluations of physical events. In the latter case, interpretation and reflection is inserted between the physical stimulus and the bodily response.

Most traditional theories begin with the premise that there are certain happenings or events which in and of themselves (organismic theories) or on interpretation (cognitive theories) give rise to physiological and bodily responses which are characteristic of emotions or, in many theories, equated with emotions. From these theoretical perspectives, emotions happen to one. Once triggered, emotions overcome one; they are passions. The emotional response, the expression of the emotion, communicates the felt emotion to others. This expression is, according to the organismic theorists, likely to be 'hard-wired'.

These theoretical approaches are individualistic and essentially asocial. Although it may be recognized that emotions serve a social function in that they communicate or signal to others, the 'function' is universal and biological.

In these accounts, there is little dispute that:

emotions involve affect or feelings, often equated with certain physiological events;
emotions also involve cognition, however fleeting, in the form of remembering or appraising;
emotions are expressions of inner feeling;
emotions communicate our feelings to others;
emotions overcome us.

Lazarus (1984) and Zajonc (1984) may argue about the primacy of affect or the necessity of cognition, Izard (1977) may stress the communicative function, but most psychologists and sociologists, indeed most people, would agree with the five points above. Averill would list all of them – they are part of the syndrome 'emotion'. Happiness, for example, may be experienced as a warm feeling of safety, reminiscent of early experiences of being loved, and communicated by smiling. It might also be experienced as an excitement, a thrill, accompanied by and so communicated to others by an exuberant shout.

Emotions, as we have demonstrated in the previous chapters, are more than this, however. Emotions are constituted in the ways in which we interpret and make sense of happenings and events in our environment, particularly our actions and the actions of others, and in the ways we communicate those understandings to others. The dynamic aspect of emotions is clearly seen in our data and analysis. Apprehension turns to exuberant joy and release and then a sense of pride in skilling and competence in some of the 'happiness' memories. Puzzlement turns to hurt and a sense of injustice and righteous indignation in many of the 'saying sorry' memories.

Emotions are produced, socially, in contradiction and conflict. Puzzlement and apprehension are the outcome of contradictions or disagreements about the way the world is apprehended by self and others. For example, Ann, in the memory of the tickling game reported at the beginning of chapter 4, expected her father to reciprocate the game; instead he responded by hitting her and shouting. Margaret expected her grandmother to be pleased when she insists on saying prayers before bed; instead she is asked to apologize. Shirley (chapter 10), while in hospital, is asked by the supervising nurse to turn the light out before the agreed-upon hour. The expectations of Ann, Margaret and Shirley are not met, their understandings of the situations and events are called into question and their appraisals and actions invalidated. In the reflection which occurs subsequently, both at the time of the episode and later in the remembering and collective discussion of them, there is a search for intelligibility and meaning. Emotions of fear, anger and righteous indignation are constructed.

These emotions are constructed by Ann, Margaret and Shirley in their self reflection, in the secondary and tertiary appraisals and evaluations of their actions and the actions of others in the situations and episodes in question. In this construction process there is more than intuitive appraisal and the triggering of affective memories and the replaying of emotional expressions, there is deliberate reflection in an attempt to make sense of the episode. This deliberate rather than intuitive appraisal (to use Arnold's terms) is paramount; a self-conscious evaluation is implicated. Our data and analysis show that this deliberate reflection is undertaken in a search, in the first instance, for a match between appraisals by actors and others in the memories. As Shotter (1984) argues, agency is expressed in this search for intelligibility, which is a search for a 'common' sense, a sense of the common or social meaning.

As we shall show below, this active search is not simply a matter of finding and appropriating the 'common' meaning. There are many 'common' meanings and meanings can be and are disputed. Our data demonstrate that on many occasions the actors chose not to accept the meaning offered by the other/s in the remembered episode. Shirley disputes the nurse's command that she turn out the light, Margaret disregards the teacher's authority and swallows the bits of balloon. The children of the memories search amongst the available meanings and select and decide; they make moral choices. They interrogate the meanings available to them, within the interpersonal context and more widely. The emotions are constructed in the reflection, in the making of the choice.

The data and their analysis presented in chapters 4, 5 and 6 lead us to conclude that the characteristics of emotions, which we have outlined above, need augmenting by three other important ones: dynamic process, a strong rather than weak sense of social, and agency. Our analyses point to how, on some occasions, we resisted when our sense of worthiness as autonomous individuals was invalidated and how, on others, an acknowledgement of the other's competence and power acted as a measure of our own social incompetence. Our happiness memories show how happiness is dependent on the attainment of selfhood, while our analysis of 'fear' and 'danger' memories indicate the central position of gender in the construction of emotions. Social meanings are appropriated according to the power relations in which our actions are situated; emotion is gendered.

The remainder of this chapter develops a theory of emotion grounded in our data and the various issues raised by them. We shall focus on the importance of memory and reflection in the construction of emotions, and the fact that any treatment of emotion necessarily involves the moral order.

Emotion as Process

The most important concepts with regard to emotion as dynamic process are appraisal and reflection, both intuitive and deliberate. Once an emotion is constructed, intuitive appraisal may be all that is necessary to elicit the emotional response, but we argue that in the construction of that emotion, self-conscious, deliberate reflection is necessary.

In this we do not differ from Arnold (1969), Averill (1980, 1985), or Levy (1984). Arnold (1969, 1970) indicates that in an emotional response, although one may be unaware, 'our here-and-now appraisal is really a prejudgment (literally, a prejudice) dictated by affective memory', one may be (and we would add often is) aware of the 'prejudgment' and reappraise and reflect again. Averill notes (1980, 1986) that in adults emotions are likely to proceed automatically and appear as if there were no necessary prior reflection. Although emotion may be present in habitual action, it is not constructed there.

Why does one reflect in this deliberate manner and in what way is this reflection related to emotions? Oatley's explanation (1989, p. 20) quoted in chapter 2, which we repeat for emphasis, refers to the unexpected and to conflict, as follows: 'They [emotions] arise when something unexpected happens, a situation to which we are not fully adapted, an event at which two different concerns clash, or when someone else does something more or less than we expected.' As clearly shown by our data, it is in the attempt to make sense of and resolve the contradiction or conflict that reflection is involved in the construction process.

Oatley, however, does not address the issue of what is unexpected or why it is unexpected. Terms such as 'the unexpected' or 'conflict' can only, as we show below, be defined socially. The patterning of expectations is social; children not only acquire appropriate forms of behaviour in and through their interactions with others, such interactions define behaviour itself (their own and others') and make it intelligible.

Humans do not, however, construct and reconstruct a 'new' emotion for every occasion; many emotions do appear to 'proceed automatically'. For example, the puzzlement, shock and hurt felt by Ann as a child in the tickling game, and, on reflection, constructed as fear is, if not the same, at least similar to fear experienced later by her as an adult. She recognized and interpreted then and recognizes now the complex of feelings as 'fear'. Averill makes a similar point:

> If we compare anger in an adult with a temper tantrum of an infant, there seems little in common. Yet, there is continuity, and it is not possible to say at any given point in time that now the infantile emotion has ended and the adult emotion has come into being. Because of this, we are tempted to conclude that there must be something, like a thread through time that lends unity to the whole sequence. (1986, p. 111)

That something, we argue, is the affective memory, not only the memory of puzzlement and shock but also of the fear. Any 'new' or modified emotion must develop out of elements already present. Appraisal continues, and these reappraisals are, likewise, dependent on a knowledge of social meanings and understandings. Without denying the possible innate beginnings of emotion, emotions finally are the product of an evaluative process. In the appraisal and reflection, the bodily feelings, one's own actions as well as the actions of others, the context of the episode and other relevant components are all evaluated in light of memories and knowledge of similar past episodes and their meanings, both interpersonal and social. One way of thinking about the innate beginnings, the 'hard-wired' or 'basic' emotions as some psychologists call them, is to distinguish, as Vygotsky did (Wertsch, 1985) between elementary and higher mental functioning; the hard-wired affective responses are 'elementary' and voluntary, 'higher' mental functions are associated with appraisal and reflection.

Emotions are not only constituted in dynamic processes but in social processes. Reflection is itself essentially social. Vygotsky believed that to possess 'logical' memory, which he related to voluntary higher mental functioning, requires the ability to engage in one specific practice, social in origin; namely, the production and interpretation of narrative forms. Vygotsky used the word 'logical' to distinguish patterned or organized memory from natural memory. The latter concept is very like Arnold's 'intuitive appraisal', but there is less similarity between patterned or 'logical' memory and Arnold's notion of deliberate appraisal. This is because Arnold failed to recognize the importance of the social realm in patterning the memory. People remember (in the sense of 'logical' memory) by patterning and organizing their appraisals and perceptions, by constructing narratives or stories.

Such narratives are what are captured in memory-work. They render intelligible the ways we as children (see chapters 4, 5 and 6) and as adults (see chapter 8), made sense of our lives and constructed our emotions. Emotions are cultural products. Averill (1986, p. 105) argues that emotional development involves the acquisition of the social norms and rules that provide the component responses of the emotional syndrome with their coordination and meaning. It is important to note, however, that that acquisition is not a straightforward learning process. Emotions are socially constructed; not in the weak dyadic sense present in much interactionist psychology, but in the strong sense, present in Mead and Vygotsky, Harré and Shotter, which recognizes that human consciousness is produced and organized in participation in sociocultural practices.

Social Regulation of the Body

Consciousness does not precede interaction, it arises in it. For Mead, the earliest social act is gesture (where gesture includes all non-verbal and bodily signs), which is the basis of human communication, which, in turn, is the basis of the social character of consciousness. Thus, intersubjectivity precedes subjectivity. The fact that human beings can be conscious of their own gestures in the same way as others are conscious of them provides the basis for intersubjectivity and for the voluntary transformation of gesture.

The transformation from the non-verbal gesture as sign to symbol is nowhere more obvious than in the process of the construction of emotion. Emotions perhaps more than other forms of communication are the link between phenomena at the social and biological level of analysis. It is through affective expression (gesture) that biologically structured bodily systems become accessible socially, and it is through the expressive feedback of others that the bodily systems become socially regulated. Indeed, it is most probable that emotions have been and continue to be seen as 'of the body' rather than 'of the mind', as physiological and irrational rather than cognitive and relational, because of the close relationships between gesture and emotion.

A particularly striking example is in the construction of happiness. Benjamin (1980) discusses the early childhood conflict which arises between the need to establish autonomous identity and the need to be recognized by the other. Our data indicate that, in the search for a resolution of that conflict, the emotions that are constructed (see chapter 5) are grounded in smell, touch and texture. In a very important sense, emotions are socially regulated gestures.

Part of the social regulation of emotions occurs through language. Narrative form provides some of the patterning to which Vygotsky refers, that is the patterning may be verbal or non-verbal. Experimental evidence (Argyle, 1975) indicates that, in certain contexts, non-verbal communication may be more important in the interpretation of others' emotions than verbal language. Indeed, with regard to emotions which are constructed early, such as happiness, the non-verbal aspects of communication are paramount.

The earliest of the memories reported in the previous chapters give us some insight into this transformation. In a transgression memory, Amy recounts stealing some money from her mother's purse and buying some sweets: 'and she felt sick in the tummy . . . and the lollies didn't taste good'. In the same memory, after she has told her mother, her mother 'yelled at her and smacked her', and again Amy's 'tummy ached with her disappointment'. A pain in the stomach in the presence of yells and a smack from a parent is transformed into guilt and disappointment; the signs of 'pain', 'yells' and 'a smack' into the symbolic form, guilt and disappointment. In another transgression memory, slinking away indicates guilt. In this memory, Lawrence's parents were silent: 'They stared at him. He was beneath contempt.'

The beginnings of happiness are tied to smiling, warm and resonant voices, being held. Screaming occurs in many of the 'fear' and 'danger' memories reported in chapter 6. Philip reports that 'he was terrified. He screamed more and more'; Howard that 'he screamed for hours'; Ann that 'she was terrified and began to scream'. Screaming is a gesture of fear as is gasping for breath. Robert reports that he 'began to . . . gasp for air' and Dougall that he was 'running short of breath'.

These non-verbal bodily responses and gestures, the signs of affect, take on meaning. The transformation from sign to symbol takes place in reflection and a consciousness of self as fearful, guilty or happy develops in the context of the search for intelligibility in terms of the meanings shared in the episode and from common-sense meanings of the wider sociocultural realm.

> It is evident that but for the original situation of social interaction the bodily and vocal gestures could never have attained their signification. It is their reference to other individuals that has turned expression, as a mere outflow of nervous excitement, into meaning, and this meaning was the value of the act for the other individual . . . (Mead, 1909, pp. 406–7)

Because, as noted above, the self is able to 'take the role of the other' and view her/his own gestures as others view them, the subject constructs her/his own emotions with reference to the evaluations of others. The actor assumes that her/his actions have the same or similar meaning for the actor as for the other. The self discovers through others, intersubjectively, what it is to feel 'happy', 'fearful', or 'guilty'.

Thus, the interpretation of the actions and feelings as emotion has its roots in the relations among actors (subjects) that are established through their cooperative actions. Mead insists that, as well, the situation must be functional for the actor, that is, that the conflict must arise in the presence of other actors. As Joas, in his explication of Mead, notes:

> This kind of situation is given only in the case of interaction between or among individual actors. Only then is one's own action responded to by the immediate responses of others in such a way that one is compelled to assume an attitude of self-reflective attentiveness. Only when we are

ourselves the stimulus for the responses of another, responses which are in turn stimuli for us, must we concentrate our attention on our character as a source of stimulation. (1985, p. 104)

Following on from Mead, we argue that the model of emotion (as set out in chapter 2), that is,

meet bear $\longrightarrow$ appraise as dangerous $\longrightarrow$ feel fear $\longrightarrow$ flight

is valid if and only if the concepts of 'danger' and 'fear' were socially acquired and understood. The construction of emotion can only occur in the context of others, intelligibility must be sought from others. The growl or menace of the bear is not experienced as fear unless the 'meeting with the bear' is reflected on and that reflection presupposes others; the actor can only appraise or evaluate the episode in the light of others' evaluations of the episode. Emotions are social processes; intersubjectivity, where actors share some aspect of their situation definition, lies at the heart of their construction.

- happiness – is constructed in the awareness that we are the object of others' love;
- joy – in accomplishment which is recognized and acknowledged by those we love;
- guilt – in the knowledge that what we have done offends, hurts, upsets others;
- indignation – in the misconstrual of one's actions or intentions by others;
- fear – in anticipation of an assault on self or special others;
- anger – in the invalidation of self by others.

Common Sense of the Collective

So, as pointed out above, although reflection is an individual process, the capacity of human beings for reflection is premised on intersubjectivity. The embracing of subjectivity, as in memory-work, does not necessarily lead to individualism; indeed, it uncovers the social in human experience. Memory is central – not only in the sense of self-reflection but in a collective sense.

In a manner which is reminiscent of Mead and similar to that adopted by Shotter (1984), Haug recommends building upon the human ability to recognize the commonality of experience. Inter-subjectivity is thus central to memory-work. As Haug says:

As we adopted the standpoint of others, we came to know ourselves and each other as historical contemporaries engaged in reconstructing the mosaic of experiences . . . we learned nothing if we did not pause and reflect on the attitude of each individual in her place within the social whole . . . Reflection made it possible to reinterpret those taken-for-granted aspects of our lives . . . (1987, p. 58)

The recognition of the importance of intersubjectivity and of the importance of the commonality of experience has an important corollary. As we discuss in chapter 11, there is not one common sense but many. Cultures vary in their collective understandings, as do women and men.

Gender differences of the kind we have found in our data occur because intelligibility is found in a common sense, where common sense is searched for interpersonally, between the players in the scene, and socially, in the wider sociocultural realm. As shown in the previous chapter, fear is constructed in situations where danger is socially acknowledged – a deadly spider, a fierce dog about which it 'was common knowledge . . . that he was dangerous'. It is intelligible even appropriate to scream when confronted with a deadly spider or a dangerous dog.

Fear is also constructed in situations where, in the presence of peers, danger is courted and bravery tested. This construction of fear is something with which men are more familiar than women. There is a moral imperative to swim to the nets and back, to climb onto the shed roof. Here, the fear of loss of face is greater than the fear of not being able to complete the swim or of falling from the roof.

Anger, too, is gendered. Men and women share much in their construction and experience of anger, but there are important differences, as discussed in chapters 10 and 11. In chapter 4 we noted that the transgressions of female children often produced anger in adults and anger and indignation in the children themselves. In male children, on the other hand, the predominant emotion triggered by 'transgression' was glee and delight in rule-breaking, in testing the boundaries. As was the case with the danger and fear memories, the boys appeared to be exhilarated by the risk-taking.

Not only does common sense vary from culture to culture, from men to women, but also over time. As Shotter (1984) has noted, memories locate persons within their world in relation to others with whom it is shared. One of our memories exemplifies the importance of one's changing position in the world. It is a memory of Ann's concerning a 'medical' treatment and is discussed fully in chapter 9. The memory, an elaborate one of unpleasant electrical treatment in childhood, is set in motion when she is in an emotional (angry) state as a young woman by association to a psychological experiment involving electricity that she had just heard about. But the actor in the memory modified her emotion only in a reappraisal made some thirty years later in the context of recent public discussion of the facts about sexual assault.

In this book we have focused on gender differences rather than other differences such as those arising from class and age. Gender differences, as all differences, are, however, constructed with a hegemonic set of meanings. One of the very interesting findings of the memory-work, both in our own memory-work group and in others, was the similarity of the memories. There was never any doubt that group members understood each other's emotional experiences and, in an important sense, could elaborate each others' experiences. There is a dominant set of understandings and meanings to which human beings, at any one moment in history and in any one culture, subscribe. Much of the conflict and contradiction which memory-work lays bare is caught up in these hegemonic understandings, the taken-for-granted. Thus, the power of memory-work lies in deconstructing the taken-for-granted, in questioning the moral order. And, to explore the moral, which we do below, there is no better topic than emotion.

Passions or Actions

If reflection and self-reflection are part and parcel of the construction of emotions, then why is it that emotion is experienced as a passion, that is, as something that overcomes us. Are emotions processes over which we have no control and, if so, how can humans 'educate them', to borrow a phrase from Peters (1970).

Related to these questions, is the issue of motive. What is the relationship between emotion and motive? Almost all writers assert a relationship between motive and emotion. Izard (1977, p. 3), for example, says: 'My view is that the emotions constitute the primary motivational system for human beings.' Other psychologists, for example the influential Cannon (1927), explained motive in terms of a general arousal which was linked to affect.

If we turn to those psychologists who have influenced our own thinking on emotion, we also find a close link between emotion and motive. Many theorists claim that emotions lead to action – unless something intervenes. Arnold (in Arnold, 1970, pp. 175–6) states that 'as we appraise the situation as more desirable or more harmful, we become aware not only that we tend toward or away from it, but that it is also an emotional tendency'. Emotions, in a sense, precede motivated behaviour; indeed, in some instances, they provide the necessary energy; they 'move' one to act.

Arnold (1960), in her discussion of McClelland, however, distinguished between a wanting that is emotional in nature and a wanting that comes from the reflective estimate that a particular action is contrary to one's best interests. Here she made a distinction which parallels her distinction between intuitive and reflective or deliberate appraisals in emotions. So although an emotion triggered by an intuitive appraisal should and usually does lead to action, that same emotion may be modified or transformed by deliberate appraisal and reappraisal and the motivated behaviour may not occur. 'With the second kind of wanting there will be an action that is not dictated by emotion, a state of affairs that is completely inexplicable on McClelland's premises' (Arnold, 1960, p. 241).

To return to our example in chapter 2, Arnold (1969, 1970) distinguishes:

meet bear $\longrightarrow$ intuitive appraisal $\longrightarrow$ fear $\longrightarrow$ flight
$\qquad$ as dangerous

from

meet bear $\longrightarrow$ intuitive $\longrightarrow$ fear $\longrightarrow$ reflective
$\qquad$ appraisal $\qquad\qquad\qquad$ appraisal $\longrightarrow$ fear? $\longrightarrow$ no flight

In the former case, an affective memory is produced by the presence of a bear and the person feels fear and a tendency to flee. Unless something intervenes, the person will flee. In the latter case, the person reappraises the situation, deliberately reflects, and decides to stand her/his ground. The person may feel fear but, for example, may consider that it is cowardly to run away, or that she or he stands a better chance of surviving by defending her- or himself.

What is distinguished here is the motivated behaviour of 'flight', behaviour which many psychologists would view as caused by the motive 'fear', from the action of 'standing one's ground', which is a product of reflection and reappraisal. The latter as an action assumes some notion of agency and choice. However, it is a misleading distinction – or at least a muddled one. We argue that in the case of 'fear' leading to 'flight', the possibility of choice exists; the actor in the situation, on reflection, may decide that flight is the preferred option. Arnold is correct in stating that McClelland cannot explain the lack of flight, but in neither case would we argue that the behaviour 'flight' or 'standing one's ground' is caused by the emotion. In a very important sense, as we argued in chapter 2, the flight or other behaviour is part of the emotion. 'Flight' as well as 'standing one's ground' are all actions in that they were, at some stage in the person's history, intelligible responses to an appraisal of the situation and the meanings relating to such situations.

The important point here is not the assumed distinction between caused behaviour and reflected-upon action, but that emotions are syndromes and that fear can be constructed in a variety of situations within a set of understandings and meanings, some of which will contain references to bravery and others not.

Further, the emotion of which the action, be it 'flight' or 'standing one's ground', is part, is not something which simply overcomes the person. She or he may feel fear, but other emotions, such as pride or defiance, may also be present. The emotion is constructed and modified or transformed as the situation unfolds and in reflections on it.

Peters (1969, 1970) has an account of the relationship between emotion and motive that is somewhat akin to that of Arnold. His model is:

meet bear $\longrightarrow$ appraise as dangerous $\longrightarrow$ fear

meet bear $\longrightarrow$ appraise as dangerous $\longrightarrow$ flight

The influence of Arnold is evident. Peters argues that, for example, one may respond in fear (sweating, shaking knees, trembling legs . . .) and one may act from fear (attempt to escape from the bear). One is logically independent of the other but there is a *de facto* relationship between them and they usually accompany one another. An appraisal may produce an emotion with associated feelings (sweating, etc.) over which humans have little control, as well as a reason for action (or motive), in the above example, flight. Emotions, according to Peters, are feelings which overcome one. Motivated actions are actions over which we have some control.

His distinction between actions and passions (which come over us) while important, is not one with which we fully agree. The distinction is clear in our language, as Bedford (1962) and Oatley (1989) in their different ways point out, but the distinction we believe refers to the difference between expressive and practical actions.

The physiological sensations of sweating, increased heart rate, trembling, etc. seem different from 'running away', although James (1890/1922) was loath to make much of the distinction. 'Standing one's ground' certainly seems to be different from sweating and trembling for the very good reason that it is difficult if not impossible to control the sweating and trembling but perfectly possible to decide not to 'stand one's ground'.

Further, although one may seek out happiness or put oneself in the way of experiencing happiness by, for example, catching another wave when surfing or remembering happy events, one cannot act to make 'the face glow'. One can, however, build a bomb shelter out of fear of war, make reparation out of guilt, and give money to the poor out of pity.

The sense of agency and action appears obvious in some of the above examples and absent in others. The distinction which Peters makes is not, however, a watertight one. One may flee the bear or stand one's ground, for example, with or without deliberation. Running from the bear or standing one's ground (because one is rooted to the spot) may be as much beyond control as blushing with shame or shouting in anger. James may have been correct: running from the bear may be as expressive of fear as sweating or trembling, or, one may sweat and tremble as much, if not more so, when standing one's ground rather than fleeing from the bear. One may deliberately shout in anger and at the same time be unable to control the tears in one's eyes.

Peters' problem is in equating the emotion with the physiological and expressive feelings. As noted earlier, these are the gestures which are transformed by narrative and other social forms and become part of the constructed emotion. We would argue, as does Averill, that the practical actions are just as much a part of the emotions as the expressive ones.

It may appear that, once constructed, emotions overcome us and that motives cause behaviour. But it should not be forgotten that the emotions and motives were constructed and actively produced in human beings' attempts to make sense of their world, including their own physiological responses. There is always room for deliberation and therefore always room for the modification or education of our emotions and action. Indeed, as we shall argue below, it is in these deliberations that we construct ourselves as agents.

Morality

In the resolution of conflict and contradiction, choices must be made. In order to avoid the bear, people choose actions which are intelligible to others in the sense that they bring about the desired end, whether that be escape or acting bravely. Both actions are intelligible in our society, both are usually accompanied by a number of expressive actions over which humans have more or less control. Only one of the actions, however, may be considered appropriate. On some occasions it may be considered appropriate to flee the bear and foolhardy to stand one's ground, on other occasions it may be considered cowardly to flee and brave to stand one's ground. In the latter case moral sense is obvious, although we argue that morality is present in both.

Many situations call for particular emotional expression. In such situations one might expect to feel morally inferior if such emotions were not genuinely experienced. For example, death and the loss of loved ones are appraised as occasions on which it is both intelligible and appropriate to mourn. Indeed, one ought to feel sad and cry at the death of loved ones.

There are rules which govern our expression of feeling; we learn to enact the 'emotional role'. The rules both enable and constrain action. Happiness is associated with being with one's loved ones, it is expected at Christmas and on birthdays; pride is associated with skilled performance and accomplishment; anger justified by injustice; and guilt expected for wrongdoing. Here we are in agreement with Averill's definition of emotion as 'a transitory social role (a socially constituted syndrome)' (1980, p. 312). Emotions confirm societal values.

Many authors have commented on the close relationship between the moral order and emotions. Bedford (1962) argues that emotion words form part of a vocabulary of appraisal and criticism and he points out that a number of them belong to the specific language of moral criticism: 'there is an overlap between the list of emotions and the lists of vices and virtues that are given by philosophers' (p. 119). Emotion concepts belong, he says, to systems of judgement, moral, aesthetic and legal.

Emotions are not, however, culturally imposed. They are appropriated from the social and cultural realm in interaction. The construction of emotions by children occurs as part of their developing moral sense. Emotions are produced in their interaction with others and much of this interaction is likely to be with adults – parents, teachers, nurses – although sometimes 'others' may be peers. The institutions of family, school, hospital make themselves felt. It is intelligible to feel fearful of the dark, but appropriate for only some, for example very young, children. As noted in chapter 6, there are occasions where it is not appropriate to feel fear. The spider which frightened the boy had to be a dangerous spider, the dog menacing and fierce.

Thus the moral sense is evident where institutional and adult authority is accepted and where it is resisted. The child who accepts the teacher's appraisal that it is rude to call women 'old hags' upholds the moral order in her guilt. Guilt (and shame) is logically dependent upon the notion of wrongdoing. In resisting, the sense of the moral is perhaps more obvious. The child who does not feel guilty challenges the everyday understandings, the taken-for-granted, the dominant common sense; one challenges the moral order.

In many of our memories, morality is revealed in the questioning and resisting of authority. Shirley (chapter 10) questions the authority of the nurse who Shirley knows has broken the hospital rules. Indeed, the dominant emotional response to 'saying sorry' and wilful 'transgression' was a sense of righteous indignation, a sense of injustice and betrayal. In these memories, the children's sense of worthiness as autonomous individuals, as competent, trying to be 'adult', was invalidated. Responsibility and autonomy were the social values underpinning the emotions constructed in these episodes.

There are occasions, however, when contesting an authority is applauded. As described in chapter 5, the early transgression memories of men were gleeful; rebelliousness is sometimes considered an appropriate response – at least in young boys.

Emotions such as guilt or shame or pride or jealousy are not the only emotions associated with morality. Happiness has a moral sense, as do other so-called basic emotions, such as fear.

With regard to happiness, we found that it is constructed at the intersection of freedom and autonomy, on the one hand, and recognition, which is grounded in security and love, on the other. The named emotion 'happiness' produced memories which showed how happiness is dependent on attainment of selfhood. Happiness is produced in security and warmth and through extending the competence and skills of the body in play and being recognized and praised for that competence.

As noted above, the data on 'fear' also reveal the moral order. Fear is related to the moral order in the sense that behaviour may be controlled by fear. Fear is clearly related to cowardice and bravery, especially in men. As Armon-Jones (1985, p. 10) noted, even the allegedly 'natural' emotion 'fear' is conceptually related to morally significant objects and is for this reason instrumental in sustaining social norms and values.

Morality is implicated, it seems, in two ways. First, the emotions are constructed within commonsense understandings of how people behave. In this 'normative' sense rules of behaviour are set down. They prescribe behaviours and make sense of our own and others' actions. One smiles and is happy when loved; and one weeps and is sad at the loss of that love. Second, it is not only intelligible to smile, it is appropriate and one ought to do so. The moral is implicated in the way in which one not only appraises and makes sense of one's actions but evaluates one's actions and those of others.

Taylor (1977), in his account of what constitutes human agency, distinguishes what he calls 'first-' and 'second-order' desires. Simple preference is distinguished from what one ought to prefer. To return to the example of 'the bear': a person may prefer to flee the bear, but because flight entails the abandonment of a child the person reappraises the situation as one which morally demands the standing of her or his ground. The ability of people to evaluate morally, to desire the desirable (what ought to be desired), is what makes us agents.

Averill's distinction (1980) between impulsive and conflictive emotions is somewhat similar, but is not an entirely satisfactory one. 'Impulsive' emotions represent 'straightforward desires and aversions that have become so "second nature" that they are not regarded as self-initiated . . . [they] are like states of strong motivation that (for any of a variety of reasons) are not completely identified with the self-as-agent' (p. 311). Examples that he gives of these impulsive emotions are grief, joy, hope, sexual desire and many common fears.

'Conflictive' emotions are produced in response to conflict between two sets of social norms. In the case of anger, says Averill (p. 333), the underlying conflict stems from two norms, one which condemns violence and the other which calls for the retribution of perceived injustice. The conflict is resolved by a third set of norms that allow aggression to be expressed in the form of anger, thus preserving the strictures against deliberately harming another. Averill likens his conflictive and impulsive emotions to Arnold's (1960) distinction between unhindered and frustrated tendencies.

Averill leaves little room for agency. Because his conceptualization of the social is too cohesive, there is little room for contradiction or conflict and hence little room for moral choice. Socialization is reduced to a reinforcement history where the active and agentic nature of the appropriation of the social is relegated to the background or forgotten completely. Social life is plural, even divisive, as well as cohesive. Cultural meanings are not only given and shared; they are also fragmented and contested. It is at the intersection of the personal and the social that emotions and the moral order coincide.

Taylor's discussion (1977) is more in keeping with our position. He places choice at the centre of his account of desire; agency is constituted in the self-reflections and deliberations of humans and in the choices they make between the competing and conflicting demands of self-interest and society.

Self as Agent

Morality is constituted in deliberation and choice. It is here also, we argue, that emotions are constructed. And as humans construct their emotions, they construct themselves. Memory and reflection is implicated in those processes. Emotions are the markers of the construction of the self, the personality.

Shotter (1984) argued that human agency depends on persons being both conscious and self-conscious. Consciousness he deals with as follows:

> The actions of intelligent agents must continually be mediated by mental activity, activity which must link their present action both to its possible future consequences and their own past experience. In other words, unlike instinctual organisms, they must show both foresight and memory, for they have to act without the support of their environment, but in a way appropriate to it nonetheless. . . . they must sense themselves as 'situated' . . . (1984, p. 214)

He claims memory is 'the process by which past specificatory activities are linked to current specifiability – which makes for intentionality, and gives a "directionality" to mental activities' (p. 208). Our memories contain the conditions for agents' further self-development. People 'grow into' their emotions which they construct in their attempts to be agents. In their appraisals of the situations in which they find themselves they appropriate the cultural rules and norms, but not in a passive way. They reflect in order to resolve contradiction and to produce intelligibility as they construct their identities. Individuals reproduce the social structure because they have freedom of action. In addition, as members of collectivities, they have the chance to transform the social structures. Emotions are the markers of agency.

8

Holidays: Emotions in Childhood and Adulthood Compared

A holiday, when you stop to think about it, is an interesting phenomenon. A holiday is time set apart from ordinary life, a change of pace, usually a change of place, an opportunity for re-establishing old ties or exploring new ones, for having an adventure, for pleasure, for doing whatever you want to do, or for doing nothing at all. There is a sense that the normal rules of everyday life are set aside and new ones operate for a time.

We thought that the topic of holidays potentially provided an ideal situation for exploring the everyday – the kind of exception that throws the rules into high relief. It was chosen as one of the later themes, and followed our analysis of transgressions, anger, crying , and play. Holidays are also one of the ways that our society provides for emotional experiences, in this case supposedly the experiencing of pleasure or happiness.

We hoped that by looking at what was different in our lives, we would see more clearly what was ordinary, the taken-for-granted. In fact we found many of the same patterns of our other memories re-emerging, often in exaggerated form, in the holiday memories. They provided us with material for theorizing that was very rich indeed.

For the first time, we departed from our usual practice by deliberately writing adult memories. What do holidays mean for us as adult women, we wondered? Do we continue to construct our emotions as women? If so how? What emotions? What can holidays tell us about our lives as adult women? As to that, what will it be like to write a memory of ourselves as we are now? We decided to write at least two adult holiday memories each, one about starting a holiday, and another about a later event on the same holiday. In fact, we ended up with an abundance of holiday memories, for contrast with these first ones. Later we also obtained five childhood memories from a memory-work group of young men.

The full texts of all memories are too long for complete reproduction here. We report one memory in full, to give one complete example; the others are reported in summary or excerpt form:

'Women lifesavers, Coffs Harbour NSW, 1931', photographer
unknown. Mavis Kerr, M. Lake, Doreen Shea and Iris Mills of
the Coffs Harbour Jetty Surf Lifesaving Club, practising on
Jetty Beach. From the original photograph in the Mitchell
Library, State Library of New South Wales. Reproduced by
permission.

They were living in the USA. She and her husband and two little boys
were on holiday. They had been staying just outside of Boston for a few
days while D attended a conference. Today the conference was over and
they set out on their holiday proper – to see the autumn in the New
England area, . . . and back to New York where they had been living for
a year. This 'fall in New England' trip was one of the 'dreams of her life'.

They left the motel in the afternoon. Margaret had decided they would
get onto route 128 and follow it to its end. It was a huge highway which
circled Boston . . . and ended in a little town called Rockport . . . on the
coast . . . They had no idea what they would find there.

It turned out that Rockport was a charming holiday resort which had originally been a fishing village. They arrived about 3.30 p.m. Rockport was a very touristy place, what we would now call trendy. It had lots of tourist accommodation, the only problem was that it was a summer resort, now closed for the winter. They really liked the look of the place. So they found an information bureau which found accommodation for them in a small guest house. They were only planning to stay for one night.

They made their way to the guest house and found it to be a romantic Cape Cod style wooden house. It was run by two elderly sisters. The room was large, with an adjoining annexe for the children. They had to share a bathroom with other guests, but there were few of these at that time of year.

They decided to go for a walk to explore the village before it got dark. They put the baby in the stroller and set out. They went down by the waterfront, where the water was beginning to turn pinkish as the sun went down. There were old small cottages which had been fishermen's cottages but were now arty crafty shops. For example, one was full of glass objects.

As they strolled along, suddenly they were greeted by a man and a woman. This couple seemed very glad to see them, though Margaret for once was at a bit of a loss to remember who they were. She soon remembered that they had met about six months previously . . . at the university . . . it turned out that P and his wife H . . . were on their way to Montreal and were staying the night with H's parents who lived in Rockport. Margaret felt so happy, overjoyed almost – certainly out of all proportion – to see them. She had been lonely in Boston, and this meeting was a lovely surprise. It was the sort of thing that might have happened back in Australia, but in this context it was quite overwhelmingly surprising.

Another thing that made this meeting special was that it was one of the few times Margaret had experienced being recognized and remembered by people whom she remembered only vaguely – the opposite was a more common occurrence. To make things even more delightful, H invited them to dinner at her parents' house. Margaret felt that this was special! She would have given anything to have been able to accept. However, there was no way they could take the children with them and the whole idea seemed impossible. Nonetheless, always being one who liked to have her cake and eat it, she suggested that if she and D could find a babysitter they might visit H parents' house for a drink after dinner. H and P thought this was a good idea, and gave them the phone number and address . . . To cut a long story short, it turned out that the elderly sisters who ran the guest house had a niece who was willing to babysit. Margaret and D bought some food and fed the little boys and then put them to bed. They then went out to dinner at a seafood restaurant. They ate beautiful fresh seafood, lobster for entrée and Margaret had deep fried clams (delicious) as a main course. They had been missing seafood . . . Margaret had never lived far from the sea. After dinner, they drove to H's parents' house.

The house was large, elevated, on the side of a hill overlooking the ocean. It was quite late by now, about 9.30 p.m. H's parents were warm and friendly. They seemed very pleased to be entertaining this young(ish) Australian couple. They offered drinks, and Margaret accepted a whisky sour . . . The conversation was lively, and Margaret felt this experience was one of the nicest things that had ever happened to her. The spontaneity and warmth of the occasion seemed to give it a certain special quality. The people were interesting and conversation was stimulating. P was a fairly famous scientist, H was a bright and lively person, her father was a retired sea captain, and her mother a warm and charming person.

In the midst of this happy glow, Margaret began to feel ill. She slowly realized that she was experiencing increasing nausea. Eventually she realized she was going to be violently ill. She also knew that she should have mentioned it long before it got to this stage, and she and D should have left. But she had been reluctant to spoil the evening, for her own sake, not the others' since she believed that she was the one who was enjoying it the most.

The sicker she felt the more embarrassed she felt. Eventually, she excused herself and went to the bathroom. Fortunately the bathroom was quite a distance from the front room . . . where the rest of the people were. She just managed to reach the toilet bowl before she was violently ill. She was terribly embarrassed, upset, and felt guilty as well as nauseous. She realized she was noisy and smelly. She took some time to clean the bathroom – a large American bathroom with the toilet bowl in the same room as the bath, basin, etc. She found clean and sweet smelling bathroom cleaners and cleaning cloths and was grateful that she could clean the toilet bowl and basin quite thoroughly. She found sweet smelling soap and hand lotion and cleaned her hands and face thoroughly. She seemed to be absent for a long time, but fortunately felt reasonably well again. The nausea had gone.

Eventually she returned to the others, feeling more embarrassed than ever. She feared they would think she was drunk, though she had nothing to drink except about one third of the whisky sour. She said nothing about her illness. D asked if she were all right, and she smiled sweetly and said 'yes, thank you'. The rest of the evening was spoiled for her. She felt that everyone must be judging her badly, if not as a drunk then as someone discourteous. She remembers the occasion as one of the happiest and one of the most embarrassing of her life.

A subsequent event from the same holiday was the topic for another memory-work session. Margaret wrote:

In some respects the holiday was disappointing, mainly the weather . . . the days were misty and moist when they were not pouring with rain. It was also very cold . . . Some friends had told them not to miss Lake Winnepasauke. The name means 'mirror lake' . . . They debated on one very wet afternoon whether it would be worth taking the detour to the lake and decided they might as well. The roads were steep and slippery . . . It was getting dark and they caught glimpses of a dirty grey not very mirror-like lake from time to time. On arrival they found a very small settlement, . . . The lake was surrounded by private holiday houses which prevented anyone from seeing it at close quarters. They went into the store and asked whether they could get any accommodation. The storekeeper was friendly . . . he offered to rent them one of the cabins for the night, though he warned it was not very comfortable in cold weather. The cabin was made of timber. It was spacious, but sparsely furnished . . . no central heating. But there was an open fireplace and a stack of wood . . . By this time it was dark, but Margaret was excited to see that there was one large window facing the lake. It was still raining. They ate dinner and put the boys to bed. The fire was wonderful . . . When the boys woke early next morning, there was no rain. The sun was pale but rising over the lake and the dawn light was pale orange in colour. The lake was still, and the autumn colours of the trees which surrounded it were reflected in it. The picture window revealed this superb sight. It all seemed very special, a once-in-a-lifetime experience.

Another memory from the 'beginning a holiday' set is that in which Liz has an encounter with unknown people in a hotel dining room, one of whom seems to recognize her. The memory is recorded in chapter 1. The second episode from Liz's holiday is about a trip to Minnamurra Falls. It has been slightly condensed.

They went in a tourist bus that wasn't very crowded . . . the bus went through the Jamberoo Valley and turned up a back road and in through a gate . . . and the driver indicated that this was as far as the bus could go and a walk to the falls would be entailed . . . From here on Liz's memory is of being quite alone though she realized others must have walked there too . . . The walk wasn't a long one, say fifteen or twenty minutes . . . she knew they had come to the falls when she rounded a bend, . . . and she found herself in a sort of bowl, as though a great stone had been gouged out of the hillside and she was standing at the bottom. Rocky walls and bushes ascended the sides of this bowl . . . and she felt she was looking up from the bottom of a huge bottle. Some many feet above was a circle of blue sky . . . but all the sides of this bowl were dark and wet. In the centre was a large round pool and . . . it seemed motionless and bottomless. Over on the side opposite the entrance . . . the fall could be seen. It was a thin stream of water, but falling fast . . . the splash of the fall as it hit the surface of the pool and bubbles and circles ringed themselves out toward her . . . The only sound was the splash of the water . . . If there were other people there, they made no impression . . . Liz felt alone. She remembers mostly the dazzling contrast of the blue circle of sky against the dark dank chamber of the 'bowl' in which she stood. The memory is of a feeling of awe – a mixture of delight and wonderment and perhaps a bit of fear. She stood there for a time, and was glad she had come . . .

A third pair of memories from the adult holiday series follows:

Marie arrived with the family at Durras lake. They were to stay for a week, quite a mob of adults and children. There would be a lot of noise and activity. Yet the attraction of the place, for Marie, was the peace of the beach and the bush. As soon as possible she left the others and walked down to the beach with W. It looked so inviting, the lake, the sea, long stretch of beach in the late afternoon . . . Leaving the kids behind. Just walking to the sound of the surf and the wind in her face. Not talking much. No hurry. Marvellous sense of release and freedom. The promise of empty days.

Later in the same holiday, she remembers:

On the day in question the group looked to Marie to organize the day's outings (as usual). It was a glorious day so Marie suggested the group spend the morning swimming in the lake (lagoon) below. Then after a light lunch they could go exploring down the coast. The morning went well. By late morning R discovered fish near where he had been swimming. J and C quickly joined him with fishing lines. By the time they quit for lunch it was . . . too late to go anywhere. Marie felt hurt and angry and cheated of her turn. The family had always been careful to . . . give everyone a turn, an opportunity for a treat or outing. But with the two outside males . . . the balance had been tipped. Marie was outnumbered and her wishes ignored. She hated fishing and yet had graciously given up two precious days. Now she stormed out of the hut and off down the beach, seeking solitude to express her rage and hurt – shouting at the waves 'the bastards . . . it's my holiday, I'm paying for the hut, my boat . . . and I'm supposed to serve their bloody dinner . . .'

The fourth writer remembered episodes from a recent (adult) holiday. Some details of the preliminary journey have been omitted.

The packing was done and they [Ann, partner and child] were waiting for the cab to take them to the airport. Ann felt both excited and apprehensive . . . she was looking forward to a holiday in the sun before the conference but she was apprehensive. The trip was long and uneventful except . . . she was worried that her gut problem would prove difficult during their holiday; she also hoped that the break from work might help . . . The flight was calm . . . and everything went according to schedule. They had an hour or so to wait for a ferry to take them across to Magnetic Island . . . They were all somewhat tired and hungry and very hot . . . The ferry trip was a delight. The breeze from the sea cooled everyone down and when they reached Magnetic Island a taxi was waiting to take them to their flat. The building looked like a large single storey motel. The flat was set in a tropical garden . . . with a swimming pool . . . Ann was a little disappointed in [the flat] because it had no outlook, but, in general, she was pleased by its size and its lack of pretension; it had an air of holiday comfort about it. They unpacked happily; . . . and [they] began to feel at home. Ann began to relax and they began to make plans to explore the island and to go out to the reef to have a swim.

In the second memory, some details of the walk home have been omitted:

A walk with M and R to the mangrove swamp and the mud flats to see some birds . . . It was quite beautiful – flat and a marvellous blacky-brown colour with the earthy green-khaki of the trees. There was the exposed wreck of an old boat. For the first time since their arrival, the clouds had come up . . . and the sky was black and threatening. They had old shoes on and they were soon ankle deep in mud . . . It was an extremely enjoyable walk. The mangroves were interesting and the scenery was different from anything they had seen of the island so far. The sky became more threatening and so they decided to head for home. They thought they would walk back around the rocks to the beach near their flat . . . They met a young woman who wanted to know the way to the beach so they all walked and scrambled back together around the cliff face . . . They finally climbed to the top of the cliff and were on their way down – on a path now – and they passed an old house that had lots of 'private property' notices . . . and 'beware of the dog'. Ann was extremely worried by this last sign until she realized that they had in fact been through the 'private property' and were now on their way down the path to the beach . . . They all ran up the beach as by now the rain was beginning to set in.

The last set starts with two episodes on a boating holiday. Some qualifying details have been omitted:

They hired a sailing boat on Pittwater, a 26 footer, for 5 days . . . This was a chance to consolidate/practise/learn skills. He seemed to know instinctively what to do – she joked about his nautical genes . . . she panicked and seemed to automatically do the wrong thing when quick decisions were required. She was anxious about handling this much bigger boat, assumed they'd be given instruction . . . she felt very strongly how alien this world was – the presupposed affluence required a particular personal style at which neither of them was adept – though she was more able to play at it than he. She made small talk . . . to cover her nervousness, while [the proprietor] took them to the yacht, showed them ignition . . . location of equipment . . . B remained almost completely silent except for the occasional pertinent question. After the charter operator had left she said 'Do you understand it all?' 'No, but we'll learn.' The anxiety level was high as they cast off.

A second memory is reported from several days later:

They woke early on a warm clear morning and decided to have a swim round the boat. There were a lot of jellyfish around so they took it in turns to stay on board and warn the swimmer of impending encounters. The people on the boat moored nearest to them in the small cove were fishing . . . The neighbours called out 'the fish are really biting well. You should have a go'. Fay made the polite rejoinder and said they had no bait. Immediately the man leapt into his dinghy and rowed across with a small packet of bait. Fay and B then felt obliged to go through the motions and dropped a couple of lines over the side. Almost immediately Fay felt a tug on her line and hauled up a small-medium fish. She couldn't bear the thought of it flopping around the deck . . . so she took B's bush knife . . . and cut its head off cleanly. She was hooked! From then on she caught a few fish each morning for breakfast, stopping when they had enough to eat. B occasionally caught one also but the fish seemed to leap on her line. She felt . . . a mix of contradictory emotions – some excitement and delight, revulsion at the killing, pride at overcoming squeamishness.

This last writer contributed another memory from adult life, of a holiday spent in another place with another female friend:

Fay and R drove from London to the Dales comfortably in a day. Initially Fay felt rather anxious about the prospect of the next 10 days together in a campervan. R's mood while packing combined her characteristic manic bustling with uncharacteristic indecisiveness. But once on the road they found themselves in animated conversation and the minor decisions required on a journey: shall we stop to eat here, take this side road, stop to explore this interesting ruin, all flowed equally and with positive results. Tension rose contemplating where to stop that night but they found a lay-by amongst the trees on a quiet side road, beneath a ridge with heather starting to bloom. As they sipped a post-dinner port they congratulated themselves on the ease of the first day – how well everything had worked out, the good omen for the rest of the holiday. 'This is almost perfect' said Fay. 'We just need a running stream and a pub within walking distance.' They found the site by a churchyard in a small village the following day.

As with all memories, we found a great variety of often contra-dictory or contrasting emotions, some of them hard to label. Margaret's memory of a holiday in New England contained some strong emotional contrasts. On unexpectedly meeting another couple she felt 'a bit of a loss to remember who they were' but then happy, overjoyed, 'delighted at being recognized'. Later she enjoyed the spontaneity and warmth and stimulating conversation, but then as she became ill, she was 'embarrassed, upset and felt guilty as well as nauseous'. The episode was one of the 'happiest and one of the most embarrassing of her life'. Her later memory of the same holiday was of disappointment, some excitement, and finally a sense of beauty and awe at the superb sight of the autumn colours reflected in the lake.

Liz's memories also contained strong contrasts. In the hotel dining room she felt 'taken aback' by the stranger but 'duty bound' to be civil. She was uncomfortable, 'dismayed', felt disadvantaged by not knowing who he was, and perhaps a little annoyed. Once she had successfully dismissed the man she felt 'amused' and 'relieved', satisfied with her social competence; 'she had managed to keep her end up'. Liz's second memory of the same holiday was mainly of solitude. In the walk to the falls, though other people must have been present, 'she felt alone'. The memory was of a feeling of awe 'a mixture of delight and wonderment and perhaps a bit of fear' in the presence of the canyon and the waterfall.

Marie's memories had similar contrasts. The first episode was characterized by a sense of anticipation and pleasure, 'marvellous sense of release and freedom'. The later episode began with anticipated pleasure, 'it was a glorious day' but this turned to feelings of 'hurt and anger and cheated of her turn'.

Ann began her holiday feeling 'excited' but also 'apprehensive'. Waiting for the ferry she felt anxious but then delighted. On arriving at the holiday flat she felt 'a little disappointed' but in general pleased. The episode later during the holiday was enjoyable and interesting except that the sky 'became more threatening' and Ann felt worried.

Fay's holiday began with her feeling anxious and nervous in the alien world of boats, feeling unconfident and incompetent at handling large boats and the presumed affluent lifestyle that went with it. Later in the same holiday there is an implied peacefulness and pleasure as they 'woke early on a warm clear morning and decided to have a swim around the boat'. She was uninterested in fishing, but felt obliged to go through the motions. To her surprise she was successful at catching fish, but felt 'a mixture of contradictory emotions – some excitement and delight, revulsion at the killing, pride at overcoming squeamishness'. A second holiday also described by Fay, with another woman in the Dales in England, also began with her feeling anxious. This dissolved into a sense of pleasure in lively conversation, ease and self congratulations at successfully finding their way.

Sources of Pleasure

Holidays are supposed to be pleasurable. Indeed, all the memories were set in stereotypically pleasant locations. And each of our adult holiday memories reported some sort of pleasure, though sometimes the pleasure seemed buried within what was usually a problematic event. There seem to be several main sources of pleasure.

Nearly all of us drew pleasure from the beauty of nature, and this was important to us – the waterfall in the bush, lake, the long stretch of open beach in the late afternoon, the ferry trip to a tropical island, a warm clear early morning on the boat. These scenes were described in detail; they are rich in visual images, with lots of colour, accompanying smells and feelings of cold and warmth and the movement and sounds of nature. The remembered pleasure is sensual and rounded – golden moments treasured. There was no human interaction in these images even when other people were present: 'they made no impression'. We felt a stillness, a solitude, a sense of relatedness through all our senses to the scene around us. But another source of pleasure indeed was being with people. As adults we seemed particularly to enjoy the relaxed social conviviality that sometimes occurs in holidays. We did not seem to be seeking intimacy or intensity in our relationships, but rather a warm and easy sociability with our peers.

So Margaret was delighted to meet people in New England. The warmth of the occasion seemed to give it a certain special quality. The people were interesting and conversation was stimulating. She enjoyed meeting her hosts, Marie enjoyed the 'mob of adults and children' and Fay found pleasure in the easy companionship of her friend.

Sources of Satisfaction

There were other themes, not so much of delight but of satisfaction. We all expressed anxiety, and this seems to contradict the expectations of a holiday. But much of this anxiety seemed to be deliberately courted as we set ourselves some sort of challenge. The satisfaction came from successfully meeting the challenge, resolving the anxiety.

Anxiety was expressed several times. Sometimes the anxiety was related to circumstances surrounding the holiday itself – our travel arrangements, the weather, other people's response. There was a sense of uncertainty, of apprehension. Margaret made this explicit, 'they had no idea what they would find there'. We carried a sense of not being in control, and yet somehow of being held accountable if things went wrong. When things did go well for us, we had a sense of relief. The thread of anxiety/relief occurred particularly strongly through both of Ann's memories and through all of Fay's. It was also present in Liz's first memory and in both Margaret's, sometimes implied rather than expressed.

Competence continued to be important to us. When we felt uncertain of our competence we expressed anxiety. This was evidenced by Fay on the boat, and by Ann at the airport. When we judged ourselves as incompetent, as Margaret did when she became sick, we were embarrassed and miserable. But when we proved ourselves competent – and we were our own harshest critics – then we felt considerable satisfaction. So Liz was pleased that she had 'kept her end up', and Fay was almost smug over the discovery of her fishing skills. In these cases we have not only a demonstration of competence, but through that a deeper affirmation of our identity.

In the holidays described by Fay, by Ann and by Margaret, there is a similar pattern. All were arranged by the women for themselves and others. All involved a venture into the unknown. Each presented a minor challenge, to explore a new place, to try new skills. Each challenge involved some (minor) risk. It seems that this challenge, deliberately self-imposed, was the source of both anxiety and pleasure. Perhaps this element of challenge and adventure is part of the attraction of holidays. This may be so despite the simultaneous though contradictory anticipation of peace, quiet and rest.

A further contradiction emerged from our theorizing of these memories. Two of the memories relate to incidents where the actor (Margaret, Liz) is recognized unexpectedly. In a third (Ann's) a stranger begins to relate to her as a person, and her anxiety abates, giving way to pleasure. In all three of these memories the theme of identity was important. All were holidays in unfamiliar settings. The contradiction was between the desire to get away from the familiar and to experience the unfamiliar, while at the same time finding pleasure in being 'recognized' in this unfamiliar setting. It is as if we need to assimilate some part of the unfamiliar and find our identity in order to begin to find pleasure there. On the other hand, some of us told how many of our holidays were taken at the same place with the same people year after year. Marie's memory is of such a holiday. Pleasure also comes from the familiar, from repeated contact with surroundings known and enjoyed over and over again.

The Problematics of Adult Holidays

Our adult holidays, however, were certainly not experienced simply, or primarily, in terms of the pleasure or challenge. None of us experienced the freedom from care that holidays are supposed to be about. We realized in our collective theorizing that there was good reason for this. We all felt responsible for the success of the holiday. In particular we felt responsible for everyone else's well-being. This rendered the holiday problematic in different ways. In some cases, notably Liz's, the holiday was specifically designed for another – 'she is debilitated, run down, and Liz takes a week off her annual leave to take her to the seaside'. There was no anticipation of her own pleasure, it was incidental. In other memories there was a general anxiety that things may not go according to plan, and even though 'things' were beyond control, we still felt responsible, afraid that we might let the others down. Such is implied in Ann's, Margaret's and Fay's memories. In Margaret's case 'things' did go wrong – she became ill. It was beyond her control, but she nevertheless felt responsible and at fault, 'she felt that everyone must be judging her badly'. Marie's holiday was problematic in a slightly different way. She too felt responsible for everyone's well-being. In this case there was a clear expectation of pleasure for everyone, including herself. But in providing for others' well-being, her own needs were unattended. She responded with feelings of hurt and anger, and 'stormed out of the hut'. She, incidentally, felt guilty over her tantrum.

It appears that the messages of our childhood have been well learned (see memories of transgression in chapter 4). As adult women we are expected to place the interests of others ahead of our own comfort, to be unselfish. While we may feel resentful of that burden, we none the less accept it; we take our responsibilities seriously.

Memories of Childhood Holidays

Our memories of holidays in childhood, like the adult ones, all contained some kind of contradiction or unresolved conflict. Here are the five girlhood memories:

Marie, age 6–7:

Camping, with Mum and Dad. The first experience of camping. The memory is largely a visual image. Dirt road through dense forest. The old car fording the river. A clearing by the river with big square canvas tent. Mushrooms in the long grass. Daisies? Buttercups? An uneasy feeling that Mother wasn't ecstatically happy as she should have been. Marie was joyously happy.

Liz, age 8:

She was enrolled at age 8 in a learn to swim class at the old Manly Baths and didn't make much progress. She hated being lined up with all the kids and being made to thrash the water. She didn't make as much progress as some other kids, she felt a failure and had no confidence. But by the end of the course she 'passed' by struggling across some very short distance in the shallow end of the pool. The course gave her confidence to practise in the 'big pool' at her own pace and she enjoyed extending her swim each time. She also learned by observing a private teacher with a small boy. The boy had to swim in the deep end with a float attached to a piece of string held by the teacher. Gradually the teacher relaxed his hold of the string. From this, Liz realized, 'that learning to swim was all a matter of confidence'. Still she didn't venture out in the deep part of the pool. At any rate her mother was always watching them when they swam, and had forbidden it . . . But when her father came at the end of the holiday to take them home, he went swimming and took the girls . . . On this morning, he got into his black one-piece swimming costume and swam out with his old-fashioned crawl from the shallow edge of the 'big' pool across to the ladders and the walkway in the deep water. And Liz went too, clinging to his shoulder straps and kicking behind her . . .

Margaret, age 8:

Every school holidays they went to stay with Aunty I and Uncle L. This holiday was not the first one but is one of the earliest that she can remember. She was 8 years old. Her aunt had just had a baby, he was born in December so it was probably January and he was just a few weeks old. It was a beautiful day, hot and sunny. The beach was just a short walk away, about half a mile. Margaret was dying to go to the beach, but she had to wait until her mother had done all the housework. She was asked to rock the baby to sleep. She stood by the cot and wheeled it back and forth. It was a small wooden cot. The baby was fretful, but calmed down as she found the appropriate rhythm to rock him. She watched his eyes very closely, it seemed ages before they settled down. He seemed to be restless and very wakeful. It was like a battle of wills between them. Eventually, his eyes sort of glazed over and looked as if they might close. Margaret was impatient, she wanted to get away. She felt a bit resentful that she was not able to enjoy the holiday without paying for it. She carefully stopped the rocking and tip-toed to the door. Just as she reached it, the baby cried. She had to go back and start all over again. Her aunt was one of her favourite people, but was also inclined to tease Margaret. Margaret felt that her aunt took some pleasure from her frustration and from the baby's ability to keep her a prisoner. She reluctantly returned to the task, and eventually escaped, successful at last.

Fay, age 5–6:

She was 5 or 6. Her father was working in South Australia for several months. Fay and her parents were staying with one of her father's work colleagues and his wife and daughter, E, who was about a year younger than Fay. The two families went to stay in a caravan park at the seaside. Fay and E had to share a bunk – one at each end. They were put to bed and told to go to sleep although the lights were on, their parents eating and playing cards. Neither of the girls could get comfortable. They kept complaining to the adults about the other kicking. Eventually Fay moved to another bunk, getting into trouble because she was older. Her mother was very exasperated with her . . . Fay felt dislike for E, disgruntled and tired, and that her parents were unfair to expect her to sleep in such a situation.

Ann, age 8–9:

Ann and her parents spent most of their holidays on a property in the country, with her aunt and uncle and two cousins. They usually went there in May and although the days were warm, the nights were quite cold. Ann didn't like these holidays much; she didn't like the animals . . . she didn't like riding and didn't like helping on the farm. What she really liked was curling up in the lounge room and reading. She also liked talking to her mother and aunt in the kitchen, which had a big fuel stove. It was warm and snug and there were often nice cooking smells. Breakfast was always a delight – the smell of chops, and eggs and bacon cooking. And weetbix, which Ann always covered with fresh thick cream.

She liked the house and felt warm and safe in it . . . Ann looked forward to the evenings after dinner when she was allowed to stay up for a while. There were often visitors and there would be lots of talk and laughter in the living room in front of the big log fire. They used to play cards at night . . . and again there would be lots of joking and laughing . . . She loved those evenings when everyone was relaxed and happy. There was always lots of talk amongst the adults about wool prices, and the weather and the state of the nation . . .

Ann used to get into trouble for staying inside and was always being told to go outside and get some fresh air. She hated being told to go outside and resisted as much as possible. She learned to ride but was never any good at it and was always filled with apprehension and fear at the thought of having to go any distance. Her cousins of course were good riders and so was her sister. They used to give Ann the oldest and quietest horse but Ann was still very anxious about it all. She was very frightened of the dogs who always barked a lot and were tied up a lot of the time . . . She remembers, too, the animals being killed . . . the horses being broken in . . . the cows being rounded up . . . She didn't like any of that . . . these things were noisy and nasty.

Consistent with what we found elsewhere, a single situation produces a variety of quite different, contradictory emotions. Some of the following comments about the inside/outside contrast have already been made in chapter 5. We extend the discussion here in the context of both adult and childhood holidays. The childhood memories of Ann and Margaret have already been referred to: Ann's dislike of the outside and delight at the inside and Margaret's dislike of being inside with the baby and desire to be outside on a beautiful hot sunny day. Fay's holiday was also at the seaside; she experienced discomfort, dislike, disgruntlement, a sense of injustice – all of it inside. Marie was camping and felt 'joyously happy', sensuous delight but also unease – the delight occurred outside. Liz at the pool experienced dislike, failure, low self confidence, fear, but then, with her father, an implied delight and accomplishment.

The reported emotions were not as clearly defined or as complex as the adult ones were, but they all contained similar contrasts. In each there was an element of delight – perhaps what holidays were supposed to be. But there was also strongly remembered concern – memories of dislike, disquiet, discomfort, anxiety. Perhaps it was the contradiction or displeasure in a 'holiday' that made the memories remain vivid. Our experience of holidays did not match the pleasure we were expected to find. Nor did we find comfort in clichéd descriptions of what holidays meant.

However, there was some pleasure. For the most part this lay in simple things. Sometimes this was found in inside activities – a country breakfast, curling up with a book, talking by the fire. Sometimes the pleasure was outside – a beautiful hot sunny day at the beach, clinging to the father's shoulder straps in the deep water, a forest clearing by the river.

A strong element for all of us was the pleasure found in sharing moments with adults. These might be special shared experiences or moments of closeness with a significant adult – Marie and her dad camping, Liz and her father in the water, Ann and her mother and aunt in the kitchen. These scenes were reminiscent of some of our childhood happiness memories, like Margaret with her dad after the bath. In other memories the pleasure was more generally social, moments of general gaiety like Ann's evenings with 'lots of talk and laughter in the living room in front of the big log fire'. These memories may anticipate the pleasure we found in our adult holidays of convivial company with our peers.

There were several sources of our concern, as there was with adult memories. A common source of both pleasure and anxiety in both childhood and adult memories is our perceived competence, as in learning to ride or catching a wave (see chapter 6). In these childhood memories of holidays, we were sometimes anxious about our lack of competence. Liz was anxious about her capacity to swim in the deep water; Ann felt incompetent to handle the animals at the farm. The concern with competence continued in our adult holiday memories.

Perhaps the most interesting source of concern for us as children related to our perception of what holidays were about. For all of us (except Marie) there is a sense of being constrained, of being expected to do something with or for others that we did not want to do – worse, of being expected to enjoy it. For Ann there was an expectation that 'they would all play happily together'. Margaret 'was asked to rock the baby to sleep'. Fay was not only expected to get along with a strange child, but to share a bunk and sleep with the lights on. Liz was expected to line up with other children in the learn to swim class.

Behind these tangible expectations there were others. Our collective theorizing revealed a consistent dynamic in family holidays. Parents arrange holidays in ways that simultaneously are supposed to be for the children yet where the children's wishes are not consulted. A mythology is perpetuated about children's carefree holiday enjoyment, yet the supposed freedom is curtailed by imposed restrictions and by enforced intimacy with other people. Furthermore, we as female children (would it be the same for boys?) are held responsible for the well-being of others. And we are expected to be grateful. Hence as adults we generally do not remember childhood family holidays with much enthusiasm, despite the pleasures involved.

These themes are similar to those emerging from our other childhood memories – memories of transgression, of anger, of play. Our autonomy is important, but the apparent freedom of holidays is contradicted by the enforced nature of the 'pleasures'. Our sense of competence is important to us, but it is tested in unfamiliar situations and circumstances. We are held responsible for others' well-being and are blamed or feel anxious when others are not enjoying themselves.

Gender Relations

In order to explore the gender relations implied in the memories, we re-examined the whole pool of holiday memories, childhood and adult. We also sought and obtained four childhood memories from a men's memory-work group. Though these provided a somewhat limited set, they produced interesting contrasts for our collective theorizing. Here are the men's memories from childhood . . .

Tim:

He was about 5 or 6 years old and we were on holidays at Port Macquarie on the north coast. They, he and his sister (a year and a half younger) had a favourite beach. It wasn't the main beach . . . it was a smaller beach with very little surf because it was almost entirely protected by rocks and rocky shelves. They played submarines. They went back to the flat later and drew pictures of what they had done that day. It was sort of overcast and cold but still warm. He had a favourite top with a hood with a red and white floral pattern on it. He can't remember how long the holiday was – about a week probably – but every day was fun and new.

David:

He couldn't sleep because it was Christmas Eve. He went out into the living room where the Christmas Tree was decorated and surrounded by presents. He switched on the tree lights and dragged a blanket in to sleep under. The lights lit up all the decorations beautifully. He kept thinking about what the presents might be. He woke up in his own bed and a sack of toys was at the end of the bed. He had to wait for everyone else to wake up before enjoying the toys. So he woke everyone up.

Richard:

He went camping with his father and his brother. All around were sand and pine trees. He was really excited about camping and can particularly remember being at the top of this sand dune in the shade of some pine trees with his brother and father. He was really happy playing and sliding down the sand.

Howard:

He was in Toukley with his parents and his younger brother. They were staying in a cottage. His brother and he were playing with Matchbox cars and a bucket of Lego in the sunny front room where they slept. Later they went to the beach; it had horrible grey sand and there he got stung on the stomach by a jelly-fish and cried for ages.

In our memories, as girls and as adult women, we noticed and described the work done by women, by our mothers and aunts and later by ourselves as adults. Holidays were a lot of work. The everyday tasks of cooking and cleaning and making beds, of children, of organizing outings, were not always, but mostly, done by women. These tasks were constantly referred to – in our childhood memories we were already engaged in helping perform them, and in some cases they were the source of our displeasure (note for example Margaret's attempts to get the baby asleep so that she could escape).

There is no such preoccupation in the boys' memories. None of the boys' memories mentions any work; certainly they do not appear to have done any, or to be expected to do any. Nor do they refer, or appear to be aware of the work performed by their mother. Each refers to the other people and the place as part of the given of the holiday – the backdrop against which their own private drama was played. In essence this drama revolved around their own private excitement and pleasure at play. The memories were predominantly carefree and pleasurable: 'every day was fun and new', 'a sack of toys was at the end of the bed', 'he was really happy playing and sliding down the sand'. Only Howard found his holiday somewhat problematic 'he got stung on the stomach by a jelly-fish and cried for ages'.

That the adult women do the work and that the girls but not the boys notice this, may be stating the obvious. What is less obvious are the implications of this. The boys' description of their holidays sounds more like what we expect a holiday to be – full of fun, some excitement, a freedom from care. It was not what we experienced as girls or as women. Indeed the freedom from care, the release from workday worries, was designed by the women for the men and boys.

It was the men in our stories who 'let go'. More often than not the women organized the holiday, ostensibly for everyone's enjoyment, but primarily for the comfort of the men, or for some other adult, perhaps a sister or aged parent. As girls we were made to feel responsible for the well-being of others; as adult women we clearly accepted that we were responsible. There was no sign of an imposed or accepted sense of responsibility in the boys' memories.

Fay's holiday in the Dales was particularly interesting as a contrast to the other holidays. Fay went with a woman friend. The tone of the memory was quite different from that in our other adult memories. After some initial anxiety, there was a sense of shared adventure, shared satisfaction, mutual support, that was largely absent from the other memories. Here nobody was RESPONS-IBLE. Our collective discussion led to a rush of other memories reporting similar happy tales of holidays alone or with a woman friend – and we counted these as among our happiest. Here is an excerpt from our discussion:

> *June*: Marie's first memory where you walked away from everyone . . . moments like that
> *Jenny*: In the absence of men and children!
> *Pam*: It's the kind of attention that women pay to each other without thinking – you actually take care of each other. You're aware of it – you don't have to talk it all out . . . a lot more concern is taken
> *Jenny*: You all described it in the same sort of terms. You all say 'oh it was lovely'. All so gentle, nothing remarkable.
> *Pam*: You can go off and do things, you don't have to do things together . . . you can be in the same place, go off and do things independently, come back and meet and share things . . . much more relaxed.
> *Sue*: Why is it?
> *Jenny*: Because nobody has to take responsibility for the other's well-being. You sort of share the mutual responsibility.
> *June*: It's a holiday from
> *Pam*: Taking care of other people's emotions
> *June*: And other people's well-being generally.

In summary, the memories tell us a great deal about what holidays should be, and what they are in reality for women. The overwhelming impression we had from the whole pool of memories is that holidays are a great deal of trouble, really more trouble than they are worth.

Contrasting Child and Adult Memories

Holidays remain for women, both as children and as adults, highly problematic. So why do we keep 'doing' them? Particularly, why do we keep organizing them. We struggled with this question in our collective theorizing.

Part of the answer seems to lie in the clichés. We make statements like 'the promise of empty days', 'dreams of her life', 'break from work' and 'practising new skills'. We seem to have internalized the social definitions of holidays as something desirable, pleasurable, good for ourselves and others. So if a particular holiday is problematic it must be our fault – next time we will get it right.

Secondly, in most memories we are able to retrieve sufficient pleasure to justify (to whom are we justifying?) the event. It is as though we are saying – 'yes, it was difficult, but that special moment made it all worthwhile'. The special moments are often moments of solitude or calm, enjoying the beauties of nature. Less often they are moments of relaxed socializing, or the satisfaction of achievement. We seem to hold on to these 'golden moments' in our memories as the returns we got from our investment.

But in every case the adult holidays were ones that we had initiated and organized. They were intended for our own pleasure but also, and primarily, for the pleasure of others. We hold ourselves responsible for others' well-being in general, and for the success of the holiday in particular. So if something goes wrong, it is our fault. Yet holidays, by their very nature, are out of the ordinary, ventures into the unknown. Things are likely to go wrong, things over which we have little or no control. Somehow, the increased uncertainty and our decreased control of events does not reduce our sense of responsibility, it just makes us more anxious, and renders holidays more problematic for us. But it does not stop us from organizing them. It is, after all, our responsibility to make them, for others' pleasure.

The exception to all this seems to be holidays taken without men and children. Such holidays are less memorable, less problematic, more calm, relaxed, remembered with a greater though quieter pleasure.

Our adult holiday memories all have one thing in common that sets them apart from almost all the childhood memories, including the childhood holiday memories. The adult memories are highly elaborated, the descriptions detailed. A large number of emotions are reported and they are reported clearly and in great detail. Often the emotions are quite complex and their complexity is also described. A number of descriptive phrases are added to clarify hard-to-define emotional states. The precise context of each emotional state is also described as well as a detailed explanation (justification?) of why that particular emotion was experienced at that particular time. In other words, we as adults were quite clear about what emotions were operating, how these emotions arose and why. This contrasts with many of our childhood memories which carry a sense of confusion, uncertainty, puzzlement and undefined unease. Contrast, for example, Margaret's childhood memory 'she was impatient, she wanted to get away', with her adult memory where she was 'embarrassed, upset and felt guilty as well as nauseous'. Or Marie's childhood memory, 'uneasy feeling that Mother wasn't as ecstatically happy as she should have been', compared to her adult memory where she felt 'hurt and angry and cheated of her turn'. Or Liz's childhood memory, 'she hated being lined up with all the kids and being made to thrash the water', compared to her adult memory, 'the memory is of feeling of awe – a mixture of delight and wonderment and perhaps a bit of fear'.

Our adult memories of course occurred more recently than our childhood ones and so in that sense are more accessible. Nevertheless, most of the adult memories occurred several – in some cases ten or twenty – years ago. Even in these adult memories, some of which occurred a long time ago, there is no longer any sense of struggling to understand our feelings. Our emotions as adults have already been thoroughly constructed. We know exactly what emotions we are dealing with and what they mean. Or at least we think we do.

Clichés
We were struck by the way adult holiday memories were over-elaborated in contrast to the childhood ones. They were full of clichés – or as one of us put it, 'pure Girls Own'. Haug has noted the importance of examining clichés as part of the memory-work method – working against the text (Haug, 1987). Clichés are cultural stereotypes – socially prepared ways of seeing, thinking, feeling. Therefore when we use clichés in the text of our memories, we are not only saying something about ourselves, we are also talking in culturally defined ways and thus saying something about what we have internalized of the social order – we are making standard cultural judgements.

In our analysis of clichés in general, we realized that not all clichés were of the same order. We were able to identify at least five overlapping classes of cliché. As a tentative classification they are:

1   Summary sensory descriptions like 'silky to the touch'. These stock descriptive phrases immediately evoke some sort of sensory image, an immediately recognizable one that serves to

'set the scene' in dramaturgical terms – a few broad brush strokes and that's enough – we have a preformed backdrop.

2　Summary emotional descriptions like 'happy and excited', 'shocked and hurt', 'thumping heart'. Again we are using preformed images, this time of feeling states rather than sensory images. They are stock phrases, common, instantly recognizable. They describe emotional packages, and link specific states as 'obviously' going together.

3　Summary behavioural descriptions like 'he sunk his teeth in her arm'. These are more than straight descriptions; they are dramatic and dramatized actions. 'He bit her arm' does not carry the same load of meaning as 'he sunk his teeth into her arm'. The dramatic description is highly evocative of a whole set of relations surrounding the act itself – again a preformed and instantly recognizable whole.

4　Summary social justifications or moral judgements like 'aghast at this waste'. Like the other categories, these clichés are preformed and instantly recognizable. In this case they carry a strong ideological component. There are strong messages contained within the stock phrase about what ought to be – standard ways of thinking about and judging events. They include self justification too – statements that explain our own actions in culturally prescribed ways and make evaluative judgements of our own actions.

5　Summary cultural imperatives like 'promise of empty days'. In a sense all clichés are cultural imperatives. But some seem to stand out as headlines – they are like the subtitle of a silent movie – they serve as a summary definition of a common social event. More than a description of what is, they contain judgements of what is proper. They define the ideal. As such they also carry an ideological load.

A close analysis of one adult memory may serve to elucidate the power of clichés. Margaret's trip to New England is particularly rich in these cultural stereotypes. There are a number of summary sensory descriptions: 'fall in New England', 'a charming holiday resort', 'a romantic Cape Cod style wooden house', 'beautiful fresh seafood', 'warm and friendly people'. These phrases combine to sketch an idealized setting, the sort of place in which holidays are supposed to occur. Stock emotional descriptions include: 'a lovely surprise', 'happy glow', 'terribly embarrassed', 'couldn't wait to leave'. The reader instantly recognizes and identifies with what Margaret is feeling. The emotions are highly constructed, presented in almost idealized form. The same may be said of the summary behavioural descriptions like 'she took some time to clean the bathroom', 'she smiled sweetly'.

Particularly interesting in this memory are the stock moral judgements or evaluations. There are quite a few: 'charming holiday resort', 'the whole idea seemed impossible', she 'liked to have her cake and eat it', H was 'a bright and lively person', 'her mother a warm and charming person', Margaret was 'reluctant to spoil the evening'. Very favourable evaluations are made of the place, the social event, the other people, particularly the other women. Against these standards, she judges herself harshly. Her pleasure was 'out of proportion', she 'wanted to have her cake and eat it'; she enjoyed and wanted more than she felt entitled to have. Worse than that, it was she who spoiled the evening. Her negative self evaluation was projected onto the others: 'everyone must be judging her badly'. This latter statement in particular shows that Margaret is simultaneously holding in mind her own actions and the others' response. There is an audience that is passing judgement. She knows that and knows (or suspects) what that judgement is. Furthermore she appears to accept the judgement, to agree that she deserves no better.

The cultural imperative tells us what a holiday is, how people behave on a holiday. Clichés in Margaret's memory define these imperatives: one of the 'dreams of her life', 'conversation was lively', the 'spontaneity and warmth of the occasion seemed to give it a special quality', it was 'one of the nicest things that had ever happened to her', 'she smiled sweetly and said thank you'.

Similar clichés in the other adult memories combine to provide the accepted social definition of what holidays are supposed to be. Holidays provide a 'once in a life time experience', 'a break from work', 'the promise of empty days', 'a chance to practise and learn new skills'. 'Once on the road they found themselves in animated conversation.' 'She stood there for a while and was glad she had come.' These statements may be taken at their face value – no doubt we did experience the pleasures described, and no doubt that is partly what holidays provide. But given the problematic nature of each episode remembered, and given the kind of stock expressions we used, there is probably more to it than that. We appear to be using these clichés as a kind of justification to ourselves as to why we would go to all the trouble to have a holiday – because most of the memories are primarily concerned with the trouble.

We use clichés quite often to justify ourselves – to explain to ourselves and others why we reacted as we did. Margaret was grateful to be able to clean up her mess; Marie 'magnanimously agreed' but felt 'cheated out of her turn'. Liz is 'rather taken aback' but 'she feels she has to be civil'. Fay 'made polite rejoinder' and 'felt obliged to go through the motions' of fishing. In these phrases we are explaining ourselves, but we are responding quite consciously in socially acceptable ways. We understand what is expected of us, and by and large we conform to those expectations.

This contrasts with our childhood memories where we are able to describe our own perspectives but not so well the perspective of 'the other'. We are aware of what the other is specifically demanding of us in the present (for example, to rock the baby, not to kick in bed), but we do not yet seem to have generalized this expectation into a broad standard social principle 'to keep our end up'.

But clichés are about more than accepting the social order They also provide a culturally approved way of avoiding that which is personally (and collectively) problematic. As adults we become adept at turning aside and transforming the problematic into the standard cultural formula contained in the cliché. As Haug put it (1987, p. 63), 'clichés condemn us to walk on the well trodden path of what should be . . . the cliché deliberates; it acts as an obstacle to understanding'. So, for example, Margaret's self-judgemental cliché that she 'always wanted to have her cake and eat it' contains an acceptance that we should not expect to obtain pleasure without a personal cost, that we ought not to be 'greedy' in our hopes for personal satisfaction, in this case that it was expecting too much to be invited out for a lovely evening AND to have the children safely cared for by someone else. The situation could have been re-interpreted as a problem-solving one – how to obtain childcare so that she was free to enjoy herself – and indeed she did solve the problem in this way. But that is not the way she wrote about it.

Once we recognize what a cliché is and how it is used, we can use it to re-evaluate our own responses. We may choose to accept what the cliché is telling us (holidays are 'the promise of empty days') or we may look behind the cliché to find what is being obscured. Either way we open up possibilities for questioning, for resistance, for restructuring our ways of being.

This recognition of what a cliché is and analysis of what it represents can only be done collectively, at least in the first instance. The use of cliché constrains our thinking and prevents us from recognizing that change is possible. This effect is so pervasive that we need group support. The collective is important in seeking out and identifying cliché, in suggesting the ideology that the cliché represents, and in structuring and supporting alternative constructions of the events in question. We can change our own constructions, but change can be threatening, and so we need to do it together. As we progress, finding clichés, and reconstructing our thinking becomes almost second nature, and we are empowered. We may end up with a new set of clichés, however, and so we will always need the critical balance that a collective provides.

Our analysis of clichés and their function helps to point to why in general, though written by adults, memories from childhood contain very few clichés. Particularly absent are clichés of self-justification. It is as if as children we have not yet internalized the cultural imperatives, the standards of acceptable behaviour. We are only just learning the obstacles to our own being; we have not yet learned to impose them on ourselves.

These are the differences between adult and childhood emotions. We accept Averill's statement about adult emotions: 'as adults emotional reactions are likely to proceed automatically and in the absence of any verbal mediation. It is therefore easy to overlook the amount and kind of prior experience that is required for the proper enactment of an emotional role' (1980, p. 321). Adult emotions are possibly over-constructed, over-determined. In our adult memories, we describe our emotions in stereotyped terms, accepting limitations on what emotions are experienced and how they are expressed. Our use of childhood memories allows us to see how we come to understand these limitations, to examine the process by which we construct ourselves.

But, as well as differences between adult and childhood memories, there are also similarities. Although in our adult memories the emotions are understood better than childhood ones, are more firmly fixed, and are experienced in more predictable situations, they are still complex, possibly even more so, and difficult to disentangle. Adults still experience contradiction; the process of reflection, reappraisal and reconstruction continues. Emotions are being redefined, the self is ever changing.

9

Remembering and Forgetting

This chapter examines some of the theoretical issues regarding remembering and forgetting that we encountered during our work. The fundamental problem that we address in this chapter concerns the selectivity of memory itself and the selectivity of the memories we produce as part of the collective. Do we remember the problematic experiences of our lives and forget the unproblematic ones? Or do we remember only those things that 'fit' and forget the ones that do not 'fit' some preconceived notion of our subjectivity – our theory of our self? Or do we forget (repress) exactly those experiences which are problematic – too problematic to think about?

In addition to these questions about our memories, other issues which we raised and which others have raised with us concern the accuracy of our memories and related notions of veracity and reality. We shall deal first with the issue of accuracy. We point out that there is a distinction between real events and real memories. Our view is that the memories are 'true', in the sense discussed below; whether the events which form the basis for the memories are accurately described or not is irrelevant. The focus of memory-work is the process of construction. We endeavour to capture the process of negotiation of meaning, the search for intelligibility, not the actual event.

Veracity refers to whether the writer of the memory believes the memory to be true, a real memory as opposed to an invention. We deal with this issue simply by asserting that the memories are real – they are not fantasy, they are not lies, they are not imaginary. We would point out that one might ask questions about truth or fantasy of any self-report data. How do we know whether the person who puts a mark on a Likert scale that rates him- or herself as 'Never . . . . Always' happy, responsible, or whatever, is reporting 'truthfully'. We do not know this. We trust respondents to report as truthfully as they can. We ask no more of ourselves.

Next, we can consider the question of reality versus construction. Here, the answer is unequivocally and self-evidently that memory is a construction (or reconstruction) of a past event. This is not to say that constructions are not real. It is the nature of this construction that forms the basis of our work. The rules of memory-work try to ensure that we report as much detail as we can remember, that we do not impose censorship on the material, that we allow contradiction, incompleteness, incoherence to remain. In analysing these features of the construction, we reveal the processes by which we come to understand our selves.

We are not seeking to uncover the nature of the event itself but rather the meaning that the event had for us both then and now. As mentioned in chapter 2, it is possible that we remember only events which have an emotional component – Arnold's (1970) 'affective memory' – and that we understand emotion only because we remember past events where that emotion occurred. Arnold's analysis suggests that we may remember only the emotion or the affective component of the event and not necessarily the event itself.

Arnold supposes that our emotions are learned and re-learned – learned when we experience an event which is similar (in an unspecified way) to something previously experienced so that the memory traces of the affect associated with the previous event cause that affect to be reawakened. The reawakened affect is then attached to the new experience, and thus the learning and maintaining of emotion depends upon the memory traces of previously experienced affect. Arnold's theory suggests that it is unconscious processes which are of primary importance in the development of emotion, and that the nature of the events is forgotten.

We accept that unconscious processes contribute to our emotional life. However, agency is central to our theory and thus we focus on our active participation in our own formation. We find that we do remember events or episodes, together with their affective components. We examine the ways in which we have constructed and reconstructed such events, largely at a conscious level. Thus the memories are not accurate, but this does not mean that they are not real.

We consider the question of reality by using an analogy with a famous experimental method. One of the most influential works produced on memory was Bartlett's book *Remembering* (1932). He describes many experiments carried out to explore the nature of the constructions and reconstructions of material that take place as it is repeatedly reflected upon. He used a variety of materials; one of the best known of his experiments used an American Indian folk tale as the source ('real') material. By using material from an unfamiliar culture, with unfamiliar events, connections and expectations, he hoped to examine processes of assimilation and accommodation that take place as material is reconstructed.

In some of his experiments, Bartlett showed the story to one person, who then wrote a version of the story from memory, which was then passed to another person, and so on. In other experiments, Bartlett used the same person who saw his or her own version of the story over a number of occasions. At any stage, the written version of the story (apart from the initial stage) contained inaccuracies – sometimes gross inaccuracies, including omissions and importations. But that does not mean that there was not an original story (a 'real' event). The reconstruction represents the meaning that that event has for the person at the time it is reconstructed. This is the sense in which our memories are real.

If our theory that the self is constructed out of memories is correct, then the way the actor constructs the event is what is important. Consider Amy's memory of taking something from her mother's purse (chapter 4). Suppose Amy's mother were to read that memory and deny that the event ever happened. Such a denial (even if true) would not alter the fact that Amy's construction of the event (or an event) is what forms part of her theory of self. The event is intelligible to Amy in the terms that she wrote it, and becomes intelligible to others in those terms. The memory is real.

A problem which we found more difficult to resolve concerns the importance of forgetting. This includes a consideration of accessible versus inaccessible memories, conscious versus unconscious memory, the issue of repression.

Remembering versus Forgetting

It is accepted that we remember some episodes or events and forget others. What determines what is remembered? Freud (1901/64, in a discussion of 'screen memories') believed that we remember from childhood those events which involved strong emotion, which were of some importance, and which therefore made a lasting impression. Haug (1987) states that we remember events involving conflict and contradiction, which therefore require reflection and reappraisal. We expect to remember events involving novelty, and especially those which involve 'unfinished business'.

The memories we work with are not therefore in any sense a random sample of experience. They represent a biased selection, and it is the nature of this bias which is important. We recognize that a person's memory consists of those constructions and reconstructions of past events which are of some significance. A random selection of the events that contribute to experience would over-represent the ordinary, habitual, mundane. The selection of events to be preserved systematically under-represents such events. Habitual events are not preserved as individual episodes. Nevertheless, such events and their habitual nature form the context from which 'problematic' events derive their problematic nature.

In considering the nature of the biases represented by the remembered events, we note that some of the bias stems from socially constructed meanings whereby some episodes or events are experienced as problematic and others are not. Some of these socially constructed meanings are universal; others are limited to particular subgroups or subcultures, such as social class, gender. We attempt to uncover processes whereby common understandings are reached.

Our data consist of memories which relate to problematic events and our analysis focuses on the meanings of these events in so far as they are common meanings. We seek to examine the nature of the social world which renders the events problematic, and to acknowledge the influence of gender in the constructions we observe. We have tried to minimize biography, that is, aspects of meaning which apply to the individual. However, the example of memory used below (in this chapter) is a partial exception. Nevertheless, in theorizing this memory we have related it to social processes.

In cognitive social psychology, neo-Piagetians such as Doise and Mugny (1984) have found that children learn to solve problems when presented with instances which are wrong more quickly than when given only correct examples. They learn when they or others are seen to make errors. What we are examining in our childhood memories are episodes where we 'make mistakes' in the sense of misappraising a situation. This leads us to modify our theory of self. We reflect upon, reinterpret, elaborate on such an experience in an attempt to resolve the contradictions, as discussed in previous chapters. Some of the contradictions are between our appraisal and that of an adult, between our expectation and the actual outcome, between peer group standards and adult standards.

We experience in situations of contradiction a range of emotions – actions or passions – as they relate to long-lasting moral evaluations, as discussed in chapter 7. We engage with the social rules or barriers, thus making them explicit. We either challenge them, accept them, or disregard them. We reflect upon episodes of contradiction or conflict which are important in our growth, which challenge our accepted theory of self.

We remember episodes of 'unfinished business'. This is analogous to the Zeigarnik effect (Zeigarnik, 1927), that is, an effect of enhancement of memory for uncompleted activities observed in laboratory experiments carried out in the 1920s. This effect predicts that events which are completed, resolved in our present analogy, will be forgotten readily, whereas those which are incomplete, that is, unresolved or problematic, will be remembered so long as they remain unresolved.

We consider what happens to an event which was once problematic but is partially resolved at a later time by means of reflection or what might be called memory-work. Such events do not appear to be forgotten just because they have been resolved. Our findings are that they are remembered, possibly in proportion to the amount of work that was needed in order to resolve them. It is just such episodes that give us our sense of uniqueness as individuals and our sense of continuity. Although as theorists we recognize that we are constantly changing and growing – incorporating new experiences, new relationships, new meanings into our subjectivities – as human beings we nevertheless maintain a sense of individual subjectivity, continuity, integrity.

There is also a sense in which episodes which are remembered are always subject to possible reinterpretation. They are the stuff of which memory-work is made.

Forgetting versus Repression

In our everyday understanding of memory, our usage of language implies that there is a 'memory', like a store, a library where we can find things if we search hard enough. It is described in terms that imply that the material it contains is sitting there passively, becoming fainter over time perhaps, and representing in an imperfect way information – facts – about what has happened in the past. Forgetting is a passive process that occurs automatically, in a fairly random and non-problematic fashion.

As psychologists, we know that this is not the case. Remembering (as distinct from 'memory') is an active process, and forgetting may be equally active. The determinants of what is remembered and what is forgotten are complex, but certainly involve social processes. Remembering includes choosing which episodes and which aspects of those episodes to reflect upon. As we argue below, forgetting may happen by default, or it may be a deliberate choice.

There are two kinds of episode that we are likely to forget. One relates to the totally unproblematic. For example, if we as children did something wrong and apologized, we do not need to do any more work on this experience. It recedes into the background of the ordinary, the everyday. Even if we feel guilty and ashamed about such an episode, provided it is totally expected, understood and complete, we may simply forget about it – it is part of our non-problematic set of experiences.

It is important to note that what determines the 'non-problematic' is socially constructed, that is, the class of experience that we believe is forgotten in these terms is the trivial, the mundane, the usual, the appropriate; experiences which everyone concerned appraises as 'ordinary' or 'normal'; everyone knows what to expect, and the expected occurs. Such experiences form part of the taken-for-granted, and may indeed be influential in our lives. But they will be retrieved and revealed only indirectly, by examining those things which are remembered. The second kind of episode that we are likely to forget is the highly problematic. This is discussed more fully below, when we analyse a memory illustrating the kind of event referred to here. Such forgetting is conceived of as being motivated – we have reason not to remember painful or shameful episodes. Freud's theory of repression in non-neurotic contexts (1901/64) explains how we forget not only the painful material itself, but often details one step removed from such material, details which if recalled to consciousness would by association reawaken the memory of the repressed material.

Freud uses the analogy of a person seeking to enter his house: 'it should vanish from the conscious if it was previously conscious, or . . . it should be held back from consciousness if it was about to become conscious. The difference is not important; it amounts to much the same thing as the difference between my ordering an undesirable guest out of my drawing-room (or out of my front hall) and my refusing, after recognizing him, to let him cross my threshold at all' (1915a/64). In a footnote to this sentence, Freud goes further: 'This simile, which is thus applicable to the process of repression, may also be extended to a characteristic of it which has been mentioned earlier. I have merely to add that I must set a permanent guard over the door which I have forbidden this guest to enter, since he would otherwise burst it open' (1915a/64, p. 153 n.). What 'has been mentioned before' refers to the characteristic of repression not happening once and for all, but needing to be continually maintained, since it 'demands a persistent expenditure of force, and if this were to cease the success of the repression would be jeopardized, so that a fresh act of repression would be necessary' (p. 151).

The simile or analogy does not quite work. What is it that corresponds to the 'I', the person who is censoring. It cannot be part of the conscious, since the idea is to be excluded from consciousness. So what makes the evaluation that the idea is 'too terrible to contemplate'? How can it be known that the idea is a terrible one without knowing what the idea is? According to Appignanesi and Zarate (1979) this paradox led Freud eventually to postulate the existence of the superego.

Motivated forgetting occurs not only for material which is painful, but also for material which somehow does not 'fit' with what we want to believe. Freud refers to a quotation from Darwin's auto-biography which 'convincingly reflects his scientific honesty and his psychological acumen':

> 'I had during many years followed a golden rule, namely, that whenever a published fact, a new observation or thought came across me, which was opposed to my general results, to make a memorandum of it without fail and at once; for I had found by experience that such facts and thoughts were far more apt to escape from the memory than favourable ones.' (Freud, 1901/64, p. 148 n.)

It is possible that there are two kinds of motivated forgetting. One, which we may call suppression, is the direct and deliberate pushing aside of material relating to something that we prefer not to think about. (Scarlett O'Hara, the heroine of *Gone with the Wind*, was fond of saying 'I won't think about that today, I'll think about that tomorrow.') Such memories are not necessarily repressed, they are pushed aside rather than pushed 'down' into the unconscious. They seem to correspond to the guest who is recognized after he has entered the house.

Repression is the other kind of motivated forgetting. It happens not by an act of will, but rather automatically. The material seems to be not pushed aside or even pushed down, but is described in terms that are paradoxical. The material does not arise in conscious-ness because it is too terrible to contemplate, and so it remains in the unconscious, from where it may exert an influence.

Thus there are three kinds of forgetting. Two of these are automatic, the other is deliberate. The two kinds of automatic forgetting are the forgetting of the unproblematic, the mundane, trivial etc., and the forgetting of the highly problematic, the dangerous, the threatening. The automatic forgetting of threatening and/or painful material we shall term repression – non-neurotic repression in the Freudian sense. Deliberate forgetting of the unwanted, possibly unpleasant, material which we have chosen not to reflect upon we shall call suppression. It is thus not possible completely to separate a consideration of the material which is forgotten from the process of forgetting. In automatic ('non-problematic') forgetting, the material is deemed to be lost forever, gone from the conscious, the preconscious (Freud, 1915b/64) and the unconscious. In suppression and repression, the material is painful and/or threatening, but remains either in the preconscious or the unconscious. Repressed material is said to remain in the unconscious, since it has never been conscious – but Freud is inconsistent about this in his early formulation.

Material which has been suppressed is not necessarily in the unconscious, it seems most likely to be in the preconscious. If it has been pushed out of the preconscious into the unconscious, it would be said to be repressed. Preconscious material is potentially conscious. It may be accessible, either easily or with some difficulty. Repressed material may be retrieved from the unconscious, using methods of free association as described by Freud in 'The Psychopathology of Everyday Life' (1901/64).

The examples Freud used in his early formulation of non-neurotic repression (1901/64) are more like suppression than repression, turning away rather than pushing down of material that was certainly once conscious. Though he describes instances of repression as if they are automatic rather than deliberate, he also describes the retrieval of the forgotten material as taking place fairly easily. One of Freud's observations about repressed memories is relevant to our work. He states (1901/64, p. 274 n.) that repressed memories are preserved unchanged. They have not been reflected upon. In our terms, they have not been constructed and reconstructed. Material which is forgotten is that which, for whatever reason, has not been reflected upon. Some of this material may be retrievable (from the unconscious or from the preconscious) but some of it is not. We have postulated that the non-problematic material is not retrievable, and it is possible that some of the highly problematic is not retrievable as well.

A generalization of the above reading of Freud's early writing on repression and the unconscious would be that everything that is remembered will have involved some work – either the work involved in remembering, reflecting, or the work involved in suppressing, or the constant work required to keep repressed material from becoming conscious. Only those aspects of our lives which happen automatically and pass us by without reflection will be lost entirely. We have used 'forgetting' to refer to any process by which material is not reflected upon, and hence forgotten material will be either temporarily or permanently unavailable.

To return to the quotation from Darwin above, we may consider that what is remembered and what is forgotten may be different according to whether we are in the process of building up a theory or in the process of defending one with which we are satisfied. As children, our theory of self develops as we discover more and more about the social world that surrounds us. We transform experience into meaning as we find out about barriers and moral judgements, about emotion in ourselves and others. As children, we are gathering data for use in building our theory of self. While our theory remains in a fairly fluid state, we have no need to behave as Darwin described. We do not forget, but rather are more likely to remember, those very episodes which require us to modify our theory, since it is not so rigid that we are intent on maintaining or defending it.

As adults, we may act more in the theory-defending mode, and may therefore forget (suppress) episodes which threaten our theory. The metaphor of defending a theory (of self) fits with the metaphor of ego-defence, repression being the chief defence mechanism. Adults may well repress or suppress experiences which threaten a strongly held theory. Such experiences may be childhood ones or more recent ones.

This analysis suggests the ways in which the memories we produce in our memory-work, the building blocks for our theory of self, represent a biased selection of all the experiences that ever happened to us. The bias is a meaningful one, as mentioned earlier. Nevertheless, in theorizing our memories, we were concerned at the possibility that there were experiences which we do not remember and therefore do not produce in memory-work which were important in our construction but which were not reflected upon, as were those which we produced.

An Illustration

We considered whether such experiences might represent significant absences. They could be absences from the social world because they represent possibilities too terrible to contemplate at a social as well as at an individual level. To illustrate both the problem and the basis for our theorizing of the problem, one of us produced the following memory.

Ann:

She was a second year student sitting in a statistics class in psychology. The lecturer was a person of whom she was very fond; a person who as a teacher seemed to be on the same wavelength. She always enjoyed statistics classes . . . It was a warm and sunny afternoon. The statistical technique being taught was analysis of covariance . . . lots of fairly tedious calculations. No computers then. The lecturer used the black-board extensively to do all the calculations. The example was of some rats that had been experimented on. The nerve in both legs had been severed experimentally and on one leg electrical stimulation had been used to activate the muscle in the absence of the nerve. Nothing was done to the other leg. After a couple of weeks the nerve regenerated. The muscle on the two legs was then weighed. The one on the leg without stimulation had atrophied and the one that had had the stimulation was almost normal.

During the class the lecturer from time to time made an arithmetic error. Ann felt quite irritated and pointed out where he had gone wrong. She reacted in an obnoxious manner to his errors and interrupted impatiently and spoke sarcastically. The lecturer didn't seem upset by her manner but she felt that her fellow students did not approve of the way she had acted. After the lecture had finished, Ann went to the bus to go home. It was quite a long journey, about half an hour. While on the bus she began to feel uncomfortable about the way she had behaved. She had a bit of a crush on the lecturer as a kind of intellectual father figure. She felt that she had been unnecessarily unkind to him. She thought 'how could I have been so unkind to him when I have so much affection for him and we're usually on the same wavelength?' She started thinking about Freud and his theories of the unconscious. She felt that there was something underlying her behaviour that she didn't quite understand. She got off the bus and began walking home. She was thinking of something else when suddenly she realized why she had been so uncharacteristically rude. She made the connection between the rat experiment and something that had happened in her childhood. This childhood experience was something of which she was very ashamed. She hadn't forgotten it in the sense that she would have remembered it clearly if anyone had reminded her of it. But she had pushed it away in her memory, and certainly had never spoken about it to anyone and had never even thought about it for about eight or nine years.

Ann's childhood experience:

After she came out of hospital after having polio she wore a heavy iron caliper on her left leg from hip to foot . . . Her mother was disappointed that she may be forced to wear a caliper for the rest of her life . . . After about six months, when she was almost 12 years old, her mother began to take her three times a week to a masseur who administered electrical stimulation.

He had premises a long way from where they lived . . . The room was a small room behind a shop. It was dingy and smelt horrible. The masseur was a smallish old man, not at all clean, who wore a bluish-grey singlet and long dark grey striped trousers that didn't fit him too well. He had an unpleasant crooked face, very brown wrinkly skin and dark hair. He seemed to be very unintelligent. His wife was always present and Ann's mother also remained in the room during treatment . . . The electrical stimulation was a battery wrapped around with cloths, none too clean. It was covered with evil smelling liniment. He massaged her leg from hip to toe both outside and inside. She was naked with a facecloth draped over her private parts. Every now and then he used the stimulator to stimulate her genitals, saying things like 'this is the most important part of the body. The energy comes from here'. Ann felt acutely embarrassed when this happened, but with her mother sitting there acquiescing, she was totally unable to say anything. She tried to think of other things and never even felt in the least sexually aroused. In those surroundings, it was almost impossible. She went to some effort to disengage her mind from the embarrassment and revulsion she felt. Her mother could never understand why she didn't want to go there. Ann's embarrassment was only partly because of the revulsion. Most of it was because of the sordid bizarre nature of the whole experience. She was ashamed that she was taking part in unorthodox or quack medical procedures, particularly ones so lacking in style and so removed from mainstream or acceptable standards.

Note made at the time of writing the above:

Until I wrote this memory, even though I've thought of it on many occasions, I never ever labelled it as child sexual assault. It never even occurred to me in the context of child sexual experiences. But it does now.

In theorizing this memory (or these memories) we considered the meaning of repression – both its commonsense meaning and the more technical meaning that Freud originally used. Commonsense understandings of repression are that it refers to a process of motivated forgetting whereby an event is forgotten – either temporarily or permanently – because it represents something that is shameful, threatening, etc. The commonsense view of repression assumes that what is forgotten is something definite that happened, such as taking an object in a shop and not paying for it, and then forgetting what happened.

As mentioned above, Freud's original formulation of repression (1915a/64) stressed that what was repressed was an idea, and that it was an idea that represented an instinct. It was not necessarily the libido (defined in 1915 as the sexual instinct) that was involved, though many of the examples derived from case histories were associated with sex.

Neurotic repression – described in his essay 'Repression' (1915a/64) and the description of 'The Unconscious' (1915b/64) – involves material that can be retrieved only with great difficulty, with the help of a therapist using psychoanalytic procedures. There are also quite severe symptoms associated with neurotic repression – such as conversion hysteria, phobias, obsessions.

Freud (1901/64) seemed to differentiate between normal and neurotic repression. In that book, Freud described several examples of non-neurotic motivated forgetting (which he sometimes called repression). He also described how the forgotten material can be retrieved, sometimes with a fair amount of difficulty. Ann's childhood memory above is similar in kind to those events which Freud described from his own life in 'The Psychopathology of Everyday Life' (1901/64). In our theorizing of this memory, we found both suppression and repression, though our definition of repression is not the same as Freud's, being more focused on the social nature of the mechanism, that is, repression may occur because there is no meaning available to make sense of the event.

We began our theorizing with a discussion of why it might be important to consider such a memory in the context of memory-work. On the one hand, the original shameful episode appears to be unproblematic in this context. It represents something that was pushed aside, suppressed, not reflected upon. It was suppressed because it did not form part of the actor's theory of herself. She regarded herself as loved, protected, innocent. This experience was tawdry, bizarre, sordid. On the other hand the experience does not really threaten her theory of self. She had no reason to feel ashamed, she was an object, not an agent. What is important to notions of self are those events which would undermine one's moral evaluation of oneself. This experience is unintelligible, it did not 'fit' or make sense; it remains unintelligible that her mother would take her somewhere to be abused, and indeed she did not, yet she did.

In terms of constructing emotion, this experience is related to many negative emotions – shame, revulsion, embarrassment. For the moment, we leave aside the sexual content. We considered whether the childhood memory referred to here was different from any of the other memories we had been examining. A major difference was that it had not been reflected upon.

We theorized about why this experience had not been reflected upon, given its contradictory nature, its problematic nature. Why were some experiences that were hard to understand reflected upon and remembered when this very problematic one was suppressed. We questioned whether it was the strong negative emotions attached to the experience that led to the suppression, but noted that many of our other memories and those of others from whom we collected memories contained strong negative emotions, including shame and guilt and revulsion.

Another member of our group remembered something that had happened in her own childhood that was triggered by this memory. It concerned a man who 'used to play with children'.

> I can remember that one of the games we used to play was to get on his shoulders and he liked us being on his shoulders and I was aware of why I liked to be on his shoulders and why he liked me being on his shoulders and it was very sexual . . . he never did anything and I always felt my parents were very edgy about him . . . slight edge of tawdriness – uncleanness, and a slight attraction, and it was dangerous, and pleasurable, that warmth – like riding a horse . . .'

During discussion one of us recalled:

someone who stopped my sister and me one day and asked us to pull down our pants. Our response to that was to run. I now wonder if we had in fact said yes, and he kept saying he'd like to show us his dick, whether my memory would be similar to yours, that is whether I would have pushed it away and not dealt with it for years, but because we said no and ran . . . it was dealt with because . . . I then told my parents and their first response was in a funny way to deny, and then my mother told my father and my father asked us to repeat it and then in fact they called the cops.

In this latter memory, the matter became one of social discourse, and therefore provided a means of dealing with the experience then and rendering it meaningful. This is in contrast with the 'repression' memory above, which remained devoid of social relativity and hence remained unintelligible.

Thus one way of understanding the 'repression' memory, particularly its evaluation as one of 'child sexual assault', is in terms of its lack of a social referent. The experience is not only problematic, it is unintelligible. The child could not construct a meaning, she had no tools with which to do so. Because there are no words for it, no discourse, no comparable events in her own or others' experience with which to compare it, there is no way to make it intelligible. It is perplexing, totally inexplicable, as well as very painful.

The elements of this experience which were intelligible – the fact that it was a pseudo-medical treatment, something she felt ashamed about, did not want to think about, embarrassing etc., were suppressed. The sexual content of the memory was also suppressed, not repressed. A psychoanalytic characterization would insist that there was some sexual pleasure involved and that that was what was repressed. It seems particularly relevant in this context to note the attraction between the student and the lecturer, and to emphasize the connection between this sexual attraction and the repressed sexual excitement and/or pleasure associated with the original episode. Any such association was strenuously denied by the writer of the memory. We acknowledge that psychoanalytic theory would regard this denial as strong evidence of what was being denied.

But there is another way of theorizing the repression. Suppose the writer of the memory had been asked to write a memory about child sexual assault. Indeed, she reported in the discussion that about six months previously she had finished supervising a student who wrote a thesis on what behaviours were judged to constitute child sexual assault. As part of her data collection, the student had asked respondents whether they had ever experienced child sexual assault, defined as any experience prior to the age of 14 years involving a person at least five years older. She reported to her supervisor that a large number of female respondents had phoned her days or weeks after the interview to tell her that they had remembered something which they had not reported at the time of the interview. The supervisor had discussed these findings with the student, and they had worked on trying to understand why such episodes were not remembered at first, assuming that some form of repression must be operating. At that time, the supervisor told the student that she (supervisor) had never experienced anything remotely of that kind.

We can be fairly sure, then, that this person would not have produced the above memory or any other memory in response to the request to provide a memory of child sexual assault. If the childhood memory had been produced by some means, a psycho-analytic interpretation would be that she had repressed it. But the memory was not repressed in the sense that it was difficult to retrieve. It was just difficult if not impossible to retrieve by classifying it under the heading of 'child sexual assault'. It became intelligible in those terms only when retrieved using quite a different trigger (in this case 'repression') and only after many years, and after writing it down. We surmise that this interpretation of the event became possible only in a social context where child sexual assault has been defined, talked about, written about.

Conclusion

From this analysis, we consider repression in the following terms. An event occurs. It is problematic. It has some immediate strong affect (most likely negative). The actor tries to construct a meaning, but is unable to do so because the social building blocks for doing so are not available. It cannot be constructed in a meaningful way and in addition it does not fit with the person's definition of self. It never does become part of the construction of self because it has not been worked on (reflected on) and neither were there available tools for doing so. It is not erased, it stays there (possibly in the unconscious) until such time as something else triggers it. It is possibly triggered by a future episode that reawakens the affect (emotional response) or the unintelligibility.

There is both suppression and repression here. Although the classic psychoanalytic elements are present, and it is possible to analyse the experience in terms of individual idiosyncratic elements (in other words, biography), it is also possible to carry out the analysis from a more social viewpoint. We contend that the analysis is incomplete without the social viewpoint. It is in part the moral judgement that the experience was sordid, bizarre and tawdry that made it both painful and subject to suppression. In addition, the experience (even without any sexual content) is relatively uncommon, not brought into notice very frequently in the normal course of events – thus confirming its shameful nature. The extreme repugnance revealed in the written childhood memory was probably sufficient to deny it reflection. It did not represent a contradiction that needed to be resolved, but rather something 'best forgotten', it did not fit.

In this example, repression is the denial of the idea of sexuality, the failure to file this memory away under the heading of sexual experience. The search for intelligibility took place in the social interactions, but there was no sense of the 'common' surrounding the *sexual* elements of the episode. This event was not understood as a sexual episode, was not reflected upon in other sexual contexts, did not enter into the construction of the sexual self, at least at a conscious level. This is the sense in which the memory was repressed. We can explain repression in classical psychoanalytic terms, but our analysis is considerably enhanced by the consideration of the lack of a social representation of child sexual assault (or of any adult–child sexual activity) at the time the event occurred.

This childhood memory may well have formed part of the construction of emotions of embarrassment, shame, guilt, revulsion. It may have been produced if certain triggers had been used. In that context, it would not have been very different from the other memories we have worked with. But it is unlikely that it would have been produced without the experience of retrieving it at the time of the statistics lecture. Much of the reflection that makes the memory retrievable now was done at that time and not during childhood. It is thus different from some of the other memories we have retrieved, but not different from all of them. What is different about this memory is that it was at one stage suppressed and/or repressed. We still do not know anything about other memories we may have that fall into such categories.

What we have found is that suppression and repression can occur for elements of the same event. We have reinterpreted repression to take into account its social nature. Events which are unintelligible will be repressed. Unintelligible events are those which cannot be related to other experience, that is, an event which appears to be unrelated to anything else that has happened to the particular individual or to anyone else, either in life or in literature, will be unintelligible. There is a failure of intersubjectivity. Adult–child sexual experiences, adult–adult sexual experiences (one case is the 'primal scene'), any experiences which adults try to keep secret from children would be unintelligible to a child who witnessed or experienced them. In our culture, sexual activities are the ones that come most readily to mind.

This discussion of forgetting, both motivated and incidental, has some implications for memory-work, and more importantly for the application of memory-work to the study of the social construction of emotion. On the whole, however, we do not regard the fact that there are some experiences which will not be produced (for whatever reason) as seriously calling into question the basis for our work.

In the context of studying emotion, we must cope with the commonsense idea that experiences associated with strong negative emotions will be irretrievably forgotten. We have not found this to be the case. Many of our own memories and those of students and others who have given us memories included experiences involving shame, guilt, revulsion. The material examined in this chapter indicates that it is possible to retrieve, reflect upon and reinterpret material long forgotten at any stage of our lives. It is the time at which the reflection is done that is important, as well as the time at which the experience happened. The relationship between the two (or perhaps more) versions of the self that are represented by these times is revealed in the way the material is constructed.

The example used in this chapter shows similarities and differences between the individual and social level of analysis. We emphasize the social level, but do not reject the importance of the individual level for purposes other than our own. In this chapter, because we have been concerned with psychoanalytic theory in particular, we have used the comparison of individual with social explanation. However, we agree with Henriques et al. (1984) that the dualism between individual and social must be deconstructed. Our view is that this may best be done by building theory in the context of true intersubjectivity (that is, an intersubjectivity which is not limited to interpersonal processes). This is what our work as exemplified more directly in the other chapters is attempting to provide.

10
Anger

In this chapter we explore what anger has meant to us as girls and as women. We argue that women differ from men in the way they experience anger, and that this is because women's and men's anger provoke different responses in others. Our data led us to explore the relationship between anger and fear, hurt, crying and injustice. We find that power underlies all of these relationships, and that our examination of anger involves an exploration of our experience of male dominance, of our subordination and resistance.

Anger has been the focus of many studies of emotion. It is seen as in need of explanation by theorists examining emotion from very different perspectives, including philosophical, physiological, psychological, psychoanalytic, social constructionist and feminist perspectives. Despite much research within and outside of psychology (reviewed by Averill, 1982 and Tavris, 1982), anger and its expression remain problematic. The connection between anger and aggression and/or violence, the nature of the anger which underlies important political movements such as protest movements of all kinds, and the connection between anger and injustice point to the importance of understanding how anger enters into social, political and moral spheres.

Anger is regarded as negative, a response to frustration, described by Averill (1980) as conflictive. According to Averill, the conflict is between two different moral judgements, the one being the right or desire to protect oneself or one's property, the other the social sanctions against harming another. As we shall show, our findings about anger question Averill's analysis, which we believe is more congruent with a male view of the world.

In terms of theory, too, anger is an important emotion because of its intimate relationship with morality or moral judgement. As discussed in chapter 7, the moral judgements involved in emotion are central to our analysis. Averill (1980) noted that if one knows what makes someone angry, one can tell a lot about that person. We would claim (with Averill, 1982) that anger always involves moral judgement, a feeling of the rightness or justice of our cause. It is experienced when someone threatens or challenges a right or breaks a social rule; for example, when someone takes your lunch from the communal refrigerator or jumps a queue.

Anger is sometimes socially acceptable and sometimes not, but it is not as clearcut as that. Whether anger is sanctioned or condemned will depend on a number of things — who is angry, how the anger is expressed, what the consequences of the anger are. Judgement about anger and its expression will also depend on who is making the judgement — one person may see the anger and its expression as justified where another might not. In some circumstances, anger is called for — the person who does not become angry in the face of gross injustice is seen as morally flawed.

Anger as a Focus

When we began our work on emotion, we did not focus specifically on anger. Indeed, our early theorizing suggested that psychological theories of emotion had been limited by being based on the emotions of fear and anger, and that some of the other emotions were more in need of theoretical investigation. However, as we analysed our memories arising out of different episodes or triggers, we found that we were very frequently led into a discussion of anger. Anger was a problem for us as children, as women, as a memory-work group, and as human beings.

Our first topic ('saying sorry') produced memories where anger was present, the anger of another person directed towards the writer of the memory. As we reported earlier, we followed this topic of 'saying sorry' by looking at a memory of a transgression – an occasion when we deliberately broke our own rules. Again, we found anger coming through from these memories. In the transgression memories, as described in chapter 4, the writer of the memory was sometimes experiencing her own anger, sometimes the anger of another directed towards her, and sometimes both of these.

As we theorized these and other memories, we became aware of the contradictions surrounding anger for us as children, and in many cases as adults. We also found anger in memories written about crying, play, holidays, praise. We decided to bend the rules and write a memory specifically about anger. In our early theorizing, we looked at these episodes one at a time.

As our work progressed, we found that we were led to theorize anger on many occasions. This chapter is the result of re-examining the memories where anger arose (very often unexpectedly) and the theorizing that emerged from this re-evaluation. We discuss our analysis in terms of the themes that we found during this process, and relate our analysis to some theories about anger that we have found relevant.

Our analysis of anger aimed to explore the processes whereby anger and its expression come to be a problem for women. Our memories about anger reveal some common understandings about anger – both our own anger and that of others. This analysis took a large number of memories in which anger was relevant and examined them in relation to a number of themes which emerged. We found the same emotion, anger, in episodes which are superficially very different but which elicit anger in intelligible ways.

Analysing Anger

The following memory from Margaret illustrates many of the themes of anger.

Margaret, age 13:

During high school she went on a two week exchange visit to another family. They were very thoughtful hosts. The daughter of that family returned to Margaret's family. Margaret was anxious to provide her with the same hospitality that she had received. Early in the visit, they were tired and went to bed early. Margaret's father and brother were playing table tennis downstairs – loud laughter and banging. Margaret was angry that they should be so inconsiderate to their guest. She went half way downstairs and asked them to be quiet. Her father had a look of thunder – came up and hit her – said something to the effect of who did she think she was – little twerp. He then returned to the game with her brother. Margaret experienced strong feelings – chaotic rage, frustration, hurt, defeat, despair, shame. She retreated to a corner and sobbed. She judged her father as having failed her yet she too had failed, not a person worthy of respect. She felt ashamed that this was witnessed by her guest though she [guest] never referred to the incident.

From this one memory, we can examine many of the important considerations used in our analysis. In the first place, this memory reveals a number of moral judgements or common social rules. Margaret is very conscious of a social rule which says that hospitality must be reciprocated – the whole setting, an 'exchange visit', carries with it a whole set of expectations. Margaret understands these expectations, believing initially that they would be shared by her father (and possibly her brother). They are also shared by those who read the memory. Nothing more needs to be said beyond 'exchange visit' in order for a reader to understand the social rules. As readers, we share Margaret's judgement of her father: she is right, he is wrong. Her anger is justified; his, while intelligible, is not.

This memory illustrates almost every theme that we found in our memories and subsequently used in our analysis of anger. We begin by examining the relationship between anger and two important emotions, fear and hurt (or feeling hurt). We continue by looking at the process of the suppression of anger, the relationship between anger and injustice. Each theme points to the underlying import-ance of power and of our own subordinate status. At the end of the chapter, we draw these common threads together.

Anger and Fear

Anger and fear are often related to one another, particularly in psychological and biological theory, the 'fight or flight' syndrome. This syndrome is described in terms of situations likely to provoke either aggression or flight – aggression being equated with a behavioural manifestation of anger and flight with fear. The physiological response associated with anger was originally believed to be different from that associated with fear, and this was what was supposed to differentiate anger from fear. However, evidence for such differentiation has never been convincing (Frijda, 1986).

Many of the memories in which we as actors expressed anger resulted in making another person angry. The memories show that the actor in the memory only rarely behaves in an aggressive manner towards another person when experiencing anger. On the other hand, a person who becomes angry towards the actor frequently punishes the actor (often physically). Thus anger on the part of another is something to be feared.

Margaret's memory illustrates the relationship between fear and anger. It also reveals some of the complexity involved in experien-cing anger (and other emotions). Although fear is not explicitly mentioned, Margaret responds with a variety of emotions to the experience of being physically punished for her anger. She also internalizes her father's judgement and possibly even identifies with his standards of behaviour, since her shame seems more on his behalf (or on behalf of her whole family) than on her own. Although not ashamed of her anger, Margaret is likely to hesitate before expressing anger again, especially towards her father or others more physically powerful than herself, at least according to common understandings of the relationship between fear and physical punishment. As well as illustrating how physical punish-ment (and by implication fear of physical punishment) is used to deter expression of anger, this memory illustrates fear of unfavour-able social consequences brought about by expressing anger, even though the expression of anger is described merely as 'asking them to be quiet'.

The connection between another person's anger and being physically hurt is also found in memories when the actor herself was not angry. One of the earliest memories from the 'saying sorry' chapter (chapter 4) illustrates the fear engendered by another's anger when the actor was not herself angry. The 4-year-old child who tickled her father while he slept 'was sobbing with fright and surprise'. In this memory, as well as Margaret's, we feel angry on her behalf at her father's over-reaction. She, however, did not mention anger as part of her experience. The fear was overwhelming; surprise, hurt, shock were what she felt.

Being the target of anger from others may involve actual physical fear. Since becoming angry with someone else often makes them angry, this fear provides a powerful sanction against anger on the part of women (especially towards the physically more powerful). One of the patterns we found in the memories was that adult women (mothers, teachers) almost always expressed their anger verbally, sometimes even by 'speaking gently but firmly' in accordance with the stereotype of the 'good' woman, whereas men (usually fathers) responded with physical violence. There is clearly a different social representation (Moscovici, 1984) of anger depending on whether it is a man's or a woman's anger. Anger in women is expected to be restrained; if it is not then it is often represented as being 'emotional' or 'hysterical' rather than being aggressive or violent. Men's anger is most frequently accompanied by violence, either overt or implied, and is expected to be so. These different representations of anger clearly point to an underlying structure of power and subordination.

Anger and Hurt

A recurring theme in our theorizing of anger was the connection between anger and depression, anger and crying. Some of us reported that one of the reasons why as adults we had difficulty in expressing anger was that whenever we became really angry we accompanied our verbal expression of that anger by 'bursting into tears'. This often resulted in our anger being misinterpreted as hurt, depression or personal incapacity rather than as the uncontrollable rage or righteous moral affront that we experienced.

When we wrote memories in response to 'crying' some of them were indeed angry memories, though not all of them were. Some were memories of grief occasioned by separation or loss. Some crying expressed frustration, with or without anger. In many memories, anger is described as being accompanied by crying. In Margaret's memory above, when her anger ('rage') at her father after he punishes her cannot be directed towards him, she 'retreated to a corner and sobbed'.

There have been many theories about the relationship between anger and depression. During our discussions, we noted Freud's definition of depression as 'anger denied' (Freud, 1917/64). This has been accepted by later theorists, therapists, writers of self-help manuals, including feminists, as Tavris (1982) has noted. However, this was not our experience. Our analysis at first suggested that anger and depression frequently co-existed, and that anger could be consequent on hurt or grief, abandonment or loss, but just as much could hurt, grief or misery be a consequence of anger or its expression.

> Clare is four years old. She is about to walk home with her mother and father after visiting an aunt. The aunt suggests that she wear a cardigan belonging to Clare's [male] cousin as it has become chilly. 'Clare did not like it [the cardigan] because it prickled her skin. I don't want to wear it', she said. She argues with her parents. Finally her mother smacks her and forces her to wear the cardigan. 'Clare cried partly in anger and partly because she was not believed. She really felt that if her mother and father had realized how uncomfortable she was they would not force her to wear this horrible garment. Her feeling was of being MISUNDER-STOOD' [her capitals].

In this memory, Clare's crying and misery are not brought about because she is punished, but because she is misunderstood. She is trying to use her tears to communicate the strength of her feelings about the garment.

In attempting to understand the complex relationship between anger and crying, one of us wrote about the relationship as follows: 'When my brother used my doll for target practice, I remember whingeing rather than anger.' It is possible that there is contradiction in such a memory, as in all our memories, namely that the memory of the brother using the doll for target practice was reflected upon *because* she didn't become angry – but cried instead. But it is also possible that the consequences of expressing anger are too frightening to contemplate. So she retreats into passivity.

There is thus a complex relationship between anger, fear and crying. Theories of social conditioning suggest that boys are not punished for aggression (presumably arising out of anger), whereas girls are. Therefore, women are socialized not to be aggressive, and hence perhaps not to be angry. But such theories suppose that anger and aggression are inseparable. These theories have been used to explain why in situations of stress men become violent and women become depressed – depression being seen as anger turned inward.

If we are afraid that our anger will evoke a violent response, we may suppress it, expressing our frustration in the form of tears or crying. However, one of the problems that we found from our memory-work was that we sometimes cry when we become angry, not as a substitute for anger. This connection between crying and anger does not seem to follow the ordinary rules of learning; if it did then crying out of anger should represent a successful way of displaying or experiencing anger. In our memories, however, this was certainly not the case.

If we define episodes of anger as successful when they were not invalidated by others, were not punished, and were viewed positively, we find that successful episodes did not involve crying, although crying may be rewarded in the long run. Those which did involve crying were not successful, they resulted in feelings of guilt and shame. The crying was interpreted by the actor as an inevitable accompaniment of expressing anger and rage; one of the uncontrollable and undesirable components of anger. Crying is not misplaced anger, nor is the crying discussed here indicative of anger which has been turned inward. It is a message used to communicate to others the strength and seriousness of the anger; it contains a strong element of the feeling of being a victim, and in particular is interpreted by the actor as a plea for understanding in the face of being disbelieved or misunderstood.

The crying we are discussing is directed at the object of our anger. It is an expression of anger, not a substitute for it. It is nevertheless frequently interpreted by the object of our anger (and by others) as an appeal for help. This misinterpretation of crying in anger has also been noted by Campbell and Muncer (1987).

A member of our group gave this biographical anecdote. At a meeting of a university committee, a male colleague moved a motion designed to avoid debate on an issue that she viewed as very important. The chair of the committee allowed the debate to be avoided. After the meeting, the group member concerned tackled the chair of the committee, saying 'I am very angry with you. How could you allow that motion that resulted in stifling the debate? It was not appropriate to do that – the committee must discuss the matter.' Whereupon she began to cry, unable to control the expression of her emotion. 'There there,' said the chair, 'you don't need to feel so hurt about it, I didn't mean to cause you to grieve [he was a psychologist]. I will allow the matter to be reopened at the next meeting.'

Note that the crying was misinterpreted as hurt, grief, loss. Note also that crying was 'successful' – possibly others may interpret it as manipulative – strong men cannot bear to see a woman cry. The actor felt not hurt, grief or loss, but fury and rage. These feelings were only intensified by the 'sympathetic' response.

This experience is not an unusual one. Many women have reported that their anger, especially when accompanied by tears, has been misinterpreted, mislabelled. Even when expressed clearly, in no uncertain terms, and without the accompaniment of tears, anger is interpreted as 'a problem'. Misinterpretation of anger sets up a vicious cycle which some of us (as adults) have experienced sufficiently often to be deterred from expressing our anger.

We have already noted that the crying we found in expressing anger is different from crying as an appeal for help. We also found that such crying is quite different from weeping and feelings of melancholia that accompany true or clinical depression. This depression is characterized in particular by an inability to feel and an inability to act. This disabling character of depression is not the same as the frustration, impotence and powerlessness that we felt as part of much of our anger. In depression, inability stems from within; knowing what activity we could and should engage in, we are yet unable to act. In situations where frustration, impotence and powerlessness lead to anger, we cannot act because action is denied us – the forces which frustrate us are too powerful.

When we cry when angry, when we 'throw a tantrum', we are demonstrating our feelings of being a victim. This aspect of our analysis supports Warner's (1986) analysis of anger. The out-of-control aspect of anger is engendered at least in part by a feeling of victimization and the failure of the other person in an angry interchange to acknowledge the victim's status as a victim.

In using the terms 'victim', 'victimizer', 'victimization' we do not wish to characterize our discussion with the negative and helpless image which the term victim often carries. We use it in the context of a person who is or perceives themselves to be aggrieved, wronged in some way, usually justly so. It is perhaps unfortunate that victim is the only term in our language which readily lends itself to fitting all of the roles and actions needed for the discussion, having both an active (victimizer) and passive (victim) form, and associated words to indicate the action (victimize, victimization).

The relationship between feelings of victimization and anger is a very important one. Warner (1986) pointed to this relationship. Her discussion of anger as 'self-deception' is a careful analysis of one kind of anger, the perseverative self-fuelling anger that occurs in verbal conflict, particularly between partners within an ongoing relationship such as marriage. The example she uses is one where there is no differential in power between the two protagonists.

Her analysis is a very sophisticated one. Although she does not discuss anger in terms of intersubjectivity, her analysis can be interpreted in the following way. Warner identifies the paradoxical nature of perseverative anger, and the self deception she speaks of refers to the strong feelings that the other person is 'causing' the anger whereas it is really self-generated.

The paradox she speaks of is that anger is generated because there is both too much and not enough of the feeling that one of the protagonists knows what the other is feeling and thinking. In our terms, this represents the result of intersubjectivity, but involves at the same time a failure of intersubjectivity. The nature of this paradox may be clearer if we examine some of our own memories, and in particular memories where a power differential exists, as in almost all of our memories of childhood. In the victim/victimizer relationship there is a strong connection between anger and power.

We take once again Margaret's memory with which we began our analysis in this chapter. Margaret became angry with her father and brother, and believed that they would cease the behaviour that was making her angry if she asked them to be more considerate. If they had shared her view of the situation – that is, she had a right to be angry, they were being inconsiderate – they would presumably have stopped their game of table tennis and that would have been the end of the episode, and in all likelihood Margaret would have forgotten all about it.

However, Margaret's father immediately became one who was wronged ('a victim') and became angry, directing his anger towards her. When he physically punished her, he turned her into a victim once more, and his own anger dissipated (we assume). She was left in the victim position, and her anger, feelings of righteous indignation, rage etc. have remained with her in the form of the memory. The power differential between Margaret and her father, both in terms of physical and social power, determined the outcome. We assume that if she had been more powerful than he, she would have retaliated, re-positioning him as victim, and feeling satisfied once he acknowledged her right to be angry. If the two protagonists had been of equal power, the argument may have gone on for a long time because there is no predetermination of who will 'win'.

Anger cannot be sustained if the angry person feels sorry for or sympathy with the person making them angry. Warner uses an example of a person who becomes angry because a friend is late for an appointment. The anger disappears when the angry person learns that the friend has been involved in a car accident or some other event that prevented them from keeping the appointment. Thus when two people are angry with each other, the anger goes on and on not only because A does not feel any sympathy with B's position but also because A knows that B feels no sympathy with A's position. Being able to 'see the other person's point of view', which should facilitate communication, in this case only serves to maintain the breakdown of the communication – hence the paradox.

Anger goes away, at least as far as the more powerful is concerned, as soon as the 'victimizer' unambiguously becomes the victim and/or the victim becomes the victimizer. Consider the father and the 4-year-old child (the story of Ann, given at beginning of chapter 4). We do not know how he felt as a result of his action, but we would expect him to have ceased to be angry and to have become at least partly sympathetic with the little girl. She says she is sorry, thus convincing him of the righteousness of his position, that is, acknowledging his victim status, validating his anger, and at the same time acknowledging her own status as a victim and hence his as victimizer. If she had become defiant and openly angry, she would have invalidated his anger, and it would have been very likely to continue at least until she retreated.

Thus crying out of anger serves two purposes, one which is not obvious to the person who cries, and one which is not obvious to the person who witnesses it. The person who cries believes that it is ineffectual, misinterpreted, a component of her anger engendered by the strength of the angry (victim) feeling and a signal of the righteousness of her anger along with the strength of the hurt. The person who witnesses it sees it as a sign of sorrow, abjectness, acknowledgement of the rightness of his anger and a signal that his anger is no longer appropriate.

The person who is crying sees this as validation of her own anger; the person who witnesses it sees it as validation of his (if he is angry) or as a cry for help. In our memories, our crying was seen as one of the out-of-control aspects of expressing anger. Further examples of the out-of-control aspect of anger are seen below in instances where the anger is discouraged or suppressed not through fear or misinterpretation but through invalidation.

Anger and Suppression

The discussion of anger and fear and of anger and hurt above gives some idea of ways in which anger and its expression are problematic. The memories and the theorizing of them suggest that women construct anger as a negative emotion. The analysis above illustrates that we learn not to express anger partly through physical punishment, actual or feared; partly through unsuccessful experiences of expressing anger. The most powerful mechanism for discouraging the expression of anger, however, comes from having it invalidated. This is illustrated by memories where we were told either directly or indirectly that anger was inappropriate in situations which we both then and now appraised as being those where anger was totally appropriate. The memory of Margaret above, as well as illustrating the operation of physical punishment, very strongly involves invalidation. The following memory from Liz (at age 12 years) is one in which invalidation without physical punishment is seen.

> on this night she went to the lavatory which was a long way from the house. On the way back, she was walking up the outside stairs to get in to the house. Her cousin Joan grabbed her by the ankles from underneath the stairs and frightened her out of her wits. Liz was filled with rage and hatred of her cousin. When she got into the house, everybody laughed at her and urged her to be a 'good sport'. They said she should grin and bear it. This made Liz even angrier, she threw an enormous tantrum which merely made everybody even more amused. She retreated to bed, unable to escape her tormentor even there, as they slept on the same verandah.

From this memory, it is clear why we interpreted Liz's anger as being invalidated. She was not allowed to express it, received no sympathy or understanding of why she was so angry, and so became even angrier (compare with Clare's MISUNDERSTOOD above). Many of the memories have this same quality of having anger invalidated, particularly if the anger was directed against an adult. In these cases, we used the cliché 'throwing a tantrum'. In trying to get her message across regarding the strength of her anger, and possibly that her anger was justified, the actor displays more extreme forms of behaviour. In most cases the tantrum itself is responded to by further invalidation.

The following memory is one in which the anger and the tantrum were not invalidated.

> Ann [7 years old] and her sister fought a great deal. One day her sister locked Ann out . . . laughed at her from the other side of the glass door . . . Ann kicked a pane of glass in . . . She had lost her temper. It was not premeditated and Ann was somewhat taken aback by what had happened. So was her sister – to Ann's satisfaction.

This is a memory (like Liz's above) involving being teased, but here there is no invalidation. Ann's parents were angry with both Ann and her sister. Ann's parents acknowledged her right to be angry, and Ann felt 'satisfaction'.

These memories illustrate some of the 'loss of control' that is one of the cultural stereotypes about the expression of anger, and is often used as a justification for violence and aggression (especially in men) (Campbell and Muncer, 1987). It is almost as if anger out of control which involves an antisocial act such as hitting someone is viewed by society with some sympathy and understanding, whereas anger expressed verbally or behaviourally in terms of frustration (throwing a tantrum) is cause for amusement or scorn. But it is not as simple as this. Whether physical violence arising out of anger is viewed positively or negatively may be related to the sex of the person experiencing it.

> Marie is arguing in the garden with a child three years younger, but about the same size. This child is in the care of Marie's mother: Marie hit her hard and she started to cry. Marie's mother came outside and comforted the other child and was very angry with Marie. Marie felt very guilty, mean and worthless. She was hot and flushed, heart pounding, mouth dry, hands and voice trembling.

Both the actor herself and society as embodied in the mother judged the violence negatively.

Most of our memories of anger involve having it suppressed in one way or another. Our experience suggests that teasing is used in our society to teach people to 'be a good sport', 'learn to take a joke', indeed as a way of teaching the control of anger. Deliberately making someone angry and then ridiculing them for expressing the anger is a definition of teasing. Teasing is almost invariably initiated by the more powerful and is directed at the subordinate. Most teasing is done by older children towards younger ones, but we observed in our discussions that teasing enters into child-rearing to a greater or lesser extent. Some mothers use it – sometimes to make children cry. Fathers, male teachers, and others do it to boys (Russell et al., 1986). Our analysis suggests that whatever the basis for the practice of teasing it is not successful in helping to keep anger under control. The suppression of anger is not the same as its control.

So far most of the memories of anger that we have examined have been evaluated both then and now as negative. There were a few memories where anger was seen as positive and socially useful, particularly when used to confront injustice.

Anger and Injustice

Anger in the face of injustice is seen by society to be justifiable, indeed to be a cultural imperative (Averill, 1980, 1982). What is problematic is the definition of what constitutes injustice. The discussion of sex differences below returns to this point.

There are elements of injustice in many of our memories involving anger. For example, when Margaret's father hit her for asking him and her brother to be quiet, Margaret's subsequent rage was in part a reaction to what she regarded as unjust treatment. Liz's tantrum after being teased speaks of a feeling of unfair treatment. However, memories in which adults break the rules they have set or impose silly rules are those most directly involving anger regarding injustice. In these memories, the actor feels somehow vindicated, even when the outcome was not directly successful.

Shirley, age 10, is in hospital. She becomes very angry when a nurse takes her magazine and orders her to put out the light before the agreed-upon time. Then Shirley sees the nurse reading the magazine:

> she could see the clock, which still said something between twenty minutes and fifteen minutes to nine. She was so angry, she shouted . . . 'You only wanted my magazine. You have no right to read my magazine. Give it back to me. You give me back my magazine . . . ' The nurse eventually wheels her into a dark treatment room and gives her a sleeping draught. But she has a pear under her pillow, and eats it after taking the medicine. She believes that this will counteract the effect of the medicine and feels 'a strange sense that she has won'.

Carol, age 4, is in hospital having her tonsils out:

> One lunch time the nurse brought some soup with vegetables etc. floating in it. Carol wanted it strained, as she had it at home. The nurse told her not to be so silly and to eat it. Carol didn't. She waited until the vegetables sank to the bottom and drank the liquid. She did not eat the vegetables. She felt angry. She didn't see why she had to eat the vegetables. She didn't like anything about the hospital and she wanted to leave . . . But she felt vaguely satisfied – smug – when she solved the problem of the soup.

Anger in the face of injustice is seen to be justified, at least by the actor herself. It is the adults in these episodes who are behaving badly, imposing silly rules or breaking rules they have set. Even though we are victims, we achieve some sort of satisfaction out of deliberately testing out the rules. We thus show the world that the rules are unjustly applied or inappropriate, and our anger is therefore justified.

Carol's anger demonstrates that it is not necessary to display strong emotion in order to be angry. Her lack of passion in this memory is related to the fact that she knew what to do as well as her sense that she was right.

Moral judgement is a strong component of anger. The angry person has 'rights' which justify the anger. Margaret became angry because she believed that she had a right to expect her family to be considerate to a guest. Her father became angry because his right to behave as he wished in his own house was challenged, and also his rights as a father: 'Who do you think you are?'. In this conflict about whose moral judgement is valid, it is the more powerful who prevails. There is no negotiation about whose view is more correct or appropriate, the episode is resolved according to the 'might is right' principle.

The way anger is experienced, therefore, is mediated by power. In the experiences discussed so far, the anger is very much of an interpersonal kind, one person angry with another person. The issue of victimization is important, but it is victimization of an interpersonal kind, fluid and changing, which is not the same as the sense of victimization engendered by structural powerlessness or inequality which we address later. At least potentially, all the protagonists in the memories discussed so far may take on the role of both victim or victimizer during the course of the episode.

Anger and Power, the Effect of Gender

Our work is concerned with how women experience anger. Despite studies which find little evidence for gender differences in self-reported anger (Averill, 1982; Tavris, 1982) we found evidence supporting the view that our experiences were different from those of men.

Our analysis indicates several key issues relating to the gendered nature of anger and its expression. Women are condemned if they show anger, if they throw a tantrum and behave in an uncontrolled ineffective way, they are then labelled neurotic. They are also condemned for suppressing or sitting on their anger, turning it inwards, and are then labelled depressed. Our analysis above also suggests that men's anger is often accompanied by violence, whereas women's is not. The absence of violence on the part of the actor in almost all of our memories involving anger provides support for the suggestion that the equation of anger with violence is not present for women. (We use 'violence' to refer to physical aggression.)

These considerations led us to recognize at least two aspects of anger associated with sex differences. These are (i) the possibility that differences exist in the social representation of anger depending on the sex of the angry person; and (ii) a consideration of power in relation to anger, as already discussed briefly above. It is possible that the power considerations are what underlie differences in social representation if such exist, and thus the two aspects of sex differences in anger are related.

We shall first consider the possibility that there are two different social representations of anger. Tavris pointed out that the equating of anger with aggression is fallacious: 'You may feel angry and express it in hundreds of ways, many of which will be neutral or even beneficial (cleaning the house in an energetic fury, playing the piano *forte*, organizing a political protest movement) instead of violent. Conversely, you can act aggressively without feeling angry at all, as a professional assassin or soldier does . . . The fact that anger and aggression *do* coexist in many situations does not mean that, like Laurel and Hardy, the presence of one automatically includes the other' (1982, p. 35). (Note that Tavris is unsure of the distinction between aggression and violence.)

A recent article by Campbell and Muncer (1987) examined specifically the social representation of 'anger and aggression' in men and women. The method used had something in common with memory-work, namely discussions of episodes of anger by a group of men and by a group of women. Campbell and Muncer do not clearly distinguish between anger and aggression, and themselves display different social representations of what they are researching depending on whether they are discussing the women's or the men's accounts. They use headings of 'women and anger' and 'men's aggression' in reporting their results.

Tavris (1982), when specifically examining the issue of sex differences in anger, concluded that there are no differences between men and women in: how they experience anger; how they express anger; how well they can identify (their own) anger; the categories of things that make them angry. She says that the widespread beliefs about sex differences in anger arise because men and women do not agree about what behaviour constitutes an offence – that is, what constitutes unjust behaviour. Such disagreement encompasses behaviour in both the private and public spheres.

Our theoretical perspective is in agreement with that of Tavris in so far as she recognizes the cultural specificity of anger. Her acknowledgment that men and women live in different cultures, and that this is the basis for the widespread belief that men and women differ in the way anger is experienced and (especially) how it is expressed, is consistent with a social constructionist view. However, it is important to take into account the fact that men's and women's cultures do not sit side by side but that one exists, largely unseen, unheard and unspoken, within and between and subordinate to the other. This is why the equation between anger and aggression is so widely accepted – it is the dominant view, largely taken for granted by men and women alike. A woman's anger is more likely to be unintelligible to a man than vice versa, and this in turn moderates her experience of anger – since he will frequently misinterpret it.

When we examined our memories, particularly as we theorized the connection between anger, fear and crying, the issue of power was a very important one. Anger is the expression of our frustration and powerlessness. A person with power does not need to be angry. Is anger therefore empowering? There is a contradiction between what the women's movement has said (based on work by, for example, Chesler, 1972) and what we observed. The messages from the women's movement are that we should mobilize our anger, channel our anger, stop sitting on anger and start using it, do not repress anger. Anger is seen as an energizing force which would enable us to empower ourselves as women (Lange and Jakubowski, 1976). What we found in our memories, though there were some exceptions, was generally the repression (which we have called suppression to distinguish it from Freudian ideas of repression) that the women's movement recognizes. However, we also found that anger was not empowering, rather it was a passion that overcame us as a result of powerlessness. What emerged was a view that if you are powerful, you have no need to be angry. If you are not powerful, and you become angry, your anger is invalidated and you are diminished in the eyes of others.

How might anger be constructed differently for men and women? We have already suggested that the social representation of anger might differ between the sexes and that it is possible that this difference reflects differences in social power. We now examine more closely the relationship between power and anger. Although our memories are almost always about being angry with peers or those more powerful than ourselves, some theorists, notably Averill (1982), have stated that anger is much more often directed at social inferiors. This is possibly because he views the world through male eyes in common with other (mostly male) psychological theorists. A social representation of anger which equates anger and violence (or aggression) is much more consistent with anger directed towards inferiors or equals than anger directed towards superiors. Indeed, it is possible that there is a strong connection between violent anger and anger directed towards inferiors. Men have less reason to feel powerless, and thus the sort of anger derived from powerlessness and frustration may not be exhibited as frequently by men.

What distinguishes anger in men as compared with women? If you have power, anger can be regarded as a way of attempting to ensure it; an empowering thing. In this sense, it is accompanied by an underlying threat, either of physical violence or of using one's power against the person who is challenging it. The violent reaction of the father towards his 4-year-old child is an example of this in a primitive form. As mentioned above, our analysis suggests that the connection between anger and aggression that characterizes much anger by men is much more likely to be found in anger directed towards inferiors – either social or physical.

In this kind of anger, the sense of victimization is scarcely present. If the angry response is successful, or if the provoking incident is redefined, this anger is quickly dissipated. The moral judgement inherent in this kind of anger is not involved with a sense of injustice or unfairness in an abstract or structural sense, but in a more personal sense of having one's own rights, property, or authority challenged or limited in some way. The frustration involved is of a temporary nature, capable of being relieved by the angry response. This kind of anger is accepted in our society as being valid and morally appropriate. It is often, though not always, experienced without passion.

However, anger arising out of a sense of powerlessness takes on the character of an ongoing passion, involving frustration of a more long-lasting kind. Anger takes on an out-of-control, passionate, ineffective character. It is a response to strong judgements about unfairness, injustice, which remains unresolved. The anger of a person without power has a strong component of victimization. It is this kind of anger, directed at trying to overcome some basic injustice or unfairness – not necessarily of a personal nature – that is frequently accompanied by 'throwing a tantrum' or 'bursting into tears'. It is more often directed against those with more power, or possibly peers. When one is unable to act, or when it is clear that anger will be ineffective and unproductive, anger builds up and is not dissipated. Under these circumstances, if anger is expressed, it is likely to provoke in the more powerful those angry reactions to having their power challenged that have been described.

This may well be why women are characterized as both more emotional and less violent. Women are more angry, less able to act to escape from the negative affect that our oppressed situation engenders. The women's movement has awakened our sense of injustice by documenting our oppression. Our anger in the face of this injustice is likely to provoke reactions which at best are likely to include redefining our problem as being 'too emotional' or as denoting depression or hurt feelings rather than rage. At their worst, they are likely to lead to political backlash.

It has been suggested that our analysis of anger (Valsiner and Harré, personal communications), and our finding that women's anger is related to powerlessness, has been brought about by the fact that we examined childhood memories. Thus our experiences of anger are characteristic of children's anger, and should be interpreted in this light and not as characteristic of women's anger.

There are two related issues here: one is the limitation to childhood memories, the other has to do with experiences of power. We do not believe that the nature of our memories, the processes by which anger was experienced and constructed, is due to the fact that we examined childhood memories. There was no reason why we should not have reported anger directed towards peers or inferiors – after all, much of childhood is spent interacting with peers, siblings, etc. Some of our memories were about anger directed towards peers (for example, those of Ann and Marie above), but nevertheless even this anger was most often invalidated by adults. Few successful experiences of our own anger were found. It must also be borne in mind that the episodes we have analysed in this chapter were for the most part responses to triggers about things other than anger – such as 'saying sorry', or 'crying'. Thus the memories are not dependent on our understanding of what anger is, but rather anger emerges from memories of diverse episodes.

The second issue concerns the relationship between gender and power. The implication is that we experience anger differently depending on our particular power in the relationship, regardless of gender. In that case powerless men would construct anger in the same way as women do. This view ignores the consistent and structured pattern of dominance and subordination between men and women. It also ignores the other dimensions of our response as women, involving issues of responsibility and agency. As we reiterate in the next chapter, the relationship between gender and power is not a simple one.

In what way can our work be empowering? Anger that is recognized and acknowledged by others is not problematic. The anger that we feel good about is that which is engendered by our sense of injustice. We must continue to document injustice and to use our justifiable anger productively. We must encourage social representations of anger which separate it from aggression – by our child-rearing practices, by challenging and questioning those media representations which reinforce the connection. We must encourage non-aggressive forms of conflict resolution. We must contribute to theoretical formulations of anger whereby women's anger, particularly in the face of injustice, is recognized for what it is, regardless of how it is expressed. Women's experience must continue to be documented in literature, media and academia in ways that render it visible and legitimate.

11

The Gendering of Emotion

Pulling the Threads Together

Our memory-work enabled us to trace the way we constructed ourselves through particular experiences in the world. We have traced the course of our self construction through transgression and play, through danger and on holiday, through happiness, anger and fear. These we have explored in detail in chapters 4, 5 and 6 and again in chapters 8, 9 and 10. Weaving in and across these very different topics were recurring patterns of gender. There now remains the task of pulling the threads together and identifying the more obvious themes of gender.

Social Responsibility
The theme of responsibility emerged from our very first memories, and continued through virtually all topics to the last. We learned at a very young age, particularly through our transgressions, whether perceived as such by ourselves or not, that we were held responsible for the well-being of others. We became aware of this responsibility when we transgressed; apologies were sought in order to oil the social mechanism. We came to realize that our trivial actions caused discomfort to others. If others were angry, it was we who caused it and it was our task to restore the broken harmony of social relations.

In our play and our childhood holidays we were aware of the role played by adult women. It was they who organized and looked after everyone and did the work. Sometimes we were required to assist, as when Margaret had to put the baby to sleep before she was free to play. Our responsibility became most clear in our adult holiday memories. We were now in charge. We planned and organized and managed the holiday. We set challenges for ourselves and others; we became anxious when the unexpected occurred. Though the unexpected was in a sense courted, we were anxious that things turn out well. We sought pleasure for ourselves as well, but were anxious not to be seen nor to see ourselves as selfish. We rarely experienced the easy relaxed freedom from care that holidays are supposed to mean.

The sense of responsibility extended also to difficult and dangerous situations. Our memories indicated that if we got ourselves into danger, we believed it to be our own fault. It was up to us to get ourselves out of it. We seemed to accept this judgement. Note for example Kelly's hitch-hiking memory: even after reworking the memory there is still a sense of excusing the man (he was drunk) and of blaming herself for accepting the lift.

Our memories thus show a double lesson – on the one hand, be self-reliant but not selfish or self-indulgent, in addition, be responsible for the emotional well-being of others. As Eichenbaum and Orbach (1983) found from their experiences in counselling women, women can expect little care from others for their own well-being, except from female friends. Men grow up and grow old knowing that they will be cared for by their mothers, lovers, wives, daughters.

Pushing the Boundaries
Because autonomy is constituted in self-reliance, we wanted, as children, to be responsible for ourselves. In many of our memories this search for autonomy involved testing the boundaries. Both negative and positive memories included this sense of pushing against the boundaries of our own limitations as children. We often seemed to be testing the rules that constrained us, extending our mastery, trying to be the equal of adults, to be adult in an adult world. The ways we did this, and the responses of those around us, were not the same for boys and girls. The lessons learned were quite different.

As girls, in our striving to be responsible and competent, we tried to behave like adults, and to be taken seriously by them. Sometimes we succeeded, and were praised for being brave or patient or clever; for being a 'good girl'. Pleasure in competence was seen in some of our play memories and in many of our happiness memories where we developed new skills, a new independence. With competence came a greater freedom to be ourselves. This was a strong theme in both boys' and girls' memories, though the type of mastery differed. For the boys it entailed a control over the material world, for girls a control of self, of the body..

Sometimes, however, when we thought we were being adult our attempts at demonstrating our autonomy were met with reprimands, slaps, removal, angry voices, a public shaming. Sometimes we accepted the judgement and constructed our own sense of responsibility and guilt. Sometimes we resisted the judgement and struggled with an overwhelming but often unspoken sense of outrage. We collectively identified a strong underlying sense of agency; a reaching for autonomy. Our autonomy was especially threatened when we were reprimanded or punished for something which seemed to us to be right and proper. Our sense of agency was confirmed when our actions were successful; sometimes alone and not noticed by others, sometimes noticed and approved.

No doubt boys too go through some similar affirmation or disaffirmation of agency. The young men's memories were, however, very different. Their transgressions were, in the main, deliberate transgressions that were punished. But their transgressions were construed as tests of daring, always with an audience of peers. The transgression was experienced with a sense of excitement, fun, glee. The punishment was 'worth it'. Transgressing adult rules (often the rules of adult women) appeared to be necessary for the construction of a masculine identity, particularly when this was in solidarity with other boys. The same pattern appeared in an exaggerated form in some of the young men's danger memories. There was a moral imperative to court danger, to test bravery.

It seems that boys achieve autonomy by breaking adult rules. They expect punishment, but at the same time seem to believe that such rule-breaking is expected of them. They are not responsible for anyone but themselves. Self reliance is established in the context of a reliance on peers – a young version of the old boys' network, the original experience of mateship. Both boys and girls experience subordination of themselves as children, but boys experience subordination secure in the knowledge that it will be transformed collectively into male dominance.

Inside and Outside

We were intrigued to discover another recurring pattern in our tapestry of memories. Much of the descriptive detail of our early memories concerned the location of the events in question. Some memories were located inside, usually inside the home, while others were outdoors. The inside/outside dichotomy appeared consistently and seemed to carry a load of symbolic meaning.

Some of our happiest early memories were inside. The memories are replete with sensory detail – 'talcum and light flowery perfume smell' comes to mind as a good example. Inside was warm and safe and secure, a place where we could feel loved and content. Outside could also be good. It was the place where we could feel free and where we experienced the exhilaration of challenge. It was outside that we developed a sense of mastery of new skills, as in learning to surf. Here we moved away from the security of home and adults, moved to embrace an uncertain world of danger and challenge.

Happiness, particularly that kind which we have identified as exhilaration and excitement, is associated with autonomy. It is the happiness of mastery and success; of pride in skilling or competence; of testing the boundaries and extending the self. Those achievements are dependent upon being loved and feeling secure, secure enough to move beyond the familiar, to the outside. Also, autonomy and self reliance require recognition; the acknowledgement that you have passed a test, succeeded, and matured. As noted in chapter 5, love and security enable the development of self as autonomous and separate which, in turn, is what makes one worthy of love.

The young men's memories, more than ours, were full of stories of daring and challenge; the challenge of adult authority, the challenge of physical daring and skill. Many but not all of these were located outside. They occur in memories of play and holidays, in transgression and danger. As Benjamin (1983) amongst others has noted, boys find it easier to separate to become an object to themselves; girls, on the other hand, rarely if ever relinquish their identification with the mother.

Given our identification of outside with challenge and danger, and inside with warmth and security, we would expect our memories of fear also to relate to outside. Some did, but many did not. A great many of the women's memories concern fear of physical or psychological harm from people, usually male, or else a fear of being abandoned. The occasion of these fears is as likely to be inside the home as outside.

We did not become aware of this contradiction during our collective theorising. On the contrary, we were constantly struck by the rich sensuous detail associated with the warmth and security of inside in contrast to the harsh and exciting coldness of outside. In our construction as children and adults, inside was safe. The contradiction lies in the fact that inside is not necessarily safe for women or for girls. The majority of crimes of violence – murder, rape, domestic violence, child sexual assault, are committed by men on women and girls, inside the home (Scutt, 1983). Many of us as girls experienced some sort of psychological or physical threat from other persons inside the apparent warmth and safety of our homes. These memories were often triggered when writing not about danger but about anger – others' anger is something to be feared.

In our memories we seem to discount, even in our adult theorizing, the potential danger of harm, physical and psychological, from other people inside the home. The contradiction reflects the hegemony which decrees that 'a woman's place is in the home' but 'a man's home is his castle'.

Support and Isolation

Another gender theme in our memories concerned the question of visibility. Many of our memories as girls were of events where we

were alone and without support. No one bore witness to our
struggles; no one was there to hear of our experience and so it was
unspoken. It may be the same for boys, but from their memories it
does not seem so.

The sense of being alone recurred in our memories of transgression, in some happiness memories, and in the danger memories. In
our transgression memories, we sometimes accepted our guilt and
sometimes resisted. But in all except one memory we transgressed
alone, or were singly held responsible, and we faced our punishment alone. Even when peers were present, they played no part in
our memory. We did not report on their reactions, nor on our
consciousness of their presence as audience, whether hostile or
sympathetic. They seemed irrelevant.

The boys, on the other hand, played to an audience of peers.
While there was seldom a suggestion of direct peer pressure, none
the less the presence and support of peers was an important
component in the way boys constructed their own transgressions.
Our sense of shame or defiance contrasted with their sense of glee
and disrespect.

There are very few examples where we as girls played to an
audience of peers. We did not seem to expect support either from
peers or from adults. Many of our transgression memories are of
our sense of betrayal and injustice when adults break their own
rules and we are punished, or when a potential ally fails to defend
us. The same is true of our danger memories. We faced danger
alone. If there were any adults present in our memories, they did
not act. We appear to accept the responsibility of dealing with
danger alone. The boys, on the other hand, were 'rescued' by
teachers or mothers or some other adult. Those of our happiness memories concerning the pleasure of mastery were all
solitary activities. The pleasure in achievement was our own, not
witnessed.

There was a collectivity of action in many of the young men's
memories that was almost completely absent from the women's
memories. Even where we as girls were involved in episodes with
other children, there was a sense of separation. We were sometimes
victimized by boys, sometimes fought other children. We were
usually held individually responsible for their welfare. Perhaps we
have again come to one of the mechanisms of male domination;
certainly the separation of women from each other is a necessary
precondition of their continued subordination. And in our struggle
for individual, personal autonomy, we cooperated, perhaps even
welcomed our own separation.

The construction of emotion, as we have argued, occurs intersubjectively. We reflect on and define our emotions in relation to

others' response and in response to others' assessment. Therefore, if we were isolated in our experience or if our feelings were invalidated by adults, we had no grounds for making the experience intelligible. Some of the memories seem to have remained problematic for that reason; the childhood search for meaning was incomplete. The strongest example is the memory of child sexual abuse involving electrical stimulation of the genitals. Here the contradiction between Ann's feelings of embarrassment, revulsion, shame and her mother's silence and acquiescence rendered her helpless at the time, and led to her subsequent suppression of the whole event. It was only as an adult woman with a feminist understanding of child sexual abuse that she could render the event intelligible. She was able to relate the experience to the experiences of others only when others were able to speak about experiences which had been subject to social and individual repression.

Silence has the power to render us helpless.

Gender and Morality

Our memory-work has shown that emotion is often gendered. In chapter 7 we explored the ways in which we construct our emotions and, through our emotions, our selves. There we identified two apparently contradictory but equally important processes. On the one hand, our memories point to a strong sense of agency, and on the other hand to a strong sense of the social. There is, of course, no contradiction. We construct our selves through the world of our social relations and the expectations of others and social rules which govern those relations.

Self is dependent on the social realm but the self actively engages in its own making. The self is constituted in the self's reflections and evaluations of its own actions and in the self's appraisals of self in relation to other. Moreover, as we have argued in chapter 7, the construction of emotions is central to this process. Agency, which is made possible by the human ability to reflect and evaluate, resides in choice. As Taylor notes, our notion of self is inextricably connected with our understanding of our moral predicament and agency.

> Our description of ourselves as selves is inseparable from our existing in a space of moral aspiration and assessment . . . Being a self is existing in a space of issues, to do with how one ought to be, or how one measures up against what is good, what is right, what is really worth doing. (1988, p. 298)

The reflection, the appraisal and the choices made take place within sets of social relations: the family, the peer group, the school class room, and wider social institutions. We move and grow into a world of taken-for-granted shared meanings, of common understandings of the order of things, that is, of the way things *ought* to be. With Mead (1934), Shotter (1984) and Haug (1987) we recognize the importance of intersubjectivity and the commonality of experience. The acknowledging of intersubjectivity, however, has an important corollary. There is not one common understanding, not one shared social world of meaning, but many. Schutz (1973) called it multiple realities. We prefer to think of intersubjectivity as layered.

The base layer we believe consists of a common set of understandings and meanings to which all human beings subscribe by virtue of our common experience as humans. Building on that basic common human layer of subjectivity, there are many different social realities constructed out of the different experiences of people in different cultures, located within different historical contexts. At any given time and place, people are differently positioned within the social matrix, by virtue of class, gender and religious affiliation, to name but a few of the parameters that define the social reality.

Nor is it simply a question of difference. At any given point in place and time there exists a matrix of common understandings that is none the less patterned by the prevailing hegemony. We, as women, grow into a social order, the meanings of which have been shaped by a male social order. We must necessarily construct our selves in terms of our positioning in that order and in relation to the hegemonic understandings. While men, too, construct themselves within the same matrix, their location within that matrix is different from women's. It is men who are dominant. We are likely to construct our selves and our emotions, not only as different, but as subordinate.

A recent adult memory of one of us may serve as a useful example:

> A television programme showed some advertisements or planned advertisements to which women had objected. One of the advertisements showed a manikin (or rather womanikin) being constructed out of metal. It was an advertisement for machine tools, sander, saw, polisher etc. The voice-over said 'when you want to rub up the little woman . . .' and showed the torso, specifically the breasts, being sanded/polished by a powerful circular machine. Further pictures showed grinding, sawing, etc. parts of the body.

One of us who was watching with male members of her family became very angry that anyone could ever have supposed that such an advertisement might be acceptable. The male family members present, while agreeing that it should be banned, could not understand the outrage, the sense of personal threat and degradation that the advertisement engendered in the woman. Women who watched the programme or who had the ad described to them had no problem in understanding the emotions evoked – whether they responded with those particular emotions or not.

There is a set of understandings shared by women (or at least by women in our society) which men do not share. There is undoubtedly a set of understandings shared by men and not by women. The male-dominated nature of our culture, and the hidden and subordinated status of women's culture, however, suggest that women are more aware of men's understandings than vice versa.

This raises an important issue. As agents, women make choices and construct emotions within a moral realm that may be different from the moral realm of men and yet is situated within male hegemonic structures.

Our research indicates, for example, that the structures that produce women's sense of responsibility situate women as the carers of others. 'Being responsible' holds different but overlapping meanings for men and women. Similarly, with a sense of justice; it is structured differently for men and women. Women's sense of justice is offended when others break the social rules or when others misunderstand their actions. Very many of the memories of women, reproduced in this book, describe the moral indignation felt by women when others acted in ways which the women thought were unjust. There was little in the men's memories which concerned justice; perhaps it is unproblematic. Men's sense of justice appears to be more intimately tied to their sense of their own place in the world and to their autonomy. Our data and their analysis indicate that many of the emotions – anger, resentment, guilt, pride, happiness, shame and fear – are constructed with reference to justice and responsibility.

Men expect and take for granted that they will be looked after and cared for; it is expected of them that they will make the world a just place to live in. Women expect and take for granted that the world is a just place; in turn they are expected to be responsible for the well-being of others. Women have little control over issues of equity and justice, and are forced to rely on others; hence their concern when those expectations are not met.

The work of Gilligan (1982; Gilligan et al., 1990) also draws attention to these aspects of morality. Gilligan examines two ethical principles, namely an ethic of justice and an ethic of responsibility or care. She does not argue that women operate according to one, care and responsibility, and men operate according to the other, justice. Rather she is concerned that the importance of the ethic of responsibility has been diminished and may be considered a less worthy ethical principle. Male hegemonic structures privilege the one over the other.

We support Gilligan's view that men and women do not operate within different moral or ethical systems. Indeed, as we indicate above, the ethic of responsibility makes the ethic of justice possible. We do argue, however, that men and women are positioned differently within these two ethical systems. This difference is reflected in the ways in which men and women construct their emotions. In their troubled acceptance of the status quo and their resistance to its structures, women construct their anger, fear and pride, and other emotions. Such emotions are the markers of their resistance.

This is not to deny that some emotions may be constructed in the same or very similar ways by both men and women. The 'happiness' memories analysed in this book indicate that happiness may be such an emotion. Further, our work shows that many of the processes of construction are quite general, applying equally to men and women. We have suggested that women understand men's emotions better than men understand women's owing to the fact that women see themselves largely through men's eyes, that is, they share understandings with men due to male dominance of culture. Such understandings are not reciprocated due to the largely hidden culture of women.

Gender and Power

Our memory-work, the data and their analysis, implicate the importance of power as well as morality in the construction of emotions. The dominant moral order supports the existing power relations. As philosophers since at least the time of Rousseau have pointed out, the moral order is integral with social relations and hence to some degree maintains existing power relations. For example, a man is entitled, even encouraged, to behave aggressively towards another man who insults 'his' woman.

Because women live their lives within the existing structures, the concept of power is caught up in their construction of emotions. In much of our discussion of the themes set in train by our memories and the memories of others, the issue of power has emerged. When we talk of gendered emotion, we are talking about the impact of gendered power relations. There are many forms of power: there is the power of silence; the power of authority; the power of competence. There is the power of physical coercion, or of the threat of violence.

Power is often manifested in the memories in terms of powerlessness. The memories are full of the pain of powerlessness. Although powerlessness is experienced by both boys and girls, it is experienced differently. There are two aspects of the gendered basis of children's powerlessness. The first is that boys dominate girls, as we saw in the episodes involving the lizard, the eel and the doll used for target practice. The reverse is hard to imagine. The second aspect is that adult authority is also differentiated along gendered lines. As girls we also experienced hurt and punishment and a lack of validation from both male and female authority. It was mainly men who threatened or used actual physical violence. Perhaps too the pain of failing to meet our fathers' approval and the joy of achieving it were experienced more acutely. Probably equally painful for us was the extent to which our mothers, our potential allies, seemed to collude or remain silent against our interests. When they took the side of the powerful male, we seemed to have little hope of resistance.

A recognition of this powerlessness brings us to a central and difficult issue for women: the issue of women as actors or victims. Within this debate, Haug (1985) has argued that every oppression which is not directly enforced from without must work with the consent of the oppressed. Such consent is organized through the process of socialization but, as pointed out above, this process is not imposed but an activity 'with consent necessary at every step' (Haug, 1985, p. 6).

Thus, the structures of women's emotions, the structures of their selves, act as obstacles to change. Private relationships play too large a part in women's emotional life, and when there is a crisis in these relationships women withdraw from political involvement. In order to secure social and political change, women must change themselves, but such change is itself conditional upon social change.

The resolution of the dilemma lies in acknowledging that people create themselves;

> Women meet the existing structures of oppression as the social relations of production in which they grow up. But these structures only go on existing if they are reproduced by those living within them. And this is the very reason why they can be altered by those living within them. (Haug, 1985, p. 5)

Her answer lies in self-socialization activity and collective resistance. The places for intervention are apparent in some of the memories reported in this book, and are marked by emotion. Our memories are full of our growing sense of power. We found a strong sense of power in our own competence and a growing awareness of the personal power of our own agency, of our ability to make a difference, to master a skill, to operate effectively within the social world. We were given responsibility for the welfare of others, and expected to look after ourselves. That was a burden, but it was also a power. Even in our memories of fear and danger we were generally able to handle the situation. Our training in self-responsibility made us remarkably self-reliant, and therein also lies a power.

These individual senses of power must be shared and collectivized in order to secure change in the social and political realm.

Our Contribution to Feminist Psychology

Perhaps the strongest power is that which is never seen or heard. The powerful define the agenda. That which is not on the agenda cannot be contested. In our own discipline of psychology, the mainstream definition of what is 'research' would exclude the kind of inquiry that we have undertaken in this book. However, feminist sociologists and psychologists – Haug (1987), Wilkinson (1986), Hollway (1989) and Burman (1990) – have both questioned and challenged traditional definitions, making it possible to do research in new and different ways.

One of our aims is to 'enrich feminism within psychology' (Fine and Gordon, 1991, p. 25), where traditional psychology is recognized by all feminists as individualistic, biological, positivist/empiricist in orientation (Wilkinson, 1986; Hollway, 1989; Fine and Gordon, 1991); and as ethnocentric and accepting the nuclear family model (Kitzinger, 1991). Traditional psychology has seen the study of women as the study of 'sex differences' or 'gender' set against male characteristics and against male-defined social norms.

The critique of traditional psychology leads feminists and others eager for a new paradigm to search for new theories, new methods, aimed at the very question of subjectivity. We believe that memory-work is such a new approach. It incorporates a method for psychology, though not a narrow individualistic psychology.

Our work is clearly situated within constructionism, but constructionism which allows a strong sense of agency (see Bhaskar, 1979). Our method and theory was developed in a feminist framework, following Haug (1987). Our work is thus truly woman-centred, that is, we are explicit in stating that our perspective is women's perspective. We do not claim to be unbiased; nor do we claim a false neutrality.

In the past, feminism and feminists have tended to disregard psychology, or at worst to relate to it very negatively. A feminist psychologist is regarded in some quarters as a contradiction in terms. Our work shows that psychology does not have to be individualistic; nor does it need to locate important processes 'within women's heads'. In our work, we have taken into account the importance of language, but have been most concerned with the analysis of practice or experience.

Although we disagree with many of the values and methods of mainstream psychology, we acknowledge that many of our insights are derived from our training as psychologists, and we do not repudiate it. Feminist scholarship now includes a growing body of research from within psychology, to which we have contributed. We believe it is important that this body of knowledge should be recognized as part of transdisciplinary feminist studies.

Memory-work has changed our lives. In doing so, it has changed the way we teach, the way we interact with the professional associations of psychologists, the way we do research, and the way we write. In documenting our experiences and our method, we make it possible for others to build upon what we have done.

The Way Forward

Through our memory-work we recognize ways in which we have participated in our own oppression. But we also find ways in which we resisted. We as girls and as women are constantly resisting, reaching out, seeking intelligibility, pushing the boundaries, asserting our agency. Through memory-work we see the contradictions, including that between actor and victim. In order to see ourselves as able to change the structures, we must first acknowledge our complicity in our own subordination, that is, that there are benefits as well as costs in maintaining the status quo. Rocking the boat may be dangerous. The unknown, the power of the oppressor, are things to be feared.

What memory-work provides is a new understanding, and it is a collective understanding. It enables us to reshape our lives, and to show others how to do so. The collective nature of memory-work situates our understandings in the intersubjective realm, and makes it more likely that our experiences and our understandings will resonate with those of other women, with their bodies and with their emotions. As individuals, we may find it impossible to resist the forces which oppress us. Collectively, we are powerful.

We must take an active part in renegotiating our responses to and our understanding of the web of power structures. This means refusing to engage with patriarchal structures, refusing to play the game by those rules. It means finding alternative ways of doing things, including alternative, women-centred ways of doing research, of doing psychology. It means developing strong new images of women, myths of women's destiny that provide the potential for positive future outcomes. It means working collectively with other women, and with those men who do not wish to work in phallocentric ways. It means developing political skills, and engaging in political action at every level of social life. If confrontation is impossible, there is always subversion.

References

Appignanesi, Richard and Zarate, Oscar (1977) *Freud for Beginners*. London: Writers and Readers.

Argyle, Michael (1975) *Bodily Communication*. London: Methuen.

Armon-Jones, Claire (1985) Prescription, explication and the social construction of emotion. *Journal for the Theory of Social Behaviour* 15 (1), 1–22.

Armon-Jones, Claire (1986) The social functions of emotions. In R. Harré (ed.), *The Social Construction of Emotions*. Oxford: Basil Blackwell.

Arnold, Magda B. (1960) *Emotion and Personality*. Vol 1: *Psychological Aspects*. Vol 2: *Neurological and Physiological Aspects*. New York: Columbia University Press.

Arnold, Magda B. (1969) Human emotion and action. In T. Mischel (ed.), *Human Action: Conceptual and Empirical Issues*. New York: Academic Press.

Arnold, Magda B. (1970) Perennial problems in the field of emotion. In M.B. Arnold (ed.), *Feelings and Emotions: The Loyola Symposium*. New York: Academic Press.

Averill, James R. (1980) A constructivist view of emotion. In R. Plutchik and H. Kellerman (eds), *Theories of Emotion*. New York: Academic Press.

Averill, James R. (1982) *Anger and Aggression: An Essay in Emotion*. New York: Springer Verlag.

Averill, James R. (1985) The social construction of emotion: with special reference to love. In K. Gergen and K. Davis (eds), *The Social Construction of the Person*. New York: Springer Verlag.

Averill, James R. (1986) The acquisition of emotions during adulthood. In R. Harré (ed.), *The Social Construction of Emotions*. Oxford: Basil Blackwell.

Ax, A.F. (1953) The physiological differentiation of fear and anger in humans. *Psychosomatic Medicine* 15, 433–42.

Bart, Pauline B. and O'Brien, Patricia H. (1985) *Stopping Rape: Successful Survival Strategies*. New York and Oxford: Pergamon Press (The Athene Series).

Bartlett, Frederick C. (1932) *Remembering*. Cambridge: Cambridge University Press.

Bedford, Erroll (1962) Emotions. In V.C. Chappell (ed.), *The Philosophy of Mind*. Englewood Cliffs, NJ: Prentice Hall.

Bedford, Erroll (1986) Emotions and statements about them. In R. Harré (ed.), *The Social Construction of Emotions*. Oxford: Basil Blackwell.

Benjamin, Jessica (1980) The bonds of love: rational violence and erotic domination. In H. Eisenstein and A. Jardine (eds), *The Future of Difference*. Boston: Barnard College Women's Center, G.K. Hall.

Benjamin, Jessica (1983) Master and slave: the fantasy of erotic domination. In A. Snitow, C. Stansell and S. Thompson, *Powers of Desire: The Politics of Sexuality*. New York: Monthly Review Press.

Bhaskar, Roy (1979) *The Posssibility of Naturalism: A Philosophical Critique of the Contemporary Human Sciences*. Brighton: Harvester Press.

Brownmiller, Susan (1975) *Against Our Will: Men, Women and Rape*. New York: Simon and Schuster.

Bruner, Jerome S. (1986) *Actual Minds, Possible Worlds*. Cambridge, Mass.: Harvard University Press.

Burman, Erica (ed.) (1990) *Feminists and Psychological Practice*. London: Sage.

Campbell, A. and Muncer, S. (1987) Models of anger and aggression in the social talk of women and men. *Journal for the Theory of Social Behaviour* 17, 489–509.

Cannon, W. B. (1927) The James–Lange theory of emotion: a critical examination and an alternative theory. *American Journal of Psychology* 39, 106–24.

Chesler, P. (1972) *Women and Madness*. New York: Doubleday.

Coulter, Jeff (1979) *The Social Construction of Mind*. London: Macmillan.

Crawford, M. and Maracek, J. (1989) Psychology reconstructs the female, 1968–1988. *Psychology of Women Quarterly* 13, 147–65.

Darwin, Charles (1872) *The Expression of Emotions in Man and Animals*. London: John Murray. Reprinted, Chicago: University of Chicago Press, 1965.

Davitz, Joel R. (1969) *The Language of Emotion*. New York: Academic Press.

Davitz, Joel R. (1970) A dictionary and grammar of emotion. In M.B. Arnold (ed.), *Feelings and Emotions: The Loyola Symposium*. New York: Academic Press.

Denzin, N.K. (1983) A note on emotionality, self and interaction. *American Journal of Sociology* 89, 402–9.

Doise, Willem and Mugny, G. (1984) *The Social Development of the Intellect*. New York: Pergamon Press.

Duffy, Elizabeth (1962) *Activation and Behaviour*. New York: John Wiley and Sons.

Eichenbaum, Luise and Orbach, Susie (1983) *What Do Women Want?* London: Michael Joseph.

Ekman, P., Levenson, R.W. and Friesen, W.V. (1983) Autonomic nervous activity distinguishes among emotions. *Science* 221, 1208–10.

Fine, M. and Gordon, S.M. (1991) Effacing the center and the margins: life at the intersection of psychology and feminism. *Feminism and Psychology* 1, 19–28.

Freud, Sigmund (1901/64) The Psychopathology of Everyday Life. In J. Strachey (ed.), *The Standard Edition of the Complete Works of Sigmund Freud*, Volume VI. London: Hogarth Press.

Freud, Sigmund (1915a/64) Repression. In J. Strachey (ed.), *The Standard Edition of the Complete Works of Sigmund Freud*, Volume XIV. London: Hogarth Press.

Freud, Sigmund (1915b/64) The Unconscious. In J. Strachey (ed.), *The Standard Edition of the Complete Works of Sigmund Freud*, Volume XIV. London: Hogarth Press.

Freud, Sigmund (1917/64) Mourning and Melancholia. In J. Strachey (ed.), *The Standard Edition of the Complete Works of Sigmund Freud*, Volume XIV. London: Hogarth Press.

Frijda, N.H. (1969) Recognition of emotion. In L. Berkowitz (ed.), *Advances in Experimental Social Psychology*, vol. 4. New York and London: Academic Press.

Frijda, Nico H. (1986) *The Emotions*. Cambridge: Cambridge University Press.

Garner, Helen (1985) *Postcards from Surfers*. Ringwood, Victoria: McPhee Gribble/Penguin Books.

Gavey, N. (1989) Feminist poststructuralism and discourse analysis: contribution to a feminist psychology. *Psychology of Women Quarterly* 13, 367–77.

Gilligan, Carol (1982) *In a Different Voice : Psychological Theory and Women's Development*. Cambridge. Mass.: Harvard University Press.

Gilligan, Carol, Lyons, Nona P. and Hanmer, Trudy J. (eds) (1990) *Making Connections: The Relational Worlds of Adolescent Girls at Emma Willard School*. Cambridge, Mass. and London: Harvard University Press.

Gow, Michael (1988) *Away*. Paddington, New South Wales: Currency Press.

Greenwood, John D. (1989) *Explanation and Experiment in Social Psychological Science: Realism and the Social Constitution of Action*. New York: Springer Verlag.

Grosz, E.A. (1988) Feminist in(ter)vention of feminist knowledges. In B. Caine, E.A. Grosz and M. de Lepervanche (eds), *Crossing Boundaries: Feminisms and the Critique of Knowledges*. Sydney: Allen and Unwin.

Harré, Rom (1979) *Social Being*. Oxford: Basil Blackwell.

Harré, Rom (1983) *Personal Being*. Oxford: Basil Blackwell.

Harré, Rom (1986) An outline of the social constructionist viewpoint. In R. Harré (ed.), *The Social Construction of Emotions*. Oxford: Basil Blackwell.

Harré, Rom, Clark, D. and De Carlo, N. (1985) *Motives and Mechanisms: An Introduction to the Psychology of Action*. London: Methuen.

Haug, Frigga (1985) Women: actors or victims? Paper presented at Macquarie University, Sydney, August.

Haug, Frigga and others (1987) *Female Sexualisation: A Collective Work of Memory*. Tr. Erica Carter. London: Verso.

Henriques, J., Hollway, W., Urwin, C., Venn, C. and Walkerdine, V. (1984) *Changing the Subject: Psychology, Social Relations and Subjectivity*. London: Methuen.

Hollway , Wendy (1984) Gender difference and the production of subjectivity. In J. Henriques, W. Hollway, C. Urwin, C. Venn and V. Walkerdine, *Changing the Subject: Psychology, Social Relations and Subjectivity*. London: Methuen.

Hollway, Wendy (1989) *Subjectivity and Method in Psychology*. London: Sage.

Izard, Carroll E. (1977) *Human Emotions*. New York: Plenum Press.

James, William (1884/1922) What is an emotion? In K. Dunlap (ed.), *The Emotions*. Baltimore, Md: Williams and Wilkins. (First published in *Mind* 9, 188–205.)

James, William (1890/1922) Principles of Psychology, chapter XXV. In K. Dunlap (ed.), *The Emotions*. Baltimore, Md: Williams and Wilkins.

Joas, Hans (1985) *G.H. Mead: A Contemporary Re-Examination*. Tr. R. Meyer. Cambridge: Polity Press.

Kimmel, E. M. (1989) The experience of feminist psychologists. *Psychology of Women Quarterly* 13, 133–46.

Kippax, S., Crawford, J., Benton, P., Gault U. and Noesjirwan, J. (1988) Constructing emotions: weaving meaning from memories. *British Journal of Social Psychology* 27, 19–33.

Kippax, S., Crawford, J., Waldby, C. and Benton, P. (1990) Women negotiationg heterosex: implications for AIDS prevention. *Women's Studies International Forum* 13 (2), 533–42.

Kitzinger, C. (1991) Feminism, psychology and the paradox of power. *Feminism and Psychology* 1, 111–29.

Lacey, J.I. and Lacey, B.C. (1958) Verification and extension of the principle of autonomic response stereotypy. *American Journal of Psychology* 71, 50–73.

Lacey, John I. and Lacey, Beatrice C. (1970) Some autonomic-central nervous system relationships. In P. Black (ed.), *Physiological Correlates of Emotion*. New York: Academic Press.

Lana, R.E. (1979) Giambattista Vico and the history of social psychology. *Journal for the Theory of Social Behaviour* 9 (3), 251–63.

Lange, A.J. and Jakubowski, P. (1976) *Responsible Assertive Behaviour*. Champaign, Ill.: Research Press.

Lange, Carl Georg (1885/1922) The Emotions. English translation. In K. Dunlap (ed.), *The Emotions*. Baltimore, Md: Williams and Wilkins.

Lazarus, R.S. (1984) On the primacy of cognition. *American Psychologist* 39, 124–9.

Levy, Robert (1984) Emotions, knowing, and culture. In R.A. Schwerder and R.A. LeVine (eds), *Culture Theory : Essays on Mind, Self and Emotion*. Cambridge: Cambridge University Press.

Lloyd, Genevieve (1984) *Man of Reason*. London: Methuen.

Lyons, William (1980) *Emotion*. Cambridge: Cambridge University Press.

McDougall, William (1908) *An Introduction to Social Psychology*. London: Methuen.

MacLeod, Linda (1985) Policy as chivalry: the criminalization of wife-battering. In S. Hatty (ed.), *Proceedings, Australian Institute of Criminology National Conference on Domestic Violence*. Canberra: Australian Institute of Criminology.

Macquarie Library (1981) *The Macquarie Dictionary*. St Leonards, New South Wales: Macquarie Library Pty Ltd.

Manicas, P.T. and Secord, P.F. (1983) Implications for psychology of the new philosophy of science. *American Psychologist* 38 (4), 399–413.

Maracek, J. (1989) Theory and method in feminist psychology: introduction. *Psychology of Women Quarterly* 13, 367–77.

Mead, G.H. (1909) Social psychology a counterpart to physiological psychology. *Psychological Bulletin* 6, 401–8.

Mead, George H. (1934) *Mind, Self and Society*. Chicago: University of Chicago Press.

Mednick, M.T. (1989) On the politics of psychological constructs: stop the bandwaggon, I want to get off. *American Psychologist* 44, 1118–23.

Messer, Stanley B., Sass, Louis A. and Woolfolk, Robert L. (eds) (1988) *Hermeneutics and Psychological Theory: Interpretive Perspectives in Personality, Psychotherapy and Psychopathology*. New Brunswick, NJ: Rutgers University Press.

Mischel, Walter (1968) *Personality and Assessment*. New York: John Wiley and Sons.

Moscovici, S. (1984) The phenomenon of social representation. In R. Farr and S. Moscovici (eds), *Social Representations*. Cambridge: Cambridge University Press.

Oatley, K. (1989) The importance of being emotional. *New Scientist* 19 August, 19–22.

Oatley, K. and Johnson-Laird, P.N. (1987) Towards a cognitive theory of emotions. *Cognition and Emotion* 1, 29–50.

Parlee, M.B. (1991) Happy birthday to *Feminism and Psychology*. *Feminism and Psychology* 1, 39–48.

Peters, Richard S. (1969) Motivation, emotion and the conceptual schemes of common sense. In T. Mischel (ed.), *Human Action, Conceptual and Empirical Issues*. New York: Academic Press.

Peters, Richard S. (1970) The education of the emotions. In M.B. Arnold (ed.), *Feelings and Emotions: The Loyola Symposium*. New York: Academic Press.

Russell, G., Rytmeister, R. and Russell, A. (1986) Play as a mediator of parent–child relationships and parental influences. Paper presented at the 4th National Development Conference, University of New South Wales, August.

Ryle, Gilbert (1963) *The Philosophy of Mind*. Harmondsworth: Penguin Books.

Schachter, J. (1957) Pain, fear and anger in hypertensives: a psychophysiologic study. *Psychosomatic Medicine* 19, 17–29.

Schachter, Stanley (1970) The assumption of identity and peripheralist–centralist controversies in motivation and emotion. In M.B. Arnold (ed.), *Feelings and Emotions: The Loyola Symposium*. New York: Academic Press.

Schachter, S. and Singer, J. (1962) Cognitive, social and psychological determinants of emotional state. *Psychological Review* 69, 378–99.

Scherer, Klaus R., Wallbott, Harald, G. and Summerfield, Angela B. (1986) *Experiencing Emotion: A Cross-Cultural Study*. Cambridge: Cambridge University Press.

Schlosberg, H.S. (1941) A scale for the judgment of facial expressions. *Journal of Experimental Psychology* 29, 497–510.

Schutz, Alfred (1973) Multiple realities. In M. Douglas (ed.), *Rules and Meaning*. Harmondsworth: Penguin.

Scutt, Jocelynne A. (1983) *Even in the Best of Homes – Violence in the Family*. Ringwood, Victoria: Pelican.

Scutt, Jocelynne A. (1985) Still the same old story: pornography and violence against women. In S. Hatty (ed.), *Proceedings, Australian Institute of Criminology National Conference on Domestic Violence*. Canberra: Australian Institute of Criminology.

Shotter, John (1984) *Social Accountability and Selfhood*. Oxford: Basil Blackwell.

Shotter, J. (1986) A sense of place: Vico and the social production of social identities. *British Journal of Social Psychology* 25, 199–211.

Solomon, Robert C. (1983) *The Passions*. Notre Dame, Ind.: University of Notre Dame Press.

Strongman, Kenneth T. (1973) *The Psychology of Emotion*. New York: John Wiley and Sons/Oxford: Basil Blackwell.

Tavris, C. (1982) *Anger: The Misunderstood Emotion*. New York: Simon and Schuster.

Taylor, C. (1977) What is human agency? In T. Mischel (ed.), *The Self: Psychological and Philosophical Issues*. Oxford: Basil Blackwell.

Taylor, Charles (1988) The moral typography of the self. In S.B. Messer, L.B. Sass and R.L. Woolfolk (eds), *Hermeneutics and Psychological Theory: Interpretive Perspectives in Personality, Psychotherapy and Psychopathology*. New Brunswick, NJ: Rutgers University Press.

Venn, Couze (1984) The subject in psychology. In J. Henriques, W. Hollway, C. Urwin, C. Venn and V. Walkerdine *Changing the Subject: Psychology, Social Relations and Subjectivity*. London: Methuen.

Walkerdine, Valerie (1984) Developmental psychology and the child-centred psychology: the insertion of Piaget with early education. In J. Henriques, W. Hollway, C. Urwin, C. Venn and V. Walkerdine *Changing the Subject: Psychology, Social Relations and Subjectivity*. London: Methuen.

Warner, C. Terry (1986) Anger and similar delusions. In R. Harré (ed.), *The Social Construction of Emotions*. Oxford: Basil Blackwell.

Wertsch, James (1985) *Vygotsky and the Social Formation of Mind*. London: Harvard University Press.

White, Hayden (1979) Michel Foucault. In J. Sturrock (ed.), *Structuralism and Since: From Lévi-Strauss to Derrida*. Oxford: Oxford University Press.

Wilkinson, Sue (1986) Sighting possibilities: diversity and commonality in feminist research. In S. Wilkinson (ed.), *Feminist Social Psychology: Developing Theory and Practice*. Milton Keynes and Philadelphia: Open University Press.

Wilkinson, S. (1991) Editorial: From critique to reconstruction. *Feminism and Psychology* 1, 5–18.

Woodworth, Robert S. (1922/42) *Psychology*. London: Methuen.

Woodworth, Robert S. (1938) *Experimental Psychology*. New York: Henry Holt.

Wundt, Wilhelm (1911) *Grundzüge der physiologischen Psychologie*, 5th edn. Leipzig: Wilhelm Englemann.

Wundt, Wilhelm (1921/73) *The Language of Gestures*. The Hague: Mouton.

Zajonc, R. (1984) On the primacy of affect. *American Psychologist* 39, 117–23.

Zeignarnik, B. (1927) Das Behalten erligter und unerligter Handlungen. In K. Lewin (ed.), Untersuchungen zur Handlungs und Affektpsychologie. *Psychologisch Forschung* 9, 1–85.

Index

accuracy, 10, 13, 51, 151, 152
action, 10, 14, 29, 34, 43, 46, 57, 62, 74, 102, 125–6
  as agency, 53–4, 187
  in anger, 174
  and choice, 122
  deliberate, 120–2
  habitual, 113
  and interaction, 116–17
  invalidated, 111
  and meaning, 38
  and memories, 38–9
  and motivation, 119–22
  see also agency
adult, compared to child, 12, 91, 154, 165
  memories contrasted, 50, 79, 89–90, 137–42, 144–6, 150
adults/adulthood, 62, 63, 65, 74, 75, 82, 104, 159, 184–5
  and anger, 169, 171, 173–4, 178–9, 183
  emotions, 113
  fear memory, 88
  holiday memories, 127–8, 131–2, 134, 135, 147–8
  holidays, problematics, 137
  interaction with children, 123, 141
  as parents, 77, 89, 90
affect, 15, 24–5, 26, 33, 110, 119, 152
  and bodily response, 114–15, 116
affective memory, 24–5, 26, 34, 111, 113, 120, 152
affiliation/belonging/caring, 76, 77, 79, 80, 90, 136
  see also happiness; love; pleasure; security
agency, 12, 13, 17, 30, 35, 39, 61, 67, 152, 184, 186, 190
  as characteristic of emotion, 112, 120
  and choice, 120–2, 125–6, 192, 194
  and morality, 124–6
  and motivation, 122
  in psychology, 53–4, 195

and search for intelligibility, 9, 111–12
  self as agent, 126, 162
  see also action
anger, 13, 26, 28, 29, 30, 67, 71
  adult, 118, 169, 171, 173–4, 178–9, 183
  and aggression, 56, 171, 172, 177–8, 181–2
  children's, 169, 172, 175, 176–7
  as conflictive, 125, 167, 180
  and crying, 171–6, 178, 182, 183
  and depression, 171–2, 174, 183
  experience of, 134, 139, 146, 169–72, 174, 176–7, 180, 183–4
  expression of, 33, 122, 167–8, 171, 173, 174, 181
  and family members, 56, 60, 169–71, 172, 177–8
  and fear, 109, 170–1, 172–3, 183
  feminist views of, 167, 182
  and frustration, 173, 174, 178, 182–3
  as gendered, 110, 118, 178, 180–3
  and guilt, 173, 178
  and hurt, 135, 139, 171–6, 183
  and injustice, 45–6, 61, 178–80, 183–4, 192
  and invalidation, 173, 176–7, 180, 182, 184
  as justifiable, 168, 169, 177, 178–9, 184
  men's, 167, 172, 178, 180–1, 184
  misinterpretation of, 171, 174, 176, 182
  moral judgements and, 167, 169, 179–80, 183
  in others, 64, 170–1, 185, 186, 188
  as passion, 182–3
  physical aspects of, 170–1, 177–8, 180, 183
  and power, 56, 60, 170–1, 174–6, 178, 180–4
  and punishment, 60, 63, 74, 170–1, 177–8